CHAMPPS: CHildren in Action Motor Program for PreschoolerS

CHAMPPS: CHildren in Action Motor Program for PreschoolerS

by

Paddy C. Favazza, Ed.D.
Saint Anselm College, Manchester, New Hampshire

and

Michaelene M. Ostrosky, Ph.D.
University of Illinois at Urbana-Champaign

with invited contributors

Melissa Stalega, M.Ed.
Hsiu-Wen Yang, Ph.D.
Katherine Aronson-Ensign, Ph.D.
Martin Block, Ph.D.
W. Catherine Cheung, Ph.D.
Yusuf Akemoglu, Ph.D.

·PAUL·H·
BROOKES
PUBLISHING C°®

Baltimore • London • Sydney

Paul H. Brookes Publishing Co.
Post Office Box 10624
Baltimore, Maryland 21285-0624
USA

www.brookespublishing.com

Picture Communication Symbols® (PCS) appear in selected figures within CHAMPPS Units 1–7 and in the Visual Support Cards provided with this book as a downloadable teacher resource. PCS is a trademark of Tobii Dynavox LLC. All rights reserved. Used with permission. PCS and Boardmaker are trademarks of Tobii Dynavox LLC. All rights reserved. Used with permission.

Typeset by Absolute Service, Inc., Towson, Maryland.
Manufactured in the United States of America by Sheridan Books, Inc.

The information provided in this book is in no way meant to substitute for a medical practitioner's or physical or occupational therapist's advice or expert opinion. Readers should consult a health professional if they are interested in more information. This book is sold without warranties of any kind, express or implied, and the publisher and authors disclaim any liability, loss, or damage caused by the contents of this book.

Research was made possible by Grant R324A150074 from the U.S. Department of Education, Institute of Education Sciences. The contents are solely the responsibility of the authors and do not represent the official views of, or endorsement by, the funding agency.

Favazza, P. C., & Ostrosky, M. M. (2015–2018). CHAMPPS (CHildren in Action: Motor Program for PreschoolerS) (PR/Award No. R324A150074). Washington, DC: Institute of Education Sciences.

Library of Congress Cataloging-in-Publication Data

Names: Favazza, Paddy C., 1954- author. | Ostrosky, Michaelene, author. | Stalega, Melissa, contributor. |
    Yang, Hsiu-Wen, contributor. | Aronson-Ensign, Katherine, contributor. | Block, Martin E., 1958- contributor. |
    Cheung, W. Catherine, contributor. | Akemoglu, Yusuf, contributor.
Title: CHAMPPS : children in action motor program for preschoolers / by Paddy C. Favazza and Michaelene M. Ostrosky ;
    with invited contributors, Melissa Stalega, Hsiu-Wen Yang, Katherine Aronson-Ensign, Martin Block, W. Catherine Cheung,
    Yusuf Akemoglu.
Description: Baltimore : Paul H. Brookes Publishing Co., [2023] | Includes bibliographical references and index.
Identifiers: LCCN 2022018977 (print) | LCCN 2022018978 (ebook) | ISBN 9781681254258 (paperback) |
    ISBN 9781681255866 (epub) | ISBN 9781681255873 (pdf)
Subjects: LCSH: Physical education for children—Curricula. | Physical education and training—Study and teaching (Preschool)—
    Curricula. | Movement education—Study and teaching (Preschool)—Curricula. | Education, Preschool—Activity programs. |
    Motor ability in children. | BISAC: EDUCATION / Curricula | EDUCATION / Teaching / Subjects / Physical Education
    Classification: LCC GV443.F38 2023 (print) | LCC GV443 (ebook) | DDC 372.86/044—dc23/eng/20220524
LC record available at https://lccn.loc.gov/2022018977
LC ebook record available at https://lccn.loc.gov/2022018978

British Library Cataloguing in Publication data are available from the British Library.

2026   2025   2024   2023   2022

10   9   8   7   6   5   4   3   2   1

Contents

About the Downloads

Purchasers of this book may download, print, and/or photocopy the Visual Support Cards, Walk-Around Cards, and other selected teacher resources for educational use.

To access the materials that come with this book:

1. Go to the Brookes Publishing Download Hub: http://downloads.brookespublishing.com

2. Register to create an account (or log in with an existing account).

3. Filter or search for the book title: *CHAMPPS: CHildren in Action Motor Program for PreschoolerS.*

About the Authors

Paddy C. Favazza, Ed.D., Senior Research Fellow, Saint Anselm College, 100 St. Anselm Drive, Manchester, NH 03102

Dr. Favazza is a senior research fellow at Saint Anselm College. She designed and co-authored *The Making Friends Program: Supporting Acceptance in Your K–2 Classroom* (2016), the *Acceptance Scale for Kindergarteners-Revised (ASK-R),* and the *Inventory of Disability Representation,* and numerous publications in journals such as *Young Exceptional Children, Palaestra, Young Children, Journal of Early Intervention, International Journal of Inclusive Education,* and *Adapted Physical Activity Quarterly.* Her research focuses on the development of research-informed, literacy-based strategies to support social acceptance of young children with disabilities, measurement of attitudes in young children, and universal design for learning (UDL)-infused physical activities for preschoolers in inclusive early childhood classes. She has a particular interest in developing curriculum with strong theoretical underpinnings related to the inclusion of children with disabilities, viewing these as a vehicle for family, school, and community inclusion. Professor Favazza has taught and undertaken research in the United States (Louisiana, Tennessee, Massachusetts, and Rhode Island) and in the global context (Nicaragua, Bolivia, Romania, Cyprus, Kenya, Tanzania, The Netherlands, and Turkey). Additional roles in higher education include professor of early childhood special education (ECSE), director of a graduate ECSE program, principal investigator (Institute of Education Sciences), and Fulbright Scholar (Romania).

Michaelene M. Ostrosky, Ph.D., Professor of Education, University of Illinois at Urbana-Champaign, 288 Education, 1310 South Sixth Street, Champaign, IL, 61820

Dr. Ostrosky is Grayce Wicall Gauthier Professor of Education in the Department of Special Education at the University of Illinois at Urbana-Champaign (UIUC). She has been involved in research and dissemination on the inclusion of children with disabilities, social–emotional competence, and challenging behavior. Through her work at the national Center on the Social and Emotional Foundations for Early Learning, she was involved in the development of the Pyramid Model for Supporting Social Emotional Competence in Infants and Young Children and is a co-author of *Unpacking the Pyramid Model: A Practical Guide for Preschool Teachers* (2021). Professor Ostrosky is a former editor of *Young Exceptional Children* (YEC) and the co-editor of several YEC monographs. Additionally, she co-authored *The Making Friends Program: Supporting Acceptance in Your K–2 Classroom* (2016), which supports the acceptance of individuals with disabilities, and *The Project Approach for All Learners* (2018), which is a method to engage children through in-depth investigations of topics that spark their interest.

Dr. Ostrosky has been recognized for her professional accomplishments with honors such as UIUC University Scholar, Goldstick Family Scholar, College of Education Senior Scholar, and the Division of Early Childhood of the Council for Exceptional Children's Award for Mentoring.

About the Contributors

Yusuf Akemoglu, Ph.D., Assistant Professor of Early Childhood Special Education, Duzce University, Konuralp, Duzce, Turkey

Dr. Akemoglu worked with young children (birth–5 years) for several years prior to earning a doctorate in special education from the University of Illinois at Urbana-Champaign. His research examines parent-implemented language and communication interventions. Dr. Akemoglu has authored and co-authored several publications and presented his work at numerous national and international conferences in the field of early childhood special education.

Katherine Aronson-Ensign, Ph.D., Research Fellow, Global Youth and Education, Special Olympics International, 1133 19th Street, NW, Washington, DC 20036

Dr. Aronson-Ensign served as a lead graduate assistant on CHAMPPS, assisting in the development of motor activities, selecting and evaluating materials, and undertaking data collection, data entry, and analysis. She is currently a research fellow for Special Olympics International. Previously, she was a research assistant and teaching fellow at the Institute for Community Inclusion at the School for Global Inclusion and Social Development at the University of Massachusetts Boston. She is passionate about using sports programs to impact post-conflict reconciliation, which is reflected in her research on the effects the Organization of Women in Sports–Women's Soccer for Unity program in Rwanda has on participants' tolerance. She has published several articles focused on the importance of increasing physical activity levels and school readiness skills for children in inclusive settings, promoting peace through sports globally, and the experiences of Syrian refugee youth in Lebanon.

Martin Block, Ph.D., Professor, Department of Kinesiology, School of Education and Human Development, University of Virginia, 550 Brandon Avenue, Box 400407, Charlottesville, VA 22904-4407

Dr. Block is a professor in the Department of Kinesiology at the University of Virginia, where he teaches courses in adapted physical education and motor development. He is internationally known for his work on including children with disabilities in general physical education as well as his work on programs for children with severe disabilities. Among other works, he is the author of *A Teacher's Guide to Adapted Physical Education: Including Students with Disabilities in Sports and Recreation* (2016) and co-author of *Developmental and Adapted Physical Activity Assessment* (2018). Professor Block's primary consulting work is with Special Olympics, Inc., where he has worked with the Motor Activity Training Program (MATP), and Young Athletes.

W. Catherine Cheung, Ph.D., Postdoctoral Research Associate, Department of Special Education, College of Education, University of Illinois at Urbana-Champaign, 1310 South Sixth Street, Champaign, IL 61820

Dr. Cheung is a postdoctoral research associate in the Department of Special Education at the University of Illinois at Urbana-Champaign. Her research focuses on the correlation between motor, cognitive, socioemotional, and communication skills in young children with disabilities.

Melissa Stalega, M.Ed., Doctoral Fellow, Neag School of Education, University of Connecticut, 249 Glenbrook Road, Unit 3064, Storrs, CT 06269

Melissa Stalega served as the lead project coordinator on CHAMPPS, coordinating grant activities and contributing to the program's development. She has since managed and contributed to several federally and privately funded projects at the University of Connecticut, including B.R.A.I.N. Camp, the APPRISE Project, and the R.E.S.C.U.E. Project. Melissa has also supported the development of professional learning modules for the National Center on Intensive Intervention. She is currently a doctoral fellow at the University of Connecticut with a focus on bridging the gap between reading research and application in the classroom. Her research background is rooted in early childhood special education including teacher–child interactions, inclusion, and reading and literacy.

Hsiu-Wen Yang, Ph.D., Research Investigator/Technical Assistance Specialist, Frank Porter Graham Child Development Institute, 517 S. Greensboro Street, Carrboro, NC 27510

Dr. Yang is a technical assistance specialist and research investigator at the Frank Porter Graham Child Development Institute at the University of North Carolina at Chapel Hill. She received her master's degree in occupational therapy from the National Taiwan University and her doctorate in special education from the University of Illinois at Urbana-Champaign. As a former occupational therapist, she has worked with young children with developmental disabilities and their families in a variety of settings. Her research focuses on early intervention, family-centered practices, parent coaching, inclusive practices, and social–emotional development.

Preface

The idea for CHAMPPS came from several converging experiences that the lead authors, Paddy Favazza and Michaelene Ostrosky, had in the field of early childhood special education. First, as former teachers of young children with disabilities, we were tasked with "teaching" physical education with limited formal training in this content area and no access to curriculum to guide instruction. Later, as professors and researchers in the field, we had numerous opportunities to observe early childhood and early childhood special education programs where we found many programs and teachers with similar experiences (e.g., no established motor program, inadequate training, limited time dedicated to structured motor play and physical activity). At the same time, we recognized that the context of play and being physically active was central to a young child's development and that all developmental domains could be supported through intentionally structured motor play activities. The need for such a program was timely and important as we continue to see 1) an increase in the inclusion of preschool children with disabilities, many of whom have motor delays and deficits; 2) an increase in sedentary behavior, obesity, and screen time among preschoolers; and 3) a gap in preschool motor curriculum and training based on sound theory and efficacy research. Finally, Dr. Favazza had a unique opportunity to undertake research and development activities as a consultant with Young Athletes. (To learn more about the Young Athletes Program at the University of Massachusetts Boston, visit this link: https://www.umb.edu/csde/research/past_projects/young_athletes_curriculum.) Observations of this excellent community-based motor program gave insight into the gaps in school-based motor programs, specifically, the need for a motor program with

- Sound theoretical underpinnings

- Data-based motor activities that lead to increased physical activity levels and improvements in motor skills

- Programmatic links to school readiness (i.e., supports for social, communication, and pre-academic goals)

- An internal structure to ensure elevated levels of physical activity

- Lessons embedded with universal design for learning (UDL) strategies to support all children in inclusive preschool settings

- Links to literacy and language through children's motor-themed books and music videos, visual supports, vocabulary, and verbal prompts

The concept for CHAMPPS was born from these experiences and observations, leading to an exciting and daunting review of the research on motor development of young children and existing motor activities and programs. Armed with a few ideas, we turned to preschool teachers to assist us in the development and evaluation of a motor program that was responsive to the gap in programming and the current challenges faced by preschool children with and without disabilities.

Purpose

The purpose of CHAMPPS is to provide a theoretically grounded, research-based motor program to support increased activity levels and motor skills in young children in inclusive early childhood classes. In addition, CHAMPPS was developed to provide teachers and parents with activities that enable them to integrate new skills into active motor play, thereby supporting other areas of development such as social, communication, pre-academic, and approaches to learning. CHAMPPS is intended to be flexible in implementation as teachers determine the breadth and scope of content to present at any given point in time. Teachers are encouraged to adapt CHAMPPS in response to the needs and interests of their students as well as the characteristics of a school or program (e.g., half-day versus full-day, amount of time dedicated to active motor play, number of adults in the classroom).

How This Book Is Organized

This book is organized in three sections. Section I, CHAMPPS Fundamentals, provides an overview of CHAMPPS. In Chapter 1, we discuss the philosophy and instructional objectives underlying this program and outline its components, format, and structure. In Chapter 2, we present a detailed rationale for an inclusive preschool motor program. We describe key features of CHAMPPS: its sound theoretical underpinnings, its explicit connections to professional guidelines and evidence-based practices, and its grounding in UDL principles and strategies. We also present guidelines for including all children in motor play activities to support their motor development. Tips for facilitating smooth transitions, managing behavior challenges, and using verbal prompts are included.

Section II, Get Moving: CHAMPPS Motor Skills Units, is the heart of this book. It begins with guidance on the practical aspects of implementing CHAMPPS units: tips for getting started, sample unit schedules, and the like. The seven CHAMPPS units reflect the standard progression of the development of fundamental motor skills, from foundational skills (e.g., body awareness, motor imitation, visual tracking), walking, and running, to more advanced skills such as balancing, jumping, and hopping, and movement skills that involve motor play with objects (catching, throwing, striking, and kicking). Among other features, each unit includes

- Unit objectives and key vocabulary

- Guidance on setup of the learning environment and needed materials

- Space for your unit planning notes

- Lessons with warm-up, core, and cool-down activities, including songs to help children remember the movements and classroom routine

- Suggestions for children's books and music videos that correspond to each motor unit

- Suggestions for adapting activities using UDL strategies and for incorporating school readiness skills

- Walk-Around Cards as a quick reference that you can keep on hand as you lead an active motor lesson

- A glossary of verbal prompts you can use when teaching different movements

- Recommendations for Visual Support Cards to use with each unit; these are available as a downloadable resource

- Suggested variations for the lesson activities

- Home materials for families to implement a portion of CHAMPPS at home each week

Section III, Additional Resources, is intended to help teachers tailor CHAMPPS to the needs and interests of the children with whom they work; address individual children's challenges with specific motor skills; and implement CHAMPPS with the resources they have available. This section begins with a detailed Skill Leveling Guide, addressing each of the motor skills covered in the CHAMPPS units. This guide helps teachers assess a child's skill level, identify subskills to emphasize, and troubleshoot using concrete instructional strategies and verbal prompts. It also lists additional resources and references, both print and online, that teachers may want to consult for more information about the motor skills covered in CHAMPPS. Following the Skill Leveling Guide, selection criteria and recommendations for books, videos, and materials are provided so that every teacher can adapt this program to their classroom.

Finally, additional resources for CHAMPPS can be accessed online at the Brookes Download Hub. These printable and reproducible resources include

- Walk-Around Cards and Home Activities materials included in the book

- Sample of 21- and 28-week teaching schedules included in the book, along with additional sample schedules for teaching CHAMPPS over a shorter or longer time period

- Visual Support Cards, available online only, to help children learn specific movements, body parts, and other CHAMPPS concepts

- Wall posters, available online only, listing the activities and related songs for each CHAMPPS unit for easy reference during an active motor lesson

It is our genuine hope that CHAMPPS makes a unique contribution to the curricular needs of teachers of young children with and without disabilities or delays. We envision CHAMPPS serving as a fun motor play program designed for embedding teacher-selected school readiness skills within the motor play activities with additional supports through interactive motor books and videos, UDL strategies, verbal prompts, and visual supports. Get ready to get moving with the children you teach—and have fun!

Acknowledgments

This book has been a labor of love and pulling it together during a pandemic has really challenged us in ways that we could never have imagined. First and foremost, we wish to acknowledge and thank the teachers and assistant teachers who collaborated with us in creating this curriculum. They offered ideas throughout the development of CHAMPPS, they challenged us when activities did not go as planned, they offered suggestions for adapting materials and motor activities, and they celebrated small and large successes with us. We are incredibly grateful that they were willing to partner with us on this journey.

We also would like also to acknowledge all of the preschool children and their families who have shaped our work. To enter into children's play has been a gift as they have repeatedly ignited our imagination and showed us new ways of interacting, cooperating, and playing with one another with courage and excitement (and sometimes a little bit of frustration!), when gently challenged with new tasks that stretched their motor abilities and their social, cognitive, and communicative skills.

We would be remiss if we did not acknowledge the Institute of Education Science and Dr. Amy Sussman, our project officer, for supporting us as we tackled our goal to develop a motor program for use in inclusive preschool classrooms. Without your support and guidance, this would never have been possible. Also, our developmental editor extraordinaire at Brookes Publishing, Tess Hoffman, was an insightful contributor, challenger, and cheerleader as we worked through all of the logistics of pulling together a curriculum that has so many moving pieces.

Finally, we want to express our deep gratitude to our families who supported us on our journey to develop CHAMPPS. Their encouragement and interest in our work helped incredibly and kept us motivated. In the end, this book was completed with and for all of you—early childhood teachers, children, parents, and our families—and for that we are thankful.

We dedicate this book to the many teachers and assistant teachers who shared their ideas with us during the development phase of the CHAMPPS curriculum. These professionals provided thoughtful and critical feedback for improving each activity as they implemented it with their preschool students. The past few years amid a global pandemic have highlighted the incredible work you do each and every day to support children and their families. Thank you.

CHAMPPS Fundamentals

CHAPTER 1

INTRODUCTION

CHAMPPS (*CHildren in Action: Motor Program for PreschoolerS*) is a semi-structured motor program that utilizes universal design for learning (UDL) strategies to support school readiness skills (e.g., motor, social, language, pre-academics) while elevating children's physical activity levels. This class-wide program can be implemented for 21–28 weeks, depending on how it is structured, and is intended for use in inclusive preschool classes. The longer version includes 2 review days for each unit, which we have found to be very beneficial as children are learning new motor skills.

PHILOSOPHY OF CHAMPPS

CHAMPPS is based on the philosophy that *every child has the right to be fully engaged in their world, including the right to regular opportunities for motor play and physical activity.* This philosophy is consistent with the tenets of several professional organizations (i.e., National Center for Physical Development and Outdoor Play, 2010; United Nations Children's Fund [UNICEF], 2006) that emphasize the need to support children in their most important contexts for learning, during play and physical activity, which subsequently assists with all areas of development.

ALIGNMENT WITH PROFESSIONAL GUIDELINES

CHAMPPS is aligned with the tenets of several leading professional organizations that emphasize the need for young children to be physically active during school. For example, the Division for Early Childhood (DEC) of the Council for Exceptional Children recommends that teachers create environments that provide opportunities for movement and regular physical activity to maintain or improve fitness, wellness, and development across domains (DEC, 2014). Both the National Association for the Education of Young Children (NAEYC, 2020) and the U.S. Office of Disease Prevention and Health Promotion (ODPHP, 2018) stress that physical activity and play impact all areas of child development, recognizing that children learn in active and integrative ways (Parker & Thomsen, 2019). Lastly, the ODPHP (2018) guidelines indicate that preschoolers should be physically active throughout the day, engaging in at least 60 minutes of structured motor play (e.g., motor lessons, sports, dance) and at least 60 minutes of unstructured motor play (e.g., free play, recess) each day. Collectively, these guidelines support the use of programs like CHAMPPS as part of the preschooler's school day.

OBJECTIVES OF CHAMPPS

The objectives of CHAMPPS are twofold in that they focus on impacting children and teachers alike. As a result of participating in CHAMPPS, children will

- Spend more time being physically active (having elevated physical activity levels)

- Develop school readiness skills (motor, social, language, pre-academics, and approaches to learning)

Teachers will

- Gain an understanding about the importance of motor skill development and physical activity for young children

- Learn strategies for individualizing motor play for all children

- Create ways to support school readiness through intentional motor play

UNIQUE ASPECTS OF CHAMPPS

How is CHAMPPS different from other motor programs?
There are several aspects of CHAMPPS that make it unique. CHAMPPS includes:

- A strong theoretical foundation that is informed by current professional guidelines

- Semi-structured lessons to elevate children's physical activity levels

- UDL strategies to support active motor play of all children

- Suggestions for supporting knowledge and skills in motor, social, language, and pre-academics areas

- Links to literacy, music videos, and supports for family involvement

- A flexible format for use in full-day and half-day preschool programs

The sections that follow describe the components, format, and structure of CHAMPPS.

Components of CHAMPPS

CHAMPPS has seven units that focus on the most common motor skill areas acquired during the early childhood years. These standard motor skills are considered foundational to overall child development (Clark, 1994; Clark & Metcalfe, 2002) and include fundamental skills (i.e., body awareness, motor imitation, visual tracking), walking/running, balance/jumping, catching, throwing, striking, and kicking. See Table 1.1 for a summary of the components that are described next.

Lessons   Every teacher-led CHAMPPS lesson contains one whole-group warm-up activity, three core motor play activities (in small group, pairs, or independent practice), and one whole-group cool-down activity, with the teacher modeling all motor movements. Lessons include objectives, key vocabulary, and Home Activities that encourage family members to do some of the CHAMPPS activities with their child each week.

Universal Design for Learning Strategies and School Readiness Suggestions   Because preschool classes have children with varied learning needs, every CHAMPPS lesson includes a wide array of UDL strategies and ideas for supporting school readiness skills. Therefore, prior to implementing a lesson, teachers select the UDL strategies that match the needs of their students. Likewise, prior to using CHAMPPS, teachers choose which school readiness skills they will emphasize. Simply put, each CHAMPPS lesson is tailored to match the needs of the class when the teacher selects UDL strategies and school readiness skills on which to focus.

Table 1.1. CHAMPPS components

Components	Description
Units	Seven units: 1) foundational skills (i.e., body awareness, motor imitation, visual tracking), 2) walking/running, 3) balance/jumping/hopping, 4) catching, 5) throwing, 6) striking, and 7) kicking
Lessons	One lesson for each unit with the same activities repeated six times; optional variations are included for different activities. Each 30-minute lesson includes one warm-up activity, three core motor activities, and one cool-down activity. The warm-up activity, cool-down activity, and one core motor play activity include singing while doing the motor movements. Each unit includes a Wall Poster and Walk-Around Card summarizing the activities and songs for teachers to use as a quick reference while working with children.
Universal Design for Learning (UDL) Strategies	UDL strategies are included for every activity within each lesson. Teachers preselect UDL strategies or insert their own ideas for UDL strategies based on the needs of their students.
School Readiness Suggestions	Each lesson has school readiness knowledge/skill suggestions. Teachers preselect the school readiness areas on which to focus to support motor, social, language, approaches to learning, and/or pre-academic objectives from their school's preschool curriculum.
Video Link: Music Video Suggestions	Teachers preselect music videos using the criteria for music video selection to identify an interactive motor video that reinforces the motor movement from each CHAMPPS unit. See the list of suggested videos in the Resources for Musical Motor Activities–Videos in Section III, Additional Resources.
Literacy Link: Interactive Motor Books	Each unit has recommended preschool interactive motor books that correspond to the motor movements from each CHAMPPS unit. Teachers preselect an interactive motor book from the suggested preschool motor books or use the criteria for book selection to identify an interactive motor book that reinforces the motor movement from that CHAMPPS unit.
Home Activities (Family Component)	Each unit has weekly communications for families, encouraging them to implement CHAMPPS at home *after* the motor activities have already been introduced at school. The communication includes ideas for using common items from the home in lieu of specialized equipment.
Additional Resources	In addition to the lessons, UDL strategies, and suggestions for school readiness, the CHAMPPS manual provides background information on motor skill development and physical activity, Walk-Around Cards, a comprehensive Skill Leveling Guide, Classroom Inventory for Motor Play (CIMP), CHAMPPS Criteria for Selecting Physical Activity Music Videos, and CHAMPPS Criteria for Selecting Preschool Interactive Movement Books.

Suggestions for Music Videos   Music videos are utilized in CHAMPPS because they provide a unique type of visual and auditory support for children to practice motor skills introduced in the lessons while elevating their physical activity level. Music videos are added to each unit after the first two lessons in the unit are completed. Typically, after two repeated lessons, children understand the motor play activities and can transition easily from one activity to the next. Thus, once that lesson familiarity is established, a music video is inserted into the lesson. Because music videos can result in sustained vigorous physical activity levels, the duration for music videos was carefully considered and informed by research. Brown et al. (2009) found that a duration of sustained physical activities beyond 5 minutes is not appropriate for preschool children. Therefore, the duration of music video activity is gradually increased with the maximum length of the music video activity being 4 minutes.

Allowing for flexibility, teachers decide when their students are ready for music videos to be added to the lessons. Section III, Additional Resources, includes CHAMPPS Criteria for Selecting Physical Activity Music Videos, a list of recommended videos, and Resources for Musical Motor Activities. Teachers should use the criteria provided to select videos on their own. Or to easily get started, see the list of recommended video choices, which were carefully evaluated and chosen for each unit.

Suggestions for Interactive Motor Books   Interactive motor books are used in CHAMPPS to link literacy to motor play while also increasing children's physical activity levels. Some teachers use these books to introduce a new unit *prior to* the CHAMPPS lessons or to provide additional opportunities to address or review specific motor skills *after* the CHAMPPS lessons. Teachers can use one of the recommended books that were carefully evaluated from a wide array of available preschool interactive books, or they may use the CHAMPPS Criteria for Selecting Preschool Interactive Movement Books (found in Section III, Additional Resources) to select their own books.

Communications for Home Activities   Each motor unit includes a message for families describing an abbreviated version of a CHAMPPS lesson to implement at home, *after* the activities have been introduced at school. The Home Activities communication includes the opening and closing song and one motor activity. It also provides the names of interactive books and teacher-selected videos, in case families want to access these resources online or at their local library. In addition, the communication includes ideas for using common items from the home in lieu of motor materials.

CHAMPPS has an intentionally designed format and internal structure to maximize the benefits for and useability with all young children while providing the flexibility needed by teachers in a wide variety of preschool programs.

Format of CHAMPPS

CHAMPPS is intended for use in inclusive preschool settings 2 or 3 days a week for a minimum of 30 minutes each day. However, teachers may choose to implement CHAMPPS more frequently or select specific activities to implement based on the needs and interests of their students or the time constraints in their program. Each of the seven motor units has six repeated lessons, optional review days, and weekly home communications for family members to implement CHAMPPS.

Repeated lessons are important for a number of reasons. Young children with and without disabilities need multiple opportunities to do the same activities because this

- Improves their knowledge and skills (i.e., motor, social, language, pre-academic) through repeated learning opportunities

- Supports their sense of security and confidence by ensuring they know what happens next

- Eases the transition from one activity to the next as children become familiar with the activities

Repeated lessons also can lead to children's increased capacity to take on leadership and partner roles during CHAMPPS as they become familiar with the activities. Finally, self-help skills (e.g., set up, clean up) and appropriate behavior are likely to increase during independent practice when children are familiar with the routine of the activities.

The frequency of CHAMPPS lessons will vary from class to class as it is likely to be influenced by scheduling factors in each school. For example, a half-day preschool program may opt to implement CHAMPPS for 2 days a week, whereas a full-day program may implement CHAMPPS for 3–4 days a week because of differences in their scheduling needs. Consequently, the frequency of implementing CHAMPPS may impact the duration. For example, if CHAMPPS is implemented twice a week, it would take 3 weeks to complete six repeated lessons for each motor unit, whereas if CHAMPPS is implemented 3 days a week, it would take 2 weeks to complete each motor unit. Thus, each preschool program or teacher decides on the frequency of CHAMPPS lessons. Of note, CHAMPPS can be implemented more than the six repeated lessons by adding two review days per unit, depending on children's interests and needs. See Section II for sample schedules of CHAMPPS, with and without the optional review days included.

As noted above, each CHAMPPS unit includes two optional review days for teachers to pause or take a break from the repeated lessons. The purpose of a review day is for teachers to select specific activities from the current lesson to provide additional time focused on skills that children need more time mastering (e.g., throwing underhand, kicking for accuracy). On a typical 30-minute review day for CHAMPPS, the teacher uses about 20 minutes to address one or two specific motor skills that are challenging for their students, or the teacher can use the time to work with individual children. The remaining 10 minutes are used to read an interactive motor book linking motor movements to early literacy *and/or* to play the class's favorite music video to elevate physical activity levels. Teachers decide what to focus on based on the needs and interests of their students.

Structure of CHAMPPS

The internal structure of the 30-minute CHAMPPS lesson includes a warm-up activity, three motor play activities, one music video, and a cool-down activity. This structure was intentionally designed to ensure that the content and duration of motor activities and the transitions between activities result in motor-appropriate behavior *and* elevated physical activity levels for the majority of time during the lesson. In other words, the quick-paced lessons are structured to maximize engaged motor movement while minimizing sedentary behavior, inappropriate behavior, and wait time.

All of this requires adequate planning to ensure that the teacher is familiar with the CHAMPPS lesson, has preselected UDL and school readiness strategies, has the space and materials prepared ahead of time, knows which children will be in which small groups or partner activities, and so on. This is a lot to think about! So, in the beginning, a teacher might lead the warm-up activity, introduce one or two motor activities (instead of all three), and then do the cool-down activity. In other words, *flexibility is key*. Each teacher needs to determine how much time is needed for each activity within the lesson, based on the needs of their students, while remembering that CHAMPPS is intentionally quick paced to elevate physical activity levels and maintain child engagement. It is important that each teacher's goal is to implement the full lesson because it follows a very purposeful internal structure for the entire program. What is amazing is that when CHAMPPS is fully implemented, children learn the routine, or internal structure, of the motor activities across the seven units as they gradually shift from whole-group activities to small groups, to motor engagement with a partner, and to independent play.

CHAPTER 2

SUPPORTING ALL CHILDREN'S MOTOR DEVELOPMENT

This chapter includes the rationale for using CHAMPPS to support all children's motor development during the preschool years. Key features of CHAMPPS that support this development are described. Finally, an in-depth look at how you can implement CHAMPPS in ways that include all children in your classroom or program is provided.

RATIONALE

The preschool years are an ideal time to address motor development and hone those skills through engagement in physical activities. During this time, preschoolers (3–5 years of age) use their bodies in a variety of ways as they learn to jump, hop, throw, and catch, which require motor skills such as locomotion, motor planning and coordination, balance, and object manipulation. In addition, while motor development is important in and of itself, it also impacts other areas of development, including school readiness (Clark, 1994, 2005; Haiback-Beach et al., 2018; Haywood & Getchell, 2014; Oja & Jorimae, 2002). Motor skills are viewed as "building blocks" for many areas of development. As can be seen in Figure 2.1, active motor play leads to exploration and stimulation within one's environment, which supports growth in motor skills as well as social, language, and cognitive skills. Therefore, it is easy to see how motor skill development and physical activity are related to school readiness. School readiness represents a combination of *interrelated skills*: physical well-being and motor development (Trawick-Smith, 2010; Trevlas et al., 2003), social–emotional development, language development, general knowledge and cognitive skills (Fedewa & Ahn, 2011; Iverson, 2010; Piek et al., 2008; Wassenberg et al., 2005), approaches to learning (e.g., curiosity, sustained attention) (Ackerman & Barnett, 2005; Howard, 2011; Kagan et al., 1995), and adaptive behavior (MacDonald et al., 2013). CHAMPPS has different activities that reflect the interrelatedness of readiness skills. For example, one lesson focuses on different animals (their habitats, the ways they move, and what they eat). During the lesson, children hear vocabulary related to animals while they move their bodies in ways that animals move (e.g., frogs hop, birds fly, horses gallop) and use the new vocabulary, taking turns and sharing materials with peers. This simple motor activity reinforces motor, language, and social skills as well as knowledge about animals.

Therefore, motor skill development is important for *all* children. However, CHAMPPS is *especially* important for two distinct populations who are at risk for delays in motor development: children with disabilities or delays and children growing up in underresourced communities (Figure 2.2). For example, Provost et al. (Provost, Heimerl, et al., 2007; Provost, Lopez, et al., 2007)

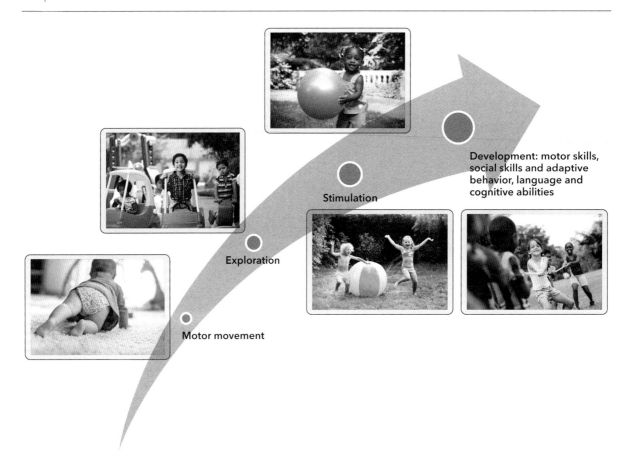

Figure 2.1.   Motor development serves as building blocks for development. (*Source*: Favazza & Siperstein, 2016.)

found that some preschoolers with disabilities had significant delays in motor skills that required balance and motor planning. Moreover, growing up in poverty can have long-term negative impacts on development (e.g., cognition, social–emotional skills, language, health, and motor skills) (Ginsburg, 2007; Goodway & Branta, 2003; Venetsanou & Kambas, 2010). These two realities are compounded by the current preschool landscape in which most children do not spend an adequate amount of time engaged in physical activities or receive intentional support for motor skill development (Figure 2.3).

In typical early childhood settings, there are three types of motor activities: *unstructured motor play,* such as daily recess monitored by teachers, parent volunteers, and other caregivers; *structured motor interventions,* such as physical therapy (PT), occupational therapy (OT), and adaptive physical education (APE) led by motor specialists for children with disabilities; and *unstructured motor and music movement,* such as brief motor breaks for the whole class led by early childhood teachers who typically lack extensive background knowledge in motor skill development. What becomes clear is that only a small percentage of children (those who qualify for OT, PT, and APE) participate in *intentional* motor movement activities designed to support motor skill development and physical activity. The interaction of these realities illustrates the need for preschool motor programs such as CHAMPPS. Moreover, these converging facts provide a rationale for CHAMPPS, a preschool motor program designed to assist teachers and parents in supporting all children's motor skill development and physical activity level while positively impacting school readiness.

Children With Disabilities

- There are about 240 million children with disabilities globally (UNICEF, 2013, 2021; U.S. Department of Education, 2014; World Health Organization, 2011).
- Children with autism and developmental disabilities have challenges with motor imitation, motor planning, motor coordination, balance, locomotion, and object manipulation, which can have a negative impact on social, language, and cognitive development and can be a predictor of later play skills (Emck et al., 2009; Favazza et al., 2013, 2021; Goodway et al., 2003; Gowen & Hamilton, 2013; Hartman et al., 2010; Ketcheson et al., 2017; MacDonald et al., 2017; McDuffie et al., 2007; Provost, Heimerl, et al., 2007; Provost, Lopez, et al., 2007; Reinders et al., 2019; Uzgiris, 1999; Vuijk et al., 2010; Wuang et al., 2008).

Children Living in Underresourced Communities

- In the United States, children under the age of 9 are particularly at risk for developmental challenges, with at least 44% of U.S. children living in underresourced communities (Jiang & Koball, 2018).
- In developing countries, more than 30% of children live in underresourced communities, resulting in lifelong negative impacts on health and developmental outcomes (UNICEF, 2015).
- Growing up in poverty can have a long-term negative impact on many areas of development, such as cognition, socioemotional and language skills, health, and motor development (Bradley & Corwyn, 2002; Buckingham et al., 2014; Choi et al., 2019; Ginsburg, 2007; Goodway & Branta, 2003; Lee et al., 2014; McPhillips & Jordan-Black, 2007; Venetsanou & Kambas, 2010).

Figure 2.2. At-risk populations.

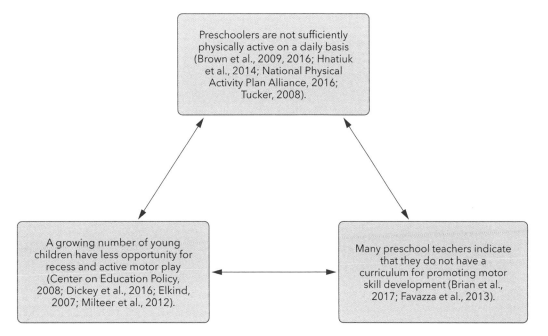

Figure 2.3. Current preschool landscape.

KEY FEATURES OF CHAMPPS

CHAMPPS includes three key features necessary to support young children's motor skill development and physical activity. It is informed by 1) sound theoretical underpinnings, 2) professional guidelines, and 3) indices of evidence-based practices. Each of these is discussed briefly.

Informed by Sound Theoretical Underpinnings

CHAMPPS is based on Clark's "Mountain of Motor Development" (Clark, 1994; Clark & Metcalfe, 2002), is rooted in dynamic systems theory (Newell, 1984, 1986), and is comprehensive in scope by addressing the seven fundamental motor skills. Adapted from Clark's "Mountain of Motor Development" (Figure 2.4), CHAMPPS represents a sequential and cumulative progression in acquiring motor skills. The five periods of motor development are described next.

- The reflexive period (birth–2 weeks) is characterized by stereotypical motor movements elicited by specific stimuli (e.g., the sucking reflex in the presence of a bottle).

- The preadaptive period (2 weeks–1 year) is characterized by the attainment of object manipulation skills needed for independent feeding (e.g., eye–hand coordination, grasp and release needed

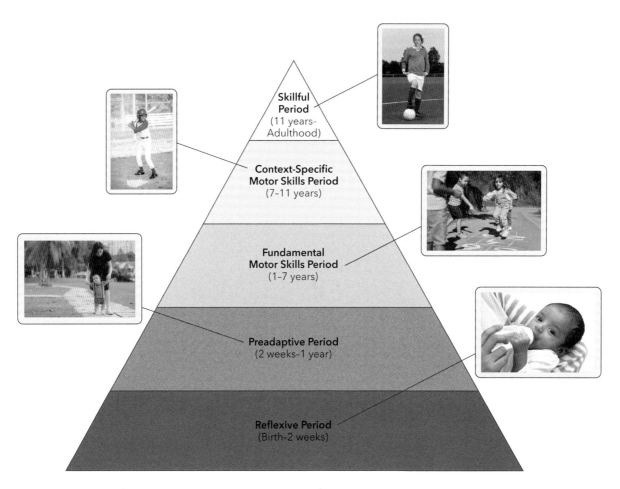

Figure 2.4. Mountain of motor development. (Adapted by permission from Springer: Springer International, "Motor skills interventions for young children with disabilities," by P.C. Favazza and G.N. Siperstein, in B. Reichow, B. Boyd, E. Barton, & S. L. Odom [Eds.], *Handbook on early childhood special education* (pp. 225–246), copyright © 2016.)

to hold a bottle, cup, or finger foods) and intentional locomotion skills such as creeping, crawling, cruising, and walking.

- The fundamental motor skills (FMS) period (1–7 years) includes the development of motor skills in locomotion and object manipulation such as walking, running, hopping, jumping, throwing, catching, and kicking. **This is the period that is targeted in CHAMPPS, which supports the development of all the FMS through motor play and physical activities**.

- The context-specific motor skills period (7–11 years) *and* the skillful period (11 years–adulthood) both involve the refinement and elaboration of FMS such as combining motor movements (e.g., run and catch at the same time) and more complex cognitive skills (e.g., learning the rules of games).

Learning to use FMS is a precursor to more advanced levels of motor movement and depends on several factors (Lerner, 1976; Payne & Isaacs, 2012). According to Newell (1984, 1986), the underlying processes through which children acquire motor skills take into account three interacting factors:

- *Aspects of the child,* such as cognitive, motor, or communication abilities or personal temperament

- *Aspects of the environment,* such as structure (e.g., space, duration, frequency), equipment (e.g., type, size, multisensory features), or instruction (e.g., use of guided instruction, prompts/praise)

- *Aspects of the motor movement tasks,* such as balance for hopping and visual tracking and hand–eye coordination for catching

Each of these aspects is addressed within the structure and content of CHAMPPS. For example, teachers model motor movements; provide guided instruction with various levels of support; implement universal design for learning (UDL) strategies by individualizing instruction, equipment, activities, and/or structure to accommodate children with diverse abilities; and provide opportunities for repeated practice of motor skills.

Informed by Professional Guidelines

As noted previously, CHAMPPS is informed by guidelines representing several leading organizations such as the National Association for Sport and Physical Education (NASPE), the National Association for the Education of Young Children (NAEYC), the Council for Exceptional Children's Division for Early Childhood (DEC), and the American Academy of Pediatrics. Examples of guidelines and recommendations from leading professional organizations that were used to inform the development of CHAMPPS are provided in Table 2.1.

Informed by Evidence-Based Practices

A critical feature of high-quality preschool motor programs is the need for them to be informed by evidence-based practices (Logan et al., 2011, 2015; Riethmuller et al., 2009). CHAMPPS meets the following key indices for preschool motor programs:

- Evidence of rigorous research that employs randomized experimental design, strong methodological quality, valid measures with the child as the unit of analysis, and demonstrated effectiveness

- Comprehensive scope and sequence linked to motor skill development theory

- An appropriate duration and intensity of physical activity levels, consistent with professional guidelines

- A family component and training component for all adults who are affiliated with the program to ensure sustainability

Table 2.1. Professional guidelines and recommendations

Organization	Recommendations for Supporting Play
National Association for the Education of Young Children (NAEYC). (2020). *Developmentally appropriate practice*. https://www.naeyc.org/sites/default/files/globally-shared/downloads/PDFs/resources/position-statements/dap-statement_0.pdf	• Play is the central teaching practice that facilitates children's development and learning. It helps children develop fine and gross motor competence, make sense of their world, interact with others, express and control their emotions, develop symbolic and problem-solving abilities, and practice emerging skills. Consistently, studies find clear links between play and success in school. • Children need daily, sustained opportunities for indoor *and* outdoor play. • Self-directed play, guided play, and playful learning, skillfully supported by early childhood educators, build academic language, deepen conceptual development, and support reflective and intentional approaches to learning—all of which add up to effective strategies for long-term success.
Council for Exceptional Children's Division for Early Childhood. (2014). *DEC recommended practices*. https://divisionearlychildhood.egnyte.com/dl/7urLPWCt5U/?	• Practitioners create environments that provide opportunities for movement and regular physical activity to maintain or improve fitness, wellness, and development across domains. • Practitioners plan for and provide the level of support, accommodations, and adaptations needed for children to access, participate, and learn within and across activities and routines. • Practitioners encourage children to initiate or sustain positive interactions with peers and adults during activities through modeling, teaching, feedback, or other types of guided support. • Practitioners promote children's cognitive development by observing, interpreting, and responding intentionally to their exploration, play, and social activity by joining in and expanding on the child's focus, actions, and intent.
Council for Exceptional Children's Division for Early Childhood (DEC) and NAEYC issued a joint position statement on early childhood inclusion: Council for Exceptional Children's Division for Early Childhood & National Association for the Education of Young Children. (2009). *Early childhood inclusion: A joint position statement of the Division for Early Childhood (DEC) and the National Association for the Education of Young Children (NAEYC)*. The University of North Carolina, FPG Child Development Institute. https://www.naeyc.org/sites/default/files/globally-shared/downloads/PDFs/resources/position-statements/ps_inclusion_dec_naeyc_ec.pdf	• Practitioners identify skills to target for instruction to help children become adaptive, competent, socially connected, and engaged. • Practitioners promote learning in natural and inclusive environments by providing the level of support, accommodations, and adaptations needed for each child to access learning within and across activities. • Practitioners use systematic instructional strategies with fidelity to teach skills and to promote child engagement and learning. • Practitioners implement the appropriate frequency, intensity, and duration of instruction needed to address each child's development and pace of learning.

Organization	Recommendations About Physical Activity
Society of Health and Physical Educators (SHAPE) America. (2020). *Active start: A statement of physical activity guidelines for children from birth to age 5* (3rd ed.). https://www.shapeamerica.org/standards/guidelines/activestart.aspx This statement can also be accessed at the following site: https://cpin.us/sites/default/files/fcab_resources/virtual/Active%20Start_2020_Final.pdf	• Preschoolers should engage in at least 60 minutes of structured physical activity per day. This can be broken down into segments lasting no more than 30–45 minutes each. During structured physical activity, caregivers should plan sessions of moderate-to-vigorous physical activity that results in an increase in heart rate and breathing. An increased heart rate will lead to these sessions sometimes lasting only 6–10 minutes long. • Preschoolers should engage in at least 60 minutes—and up to several hours—of unstructured physical activity per day and should not be sedentary for more than 60 minutes at a time, except when sleeping. This unstructured activity can be broken down into segments. • Preschoolers should develop competence in fundamental movement and motor skills that will serve as the building blocks for more advanced physical activity. • Caregivers should provide preschoolers with safe indoor and outdoor areas for performing large-muscle activities.

Table 2.1. *(continued)*

Organization	Recommendations for Supporting Play
U.S. Department of Health and Human Services. (2018). *Physical activity guidelines for Americans* (2nd ed.). https://health.gov/paguidelines/second-edition/pdf/Physical_Activity_Guidelines_2nd_edition.pdf American Academy of Pediatrics. (2020). *Making physical activity a way of life: AAP policy explained.* Healthychildren.org. https://www.healthychildren.org/English/healthy-living/fitness/Pages/Making-Fitness-a-Way-of-Life.aspx	• Preschoolers should have at least 180 minutes of physical activity throughout the day (approximately 15 minutes of every hour while awake), including 1 hour of moderate-to-vigorous activity.
National Resource Center for Health and Safety in Child Care and Early Education. https://nrckids.org/	• Preschoolers should have 90-120 minutes per 8-hour day for moderate-to-vigorous physical activity, including running. • Preschoolers should have 60-90 total minutes of outdoor play daily. The total time allotted for outdoor play and moderate-to-vigorous indoor or outdoor physical activity can be adjusted for the age group and weather conditions.
U.S. Department of Health and Human Services. (2018). *Physical activity guidelines for Americans* (2nd ed.). https://health.gov/paguidelines/second-edition/pdf/Physical_Activity_Guidelines_2nd_edition.pdf	• Preschoolers should be encouraged to move and engage in active play as well as in structured activities, such as throwing games and bicycle riding. A reasonable target may be 3 hours per day (180 minutes) of activity of all intensities: light, moderate, or vigorous intensity. • To strengthen bones, children should do activities that involve hopping, skipping, jumping, and tumbling.

INCLUDING ALL CHILDREN

This section presents additional information and guidance to help teachers implement CHAMPPS to include all children in their classroom or program. Topics discussed include

- Supporting young children's motor skill development (typical milestones for birth–5 years)

- Transitioning to small-group instruction

- Preventing and addressing challenging behaviors

- Supporting motor skill development in young children with disabilities

- Using the UDL framework

- Using prompts (verbal, nonverbal, and visual) to support motor play

Supporting Young Children's Motor Skill Development

Infants and toddlers begin learning gross and fine motor skills soon after birth. These early motor behaviors can be seen as an infant lifts their head and moves it from side to side or as a toddler stacks blocks or begins using a spoon to self-feed. CHAMPPS builds on these early skills with a focus on more advanced motor skills that emerge as children develop. Examples of some of the typical motor milestones that develop during the early childhood years are provided in Table 2.2.

Tips for Transitioning to Small-Group Instruction

During CHAMPPS lessons, children have opportunities to engage in large- and small-group motor play activities and gradually begin partnering with a peer or working independently on a motor task

Table 2.2. Typical gross and fine motor development

Age	Gross Motor or Fine Motor Skill	Explanation
Birth–3 months	Head movement	Lifts head up and turns head from side to side
	Tracking	Follows moving objects with their eyes
	Reflexes	Involuntary postures and movements
3–6 months	Rolling	Rolls from front to back and back to front
	Standing	With support
	Sitting	With support
	Pushing up from prone position	Holds chest and head up by bearing weight on hands while lying on stomach
	Reaching	Extends hands and arms toward an object
	Palmar grasp	Holds an object using the whole hand
6–12 months	Imitation	Mimics another's behavior or language independently, without support
	Sitting	Sits for brief periods of time with help getting into position, or gradually sits independently
	Crawling	Propels forward on belly
	Creeping	Crawls on hands and knees
	Kneeling	Knees rest on the floor and trunk is elevated
	Pulling to a stand	Starts pulling to stand while holding your hand or grabbing hold of furniture
	Cruising	Walks while holding onto furniture
	Standing	Independently stands, without support, momentarily
	Walking	With support
	Releasing	Opens fingers to let go of held object
	Pincer grasping	Holds an object using finger and thumb
	Transferring	Moves objects from one hand to another
	Pointing	Extends index finger, also called pointer, in direction of a person or object
12–18 months	Walking	Walks independently; wide gait
	Climbing stairs	Climbs stairs by crawling on hands and knees
	Throwing	Releases object with a slight cast
	Stacking	Stacks two to three objects
	Scribbling	Makes marks on page with little control; holds crayon with fist
	Clapping	Brings hands to midline to clap
	Drinking	Drinks from a cup independently; may spill
	Turning pages	Begins turning pages of a board book
18 months–2 years	Climbing stairs	Climbs stairs one at a time by stepping up, usually with support
	Climbing	Climbs onto/off of adult-sized furniture without assistance
	Bending	Bends over and returns to full stand without losing balance
	Turning corners	Maneuvers around corners while walking, without losing balance
	Running	—
	Stacking	Stacks four to six objects
	Turning pages	Turns multiple paper pages at a time
	Self-feeding	Grasps or scoops, bringing items to mouth; begins using spoon
	Scribbling	Makes voluntary marks on a page; holds crayon with fist

Table 2.2. *(continued)*

Age	Gross Motor or Fine Motor Skill	Explanation
2-3 years	Tiptoeing	Walks with heels raised and one's weight on the balls of the feet
	Jumping	Jumps in place, a few inches off the ground
	Climbing stairs	Climbs stairs with alternating feet
	Climbing	Climbs on jungle gyms and ladders
	Pedaling	Alternates feet while riding a bicycle/tricycle
	Balancing	Balances momentarily on one foot
	Catching	Catches object using body
	Kicking	Kicks a stationary object
	Throwing	Hurls a ball underhand
	Stacking	Stacks 7-10 objects
	Hand preference	Consistently uses same hand to manipulate objects (spoon, crayon, ball)
	Drawing	Holds item with fingers; makes controlled marks on a page; distinctive shapes visible
	Turning pages	Turns one page at a time
	Manipulation	Rolls, pounds, squeezes, and pulls/pushes manipulatives such as clay
3-4 years	Kicking	Kicks a slow-moving object
	Balancing on one foot	Balances for 5-10 seconds
	Hopping	Jumps on one foot while balancing on the other foot
	Catching	Catches using two hands
	Walking on a line	Walks placing one foot in front of the other on a sidewalk or chalk line
	Jumping	Jumps forward and/or over an object; jumps off of a low object
	Throwing	Hurls a ball overhand
	Stacking	Stacks more than 10 objects
	Cutting	Snips with scissors
	Drawing	Copies specific shapes with writing tool (crayon, pencil)
4-5 years	Dressing	Puts on socks and shoes with minimal help (e.g., shoes with zipper or Velcro closures)
	Walking backward	Walks in reverse with one foot behind the other, occasionally looking over shoulder to avoid objects
	Somersaulting (also called cartwheel)	Turns forward, moving whole body, in a complete revolution bringing the feet over the head, landing on feet
	Jumping	Jumps multiple times in a row without falling
	Throwing	Throws overhand with more accuracy and distance
	Writing	Writes name and a few letters/numbers
	Cutting	Cuts on a line with scissors

Sources: Cook et al., 2016; Kid Sense, 2015a, 2015b; Petty, 2010.

(e.g., bowling) as they progress across the units. Transitions will be easier if teachers already have an idea of which children will be in each CHAMPPS small group (or paired activity) before the lesson begins. Some teachers simply look at the whole group and spontaneously divide the group in half as they move to two different small-group activities (the children switch small-group activities after approximately 5–7 minutes). Other teachers embed an element of problem solving into the transition by posing instructions such as, "Boys go to the hurdles while girls go to the ball toss" or "Children who are wearing sandals move to the obstacle course, and children wearing sneakers go to the scarf station." It is important to consider children who might need extra time and adult support when dividing the whole group into small groups so that CHAMPPS runs smoothly and is fun and beneficial for everyone.

Tips for Preventing and Addressing Challenging Behaviors

To prevent challenging behavior, it is critical that children understand teacher expectations. Many children learn the expectations of a new setting or activity by listening to an adult give an instruction, by watching their peers, by practicing the expectations, or based on past experiences in similar situations. However, for some children, more explicit instruction and support are needed, and teachers may find it necessary to spend time carefully, clearly, and explicitly discussing how children are expected to act when given balls to toss, beanbags to carry, or other activities to perform. Teaching expectations early on during the CHAMPPS program and using simple words to describe behaviors that teachers would like to see ("hands to self," "inside voices," "soft tosses") are likely to prevent challenging behavior from occurring. Additionally, the use of UDL strategies, visual supports, and prompting strategies (all described later in this chapter), along with carefully planned transitions and enthusiasm from teachers, will result in high levels of child engagement in physical activities during CHAMPPS.

Supporting Motor Skill Development in Young Children With Disabilities

Children have unique ways of learning that reflect their diverse abilities. Prior to arranging the environment for CHAMPPS, it is important to consider the learning needs of the children who will participate in the motor program. For example, teachers should think about the characteristics of the children they teach who have disabilities and developmental delays and consider adaptations *before* starting the CHAMPPS program (see Table 2.3 for ideas about adapting activities). Teachers should remember to select adaptations *only when necessary* to support children with diverse abilities, as it is important to challenge children, not to have lower expectations of them.

Using Universal Design for Learning

The increasing numbers of young children with disabilities in inclusive preschool classes have resulted in the need to ensure that all early childhood programs incorporate the principles of UDL so *all* children have access to *all* learning opportunities, activities, and environments (Cunconan-Lahr, 2006; Horn et al., 2016). UDL strategies include *multiple means of representation* (i.e., instruction and learning activities include various formats and differences in task complexity and/or expectations in response to different ability levels); *multiple means of engagement* (i.e., a variety of ways to motivate and obtain children's attention are used in response to different learning styles, interests, and preferences); and *multiple means of expression* (i.e., a variety of response modes are used to demonstrate knowledge or skill given different ability levels) (CAST, 2018; Orkwis, 2003). Across all CHAMPPS lessons, suggestions are provided for using particular UDL strategies. In addition, teachers are encouraged to develop their own UDL strategies using a template such as the one shown in Table 2.4. The use of UDL strategies can help all children, including English language learners, children with delays and disabilities, and children who might be less confident or competent in engaging in particular gross motor activities.

Leveling of motor skill instruction is a simple and commonly used strategy to vary the motor performance expectations for children with diverse abilities (Groft & Block, 2006). For example, if a child is throwing a ball toward a target, the teacher might set up three different lines on the floor, representing three levels of distance from the target. In the same way, a teacher might vary the skill level by having various sizes of targets for children to aim toward. Another way to level a motor task is to adjust the expectations of the pattern of motor movement. As can be seen across the leveling examples in Table 2.5, a child who is just learning a skill or is less proficient may be

Table 2.3. Sample adaptations for children with diverse abilities

Disability	Setting and Structure	Equipment and Instruction
Hearing	• Minimize distractions such as music and other classroom noises. • Move to a quieter space, if needed. • Use visual signals such as a light switch (turned on/off) to gain attention or signal transition to new activity. • Use touch as a signal (e.g., lightly touch shoulder) to orient a child to a new activity.	• Use mode of communication that child uses. • If hearing aids are used, make sure that they are on. • Face child when speaking and make eye contact. • Monitor your voice; do not shout or whisper. • Demonstrate activities while giving instructions. • Use the same words (consistent language) for motor, equipment, and activities.
Vision	• If possible, use the same layout of equipment each time to support independent movement. • Use the same words (consistent language) for equipment/activities. • Walk the child around to familiarize them with the equipment and the layout. • Use touch as a signal (e.g., gentle touch on shoulder to gain attention). • If equipment, activity, or layout is new/different, introduce the new setup to the child before beginning CHAMPPS.	• Once you have established a layout for CHAMPPS, try to avoid changing the layout. • Provide clear descriptions of the layout and activities. • Use children's names and descriptive details when providing directions. • Use hand-over-hand assistance to help a child complete a movement, if needed. • Use tactile objects (e.g., beanbags, scarves) or add tactile elements (e.g., cover balls with Velcro). • Add auditory (sound) components to equipment (e.g., bells on a ball). • Enlist the help of an orientation and mobility specialist to support individualized education program (IEP) goals and strategies.
Communication	• When first setting up the environment, help the child learn the names of activities ("This is a hurdle! What is it?" "This is a balance beam! What is this called?"). This can be incorporated into a game (e.g., "I see something blue and yellow" or "I Spy"). • Label equipment with pictures of actions *and* words (e.g., a picture of a child jumping over a hurdle with the word *hurdle*). • Encourage the child to help set up and clean up, using consistent words. • Introduce first–then or visual menu of the activities for the day to help child learn the sequence of activities. • If multiple languages are used, post action words with pictures in multiple languages.	• Respond to the child's nonverbal and verbal communication (i.e., learn to recognize their body language and facial expressions). • Speak clearly with a slow pace, as needed. • Use verbal and visual cues and/or short, simple sentences and phrases. • Name and describe adult leaders' actions, in multiple languages, as needed. • Couple gestures *with* verbal directions. • Encourage the child to talk about what they are doing • Expand on what a child says, adding missing or new words ("I have a ball." "That's right, you have the blue ball."). • Praise efforts to communicate, even if they are not exactly correct. • Enlist the help of a speech-language therapist to support IEP goals and strategies.
Motor and Health	• Provide breaks to match a child's stamina. • Adjust the length and pace of activities as needed. • Provide enough space if a child uses adaptive equipment (e.g., wheelchair, walker). • Make sure the space is barrier and obstacle free. • Plan for extra time for transitions and to complete activities. • If needed, post emergency procedures and numbers for a quick response to health or medical issues.	• Ensure that all equipment is accessible. • Adapt equipment as necessary. • Use tactile objects (e.g., beanbags, scarves) or add tactile elements (e.g., cover balls with Velcro). • Modify boundaries, rules, and activities, as needed. • Enlist the help of occupational and physical therapists.

(continued)

Table 2.3. *(continued)*

Disability	Setting and Structure	Equipment and Instruction
Intellectual Ability	• Minimize distractions (e.g., extra music, noise, equipment). • Establish a consistent routine and structure. • Signal transitions (e.g., ring a bell, flicker a light, sing a song) when an activity is over. • Plan for extra time to complete activities.	• Provide instructions using short sentences or phrases. • Repeat directions, as needed. • Provide positive reinforcement (e.g., praise, high fives, clap, cheer; "Nice hopping Omeed!"). • Teach and use the same cue words or visual supports. • When possible, use the same equipment as used at home to support generalization (e.g., napkins for scarves, beach balls). • Have other children serve as role models to demonstrate activities. • Enlist the help of therapists to meet IEP goals and select the most appropriate strategies.
Attention	• Minimize visual and auditory distractions (e.g., extra music, noise, equipment). • Prepare a child for transitions from one activity to the next. • Establish a consistent routine and structure. • Provide appropriate amount of space—not too large, but not too small. • Use first-then or visual menu of the activities for the day to help a child anticipate the sequence of activities.	• Use redirection strategies when children get distracted. • Make sure the activities are varied and challenging. • Use a visual schedule (example provided later in chapter) to assist with transitions. • Provide breaks from an activity, as needed. • Have reinforcers available (child's favorite items) to maintain attention. • Enlist the help of a behavior specialist, if needed.
Social-Emotional	• Provide appropriate amount of space—not too large but not too small. • Establish a consistent, predictable routine. • Establish, post, and maintain expectations or rules in child-friendly language and with pictures. • Remove equipment that contributes to challenging behaviors. • Maintain consistency across the people who are involved.	• Provide opportunities for choice making during activities when possible. • Use a visual support schedule to assist with transitions. • Shorten or simplify activities when needed. • Teach turn taking, problem solving, and conflict management skills before situations arise. • Enlist the help of a behavior specialist to support IEP goals and select the most appropriate strategies.
Sensory and Communication Ability	• Minimize distractions (e.g., extra music, noise, equipment). • Maintain consistency across the people who are involved. • Provide a consistent structure and routine. • Provide one-on-one assistance as needed. • Plan for extra time to complete activities. • Post and use a visual schedule or menu to assist with transitions. • Post and use first-then procedures with visual prompts.	• Match the mode of communication used by the child (e.g., verbal cues, sign language, visual supports, braille). • Use brief instructions and a calm voice. • Shorten activities or allow for breaks, as needed.

Source: Brady, 2005.

Table 2.4. Universal design for learning template

	Universal Design for Learning (UDL) Strategy		
	Multiple Means of Representation	Multiple Means of Engagement	Multiple Means of Action & Expression
	Use various formats/structures within instructional and learning activities with differences in task complexity and/or expectations in response to different ability levels and different ways children learn and communicate.	Use multiple means to motivate children; obtain and maintain attention in response to different learning styles, challenges, and interests.	Plan for a variety in response modes to demonstrate skill in response to different ability levels reflecting different ways in which individuals organize and express skills and knowledge.
Activity	UDL Strategy		
Throw ball to target	Communicate using visual supports. Vary the types of prompts used.	Use sensory ball (with bell) or textured balls. Add a sound source to target. Have peers cheer for their friends. Vary target, based on child's interest and skills (e.g., tiger, truck).	Provide three distances from target. Provide three different sizes for target. Provide three sizes of balls. Provide balls with different inflation levels for easier grasping.
Two-footed jump	Hold child's hand to jump. Hold onto chair or bar to jump.	Have child jump toward or over a photo of their favorite animal, fruit, or vegetable. Have child count how many times they can jump in a row.	Place floor markers at two distances from standing position. Provide three heights on hurdle (step over, jump from a lower height, jump from a higher height).

expected to perform at one level, whereas a child who is more proficient may be challenged to perform at another level.

Using Prompts to Support Motor Play

While it is important to consider the use of cues (Buchanan & Briggs, 1998; Landin, 1994; Valentini, 2004) and prompts from a least-to-most perspective (Grow et al., 2009; Libby et al., 2008), one type of prompt that has gained popularity and demonstrated effectiveness with young children with disabilities is the use of visual supports or picture cues (Johnston et al., 2003; Massey & Wheeler, 2000; Morrison et al., 2002). For children who may benefit from seeing a picture or a visual cue of the sequence of activities for the day or for a particular activity, a picture schedule is easy to make.

Table 2.5. Examples of leveling

	Distance From Target	Size of Target	Movement Pattern
Beginner	3 feet	Large	Faces target, overhand motion
Intermediate	7 feet	Medium	Faces target, overhand motion, step and throw
Established	10 feet	Small	Side orientation, overhand motion, step and throw

Table 2.6. Prompts

Type of Prompt	Description	CHAMPPS Example
Verbal (also called verbal cue)	Direct verbal prompts tell the child what they need to do.	*Jump, Cindy!*
	Indirect verbal prompts give the child a hint about what they are expected to do.	*Time for CHAMPPS! Where do we go for Warm-Up?*
Nonverbal or gestural	Nonverbal prompts include gestures and signs that are known to the adult and the child and that cue the child about what they are expected to do.	*Time for CHAMPPS!* The teacher looks at Simon and points to his carpet square, where he should go for Warm-Up.
Visual	Visual prompts include real objects, pictures, drawings, or symbols that provide the child with a cue about what they are expected to do.	Teacher uses a visual cue, such as a Boardmaker picture, to show what is happening next.
Model	In a full model, the adult demonstrates exactly what the child is expected to say or do.	While the other children are throwing/catching scarves, the teacher models for Peter how to throw his scarf by throwing her own while explaining what she is doing (i.e., full modeled prompt).
	In a partial model, the adult demonstrates only part of the expected behavior.	Matt needs help stepping over the hurdle. The teacher looks at Matt expectantly and says the initial [h] sound (i.e., partial modeled prompt for *Help*). Matt says, "Help," and the teacher holds his hand to assist him in stepping over the hurdle.
Physical	The adult manually guides the child to perform a specific behavior.	
	• Full physical prompts: The adult provides hand-over-hand or hand-under-hand guidance to the child.	During CHAMPPS, the teacher provides hand-over-hand guidance to help Hannah catch the ball (i.e., full physical prompt).
	• Partial physical prompts: The adult partially supports and guides the child to perform a behavior.	During CHAMPPS, the teacher touches Hannah's elbow, guiding her to catch a rolled ball and bring it close to her chest (i.e., partial physical prompt).

Source: Meadan et al., 2013.

Such a schedule works best if it is made ahead of time by inserting pictures that match the sequence of the CHAMPPS activities to be completed. For children who need a simpler two-step schedule, a *first–then schedule* is ideal. To create one, a teacher prepares the first–then schedule ahead of time, with a picture of the activity in the first box and a picture of the reinforcement (or motivator) in the second box (e.g., first clean up, then outdoor play time). Another type of visual support is a *picture schedule*, which provides a sequence of multiple pictures representing the order in which several activities will occur (e.g., scarf toss, jumping game, yoga). As with the first–then schedule, it is best if the picture schedule is made ahead of time, introduced to all children at the beginning of CHAMPPS, and then placed in a location so the children and teachers may refer to it during the CHAMPPS activities (Figures 2.5A and 2.5B provide examples of a first–then schedule and a picture schedule). Table 2.6 summarizes types of prompts.

Now that you have a general idea about CHAMPPS and have been introduced to a few strategies to ensure the engagement of all children, we will look at some CHAMPPS lessons. In the next section, you will find unit lessons to begin planning CHAMPPS for the children you teach.

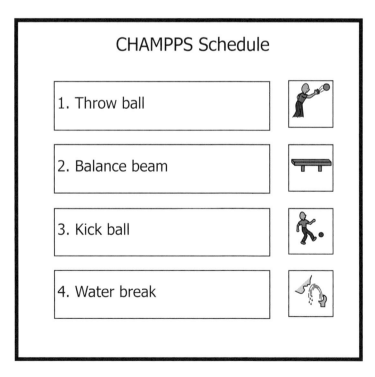

Figure 2.5. **(A)** First-then schedule. **(B)** CHAMPPS picture schedule.

Get Moving

CHAMPPS Motor Skills Units

Before you delve into the seven CHAMPPS units, it is recommended you review the information provided below. This will help you understand

- What components are included in each unit and how to use them for planning

- What teaching resources are available in this book and at the Brookes Download Hub

- How to fit CHAMPPS activities into the schedule for your learning environment

UNIT COMPONENTS AND PLANNING

Each unit begins with a Table of Contents so you can easily locate the components you need to read or review as you are planning.

Lesson Preview

Read the Lesson Preview for an overview of the unit. It includes unit objectives, key vocabulary words, and suggested time allotments for the activities. Note that key vocabulary words are shown in **bold** type here and wherever they appear in the unit.

Refer to Preparation and Materials to identify what items you'll need for each activity. This section also lists which Visual Support Cards support teaching the unit. These cards are an optional support you may use to aid children in performing specific movements or understanding related concepts such as parts of their bodies, stop and go, and so on. Whether and how you use them will depend on the abilities and support needs of the individual children you teach. If you expect to use this resource, download the PDF of Visual Support Cards at the Brookes Download Hub. Cut along the dashed lines and create the cards in advance to have on hand when you teach. You might consider laminating the cards to help with durability.

Additionally, directions and diagrams are provided that explain how to set up your room for different activities. Featured interactive movement books are listed, along with guidance for selecting videos to use for the Physical Activity: Music Video section of a lesson.

Finally, use the Planning Notes to identify concepts you will focus on, children you might pair or group together, opportunities for children to help with setup or cleanup, and so on.

Lesson Activities

The heart of each unit is a CHAMPPS lesson with a warm-up, three core activities, and a cool-down. You'll repeat the lesson six times, over the course of 2–4 weeks, to complete a unit. Starting in the second week of the unit, plan to also include brief music videos in each lesson for a period of elevated physical activity.

Repeating the lesson six times ensures children have multiple opportunities to do the motor play activities and songs so they can move and sing with confidence. However, this does not mean you have no room for variation! See the suggested Lesson Variations at the end of each unit or use these variations as a starting point to create your own lesson variations. CHAMPPS is designed to be flexible, and as you do the program, you will get a feel for what works best with the children you teach.

Each lesson activity includes

- Objectives and vocabulary to focus on in that activity

- MOVE: Motor Movements, with directions for how to guide children to do the movements. Often these directions include scripted questions or instructions for children in *italics*. Italicized words or phrases in ***color*** are from the Verbal Prompt Glossary for that unit.

- ADAPT: UDL Strategies, listing a few suggestions for using universal design for learning (UDL) within that activity

- SUPPORT: School Readiness, listing a few suggestions for building school readiness skills within that activity

Other Unit Components

Following the lesson activities are several additional unit components to aid in your planning:

- The Walk-Around Card is a summary of the lesson, with activities on one side and songs on the other. It is designed for you to keep on hand for quick reference during CHAMPPS activities. Photocopy this page from the book and laminate it, or visit the Brookes Download Hub to obtain a printable, reproducible copy.

- The Glossary of Verbal Prompts lists words and phrases, shown in ***color,*** to use when you direct children to do different movements. Also included are examples of how to work these words and phrases into your verbal instructions and modeling. The wording of these examples is not a script; you do not need to follow it exactly. Rather, the idea is that you will emphasize the colored prompts in your verbal instructions and repeat them often. That way, children quickly learn the associated movements and key vocabulary, such as knowing to spread their arms wide when they are told to "Make ***airplane arms***."

- The UDL Suggestions charts list extensive ideas for providing multiple means of engagement, representation, and action and expression within each lesson activity

- The School Readiness Skill Support charts provide detailed suggestions for building school readiness support into the lesson activities across six areas—language and literacy, mathematics, science, motor, social and emotional, and approaches to learning.

- The Lesson Variations lists provide suggestions for varying specific lesson activities, organized in categories such as music and dance, sports and games, and arts and crafts.

Finally, each unit concludes with a Home Activities component you can reproduce and send home to families. That way, family members can do simple activities at home with children that reinforce what they are learning in CHAMPPS.

OTHER TEACHING RESOURCES FOR CHAMPPS

Besides the resources included within each unit, CHAMPPS includes other teaching resources within this book and online.

Within the Book

Section III of this book, Additional Resources, includes several resources you may find helpful in implementing CHAMPPS. The most extensive of these is the Skill Leveling Guide, organized by the same motor skills featured in the seven CHAMPPS units. You can use this guide to determine a child's skill level for a given movement, such as running, and tailor your instruction to meet them where they are.

- Use the Skill Leveling charts to determine if the child is doing a movement at a beginner, intermediate, or established level.

- Use the What to Emphasize charts to identify and teach subskills, such as pushing off the balls of one's feet when running.

- Use the Resources and References lists to identify print and online resources that may help you in teaching a given skill.

The Skill Leveling Guide is followed by guidance for selecting materials, books, videos, and other materials you may use when implementing CHAMPPS.

Online

Visit the Brookes Download Hub for unit resources you can download, print, and reproduce. These include the same Walk-Around Cards featured in the book, along with an 8.5- × 11-inch wall poster for each unit and a PDF of the Visual Support Cards. Also included are the sample 21- and 28-week teaching schedules shown below, along with additional sample schedules for teaching CHAMPPS.

SAMPLE UNIT SCHEDULES

Each of the seven CHAMPPS units includes a lesson to be repeated six times with minor variations, a home component to be completed weekly, and activities for review days. (Review days are optional; if you wish to include them, plan on two per unit.)

Use the sample schedules to plan how you will allot instructional time for each CHAMPPS unit. Depending on how often children do CHAMPPS and whether you include review days, a unit will typically take 3 or 4 weeks to complete. The schedules that follow are based on doing CHAMPPS twice per week.

Sample Schedule 1: CHAMPPS two times per week, no review days (3 Weeks/Unit)

	Day 1 (30 minutes) Wednesday	Day 2 (30 minutes) Friday	Home Activities Friday
CHAMPPS Sample Schedule **21-Week Program:** **Seven Units With Six Repeated Lessons (2 Days/Week)**			
UNIT 1 Foundational Skills: Body Awareness, Motor Imitation, and Visual Tracking			
Week 1 **Date:**	Lesson 1 • Warm-Up • Core Activities 1, 2, and 3 • Cool-Down	Lesson 2 • Warm-Up • Core Activities 1, 2, and 3 • Cool-Down	• Warm-Up • Core Activity 1 • Cool-Down
Week 2 **Date:**	Lesson 3 • Warm-Up • Core Activities 1, 2, and 3 • Video 1 • Cool-Down	Lesson 4 • Warm-Up • Core Activities 1, 2, and 3 • Video 2 • Cool-Down	• Warm-Up • Core Activity 2 • Cool-Down
Week 3 **Date:**	Lesson 5 • Warm-Up • Core Activities 1, 2, and 3 • Videos 1 and/or 2 • Cool-Down	Lesson 6 • Warm-Up • Core Activities 1, 2, and 3 • Videos 1 and/or 2 • Cool-Down	• Warm-Up • Core Activity 3 • Cool-Down
UNIT 2 Walking and Running			
Week 4 **Date:**	Lesson 1 • Warm-Up • Core Activities 1, 2, and 3 • Cool-Down	Lesson 2 • Warm-Up • Core Activities 1, 2, and 3 • Cool-Down	• Warm-Up • Core Activity 1 • Cool-Down
Week 5 **Date:**	Lesson 3 • Warm-Up • Core Activities 1, 2, and 3 • Video 1 • Cool-Down	Lesson 4 • Warm-Up • Core Activities 1, 2, and 3 • Video 2 • Cool-Down	• Warm-Up • Core Activity 2 • Cool-Down
Week 6 **Date:**	Lesson 5 • Warm-Up • Core Activities 1, 2, and 3 • Videos 1 and/or 2 • Cool-Down	Lesson 6 • Warm-Up • Core Activities 1, 2, and 3 • Videos 1 and/or 2 • Cool-Down	• Warm-Up • Core Activity 3 • Cool-Down
UNIT 3 Balance, Jumping, and Hopping			
Week 7 **Date:**	Lesson 1 • Warm-Up • Core Activities 1, 2, and 3 • Cool-Down	Lesson 2 • Warm-Up • Core Activities 1, 2, and 3 • Cool-Down	• Warm-Up • Core Activity 1 • Cool-Down

	Day 1 (30 minutes) Wednesday	Day 2 (30 minutes) Friday	Home Activities Friday
Week 8 Date:	Lesson 3 • Warm-Up • Core Activities 1, 2, and 3 • Video 1 • Cool-Down	Lesson 4 • Warm-Up • Core Activities 1, 2, and 3 • Video 2 • Cool-Down	• Warm-Up • Core Activity 2 • Cool-Down
Week 9 Date:	Lesson 5 • Warm-Up • Core Activities 1, 2, and 3 • Videos 1 and/or 2 • Cool-Down	Lesson 6 • Warm-Up • Core Activities 1, 2, and 3 • Videos 1 and/or 2 • Cool-Down	• Warm-Up • Core Activity 3 • Cool-Down
UNIT 4 Catching			
Week 10 Date:	Lesson 1 • Warm-Up • Core Activities 1, 2, and 3 • Cool-Down	Lesson 2 • Warm-Up • Core Activities 1, 2, and 3 • Cool-Down	• Warm-Up • Core Activity 1 • Cool-Down
Week 11 Date:	Lesson 3 • Warm-Up • Core Activities 1, 2, and 3 • Video 1 • Cool-Down	Lesson 4 • Warm-Up • Core Activities 1, 2, and 3 • Video 2 • Cool-Down	• Warm-Up • Core Activity 2 • Cool-Down
Week 12 Date:	Lesson 5 • Warm-Up • Core Activities 1, 2, and 3 • Videos 1 and/or 2 • Cool-Down	Lesson 6 • Warm-Up • Core Activities 1, 2, and 3 • Videos 1 and/or 2 • Cool-Down	• Warm-Up • Core Activity 3 • Cool-Down
UNIT 5 Throwing			
Week 13 Date:	Lesson 1 • Warm-Up • Core Activities 1, 2, and 3 • Cool-Down	Lesson 2 • Warm-Up • Core Activities 1, 2, and 3 • Cool-Down	• Warm-Up • Core Activity 1 • Cool-Down
Week 14 Date:	Lesson 3 • Warm-Up • Core Activities 1, 2, and 3 • Video 1 • Cool-Down	Lesson 4 • Warm-Up • Core Activities 1, 2, and 3 • Video 2 • Cool-Down	• Warm-Up • Core Activity 2 • Cool-Down
Week 15 Date:	Lesson 5 • Warm-Up • Core Activities 1, 2, and 3 • Videos 1 and/or 2 • Cool-Down	Lesson 6 • Warm-Up • Core Activities 1, 2, and 3 • Videos 1 and/or 2 • Cool-Down	• Warm-Up • Core Activity 3 • Cool-Down

CHAMPPS: CHildren in Action Motor Program for PreschoolerS by Paddy C. Favazza and
Michaelene M. Ostrosky with Melissa Stalega, Hsiu-Wen Yang, Katherine Aronson-Ensign, Martin Block,
W. Catherine Cheung, and Yusuf Akemoglu. Copyright © 2023 by Paul H. Brookes Publishing Co., Inc. All rights reserved.

	Day 1 (30 minutes) Wednesday	Day 2 (30 minutes) Friday	Home Activities Friday
UNIT 6 Striking			
Week 16 Date:	Lesson 1 • Warm-Up • Core Activities 1, 2, and 3 • Cool-Down	Lesson 2 • Warm-Up • Core Activities 1, 2, and 3 • Cool-Down	• Warm-Up • Core Activity 1 • Cool-Down
Week 17 Date:	Lesson 3 • Warm-Up • Core Activities 1, 2, and 3 • Video 1 • Cool-Down	Lesson 4 • Warm-Up • Core Activities 1, 2, and 3 • Video 2 • Cool-Down	• Warm-Up • Core Activity 2 • Cool-Down
Week 18 Date:	Lesson 5 • Warm-Up • Core Activities 1, 2, and 3 • Videos 1 and/or 2 • Cool-Down	Lesson 6 • Warm-Up • Core Activities 1, 2, and 3 • Videos 1 and/or 2 • Cool-Down	• Warm-Up • Core Activity 3 • Cool-Down
UNIT 7 Kicking			
Week 19 Date:	Lesson 1 • Warm-Up • Core Activities 1, 2, and 3 • Cool-Down	Lesson 2 • Warm-Up • Core Activities 1, 2, and 3 • Cool-Down	• Warm-Up • Core Activity 1 • Cool-Down
Week 20 Date:	Lesson 3 • Warm-Up • Core Activities 1, 2, and 3 • Video 1 • Cool-Down	Lesson 4 • Warm-Up • Core Activities 1, 2, and 3 • Video 2 • Cool-Down	• Warm-Up • Core Activity 2 • Cool-Down
Week 21 Date:	Lesson 5 • Warm-Up • Core Activities 1, 2, and 3 • Videos 1 and/or 2 • Cool-Down	Lesson 6 • Warm-Up • Core Activities 1, 2, and 3 • Videos 1 and/or 2 • Cool-Down	• Warm-Up • Core Activity 3 • Cool-Down

Sample Schedule 2: CHAMPPS two times per week, with review days (4 Weeks/Unit)

CHAMPPS Sample Schedule 28-Week Program: Seven Units With Six Repeated Lessons (2 Days/Week) Plus Review Days		
UNIT 1 Foundational Skills: Body Awareness, Motor Imitation, and Visual Tracking		
	Day 1 (30 minutes) **Wednesday**	**Day 2 (30 minutes)** **Friday**	**Home Activities** **Friday**
Week 1 Date:	Lesson 1 • Warm-Up • Core Activities 1, 2, and 3 • Cool-Down	Lesson 2 • Warm-Up • Core Activities 1, 2, and 3 • Cool-Down	• Warm-Up • Core Activity 1 • Cool-Down
Week 2 Date:	Lesson 3 • Warm-Up • Core Activities 1, 2, and 3 • Video 1 • Cool-Down	Review Day • Address motor skills that are challenging for the group OR work with individual children. • Read interactive motor books or play video.	• Warm-Up • Core Activity 2 • Cool-Down
Week 3 Date:	Lesson 4 • Warm-Up • Core Activities 1, 2, and 3 • Video 2 • Cool-Down	Lesson 5 • Warm-Up • Core Activities 1, 2, and 3 • Videos 1 and/or 2 • Cool-Down	• Warm-Up • Core Activity 3 • Cool-Down
Week 4 Date:	Lesson 6 • Warm-Up • Core Activities 1, 2, and 3 • Videos 1 and/or 2 • Cool-Down	Review Day • Address motor skills that are challenging for the group OR work with individual children. • Read interactive motor books or play video.	Home Component Parents and child choose which CHAMPPS activities to do at home.
UNIT 2 Walking and Running		
Week 5 Date:	Lesson 1 • Warm-Up • Core Activities 1, 2, and 3 • Cool-Down	Lesson 2 • Warm-Up • Core Activities 1, 2, and 3 • Cool-Down	• Warm-Up • Core Activity 1 • Cool-Down
Week 6 Date:	Lesson 3 • Warm-Up • Core Activities 1, 2, and 3 • Video 1 • Cool-Down	Review Day • Address motor skills that are challenging for the group OR work with individual children. • Read interactive motor books or play video.	• Warm-Up • Core Activity 2 • Cool-Down
Week 7 Date:	Lesson 4 • Warm-Up • Core Activities 1, 2, and 3 • Video 2 • Cool-Down	Lesson 5 • Warm-Up • Core Activities 1, 2, and 3 • Videos 1 and/or 2 • Cool-Down	• Warm-Up • Core Activity 3 • Cool-Down

	Day 1 (30 minutes) Wednesday	Day 2 (30 minutes) Friday	Home Activities Friday
Week 8 Date:	Lesson 6 • Warm-Up • Core Activities 1, 2, and 3 • Videos 1 and/or 2 • Cool-Down	Review Day • Address motor skills that are challenging for the group OR work with individual children. • Read interactive motor books or play video.	Home Component Parents and child choose which CHAMPPS activities to do at home.
Unit 3 Balance, Jumping, and Hopping			
Week 9 Date:	Lesson 1 • Warm-Up • Core Activities 1, 2, and 3 • Cool-Down	Lesson 2 • Warm-Up • Core Activities 1, 2, and 3 • Cool-Down	• Warm-Up • Core Activity 1 • Cool-Down
Week 10 Date:	Lesson 3 • Warm-Up • Core Activities 1, 2, and 3 • Video 1 • Cool-Down	Review Day • Address motor skills that are challenging for the group OR work with individual children. • Read interactive motor books or play video.	• Warm-Up • Core Activity 2 • Cool-Down
Week 11 Date:	Lesson 4 • Warm-Up • Core Activities 1, 2, and 3 • Video 2 • Cool-Down	Lesson 5 • Warm-Up • Core Activities 1, 2, and 3 • Videos 1 and/or 2 • Cool-Down	• Warm-Up • Core Activity 3 • Cool-Down
Week 12 Date:	Lesson 6 • Warm-Up • Core Activities 1, 2, and 3 • Videos 1 and/or 2 • Cool-Down	Review Day • Address motor skills that are challenging for the group OR work with individual children. • Read interactive motor books or play video.	Home Component Parents and child choose which CHAMPPS activities to do at home.
UNIT 4 Catching			
Week 13 Date:	Lesson 1 • Warm-Up • Core Activities 1, 2, and 3 • Cool-Down	Lesson 2 • Warm-Up • Core Activities 1, 2, and 3 • Cool-Down	• Warm-Up • Core Activity 1 • Cool-Down
Week 14 Date:	Lesson 3 • Warm-Up • Core Activities 1, 2, and 3 • Video 1 • Cool-Down	Review Day • Address motor skills that are challenging for the group OR work with individual children. • Read interactive motor books or play video.	• Warm-Up • Core Activity 2 • Cool-Down

	Day 1 (30 minutes) Wednesday	Day 2 (30 minutes) Friday	Home Activities Friday
Week 15 Date:	Lesson 4 • Warm-Up • Core Activities 1, 2, and 3 • Video 2 • Cool-Down	Lesson 5 • Warm-Up • Core Activities 1, 2, and 3 • Videos 1 and/or 2 • Cool-Down	• Warm-Up • Core Activity 3 • Cool-Down
Week 16 Date:	Lesson 6 • Warm-Up • Core Activities 1, 2, and 3 • Videos 1 and/or 2 • Cool-Down	Review Day • Address motor skills that are challenging for the group OR work with individual children. • Read interactive motor books or play video.	Home Component Parents and child choose which CHAMPPS activities to do at home.
UNIT 5 Throwing			
Week 17 Date:	Lesson 1 • Warm-Up • Core Activities 1, 2, and 3 • Cool-Down	Lesson 2 • Warm-Up • Core Activities 1, 2, and 3 • Cool-Down	• Warm-Up • Core Activity 1 • Cool-Down
Week 18 Date:	Lesson 3 • Warm-Up • Core Activities 1, 2, and 3 • Video 1 • Cool-Down	Review Day • Address motor skills that are challenging for the group OR work with individual children. • Read interactive motor books or play video.	• Warm-Up • Core Activity 2 • Cool-Down
Week 19 Date:	Lesson 4 • Warm-Up • Core Activities 1, 2, and 3 • Video 2 • Cool-Down	Lesson 5 • Warm-Up • Core Activities 1, 2, and 3 • Videos 1 and/or 2 • Cool-Down	• Warm-Up • Core Activity 3 • Cool-Down
Week 20 Date:	Lesson 6 • Warm-Up • Core Activities 1, 2, and 3 • Videos 1 and/or 2 • Cool-Down	Review Day • Address motor skills that are challenging for the group OR work with individual children. • Read interactive motor books or play video.	Home Component Parents and child choose which CHAMPPS activities to do at home
UNIT 6 Striking			
Week 21 Date:	Lesson 1 • Warm-Up • Core Activities 1, 2, and 3 • Cool-Down	Lesson 2 • Warm-Up • Core Activities 1, 2, and 3 • Cool-Down	• Warm-Up • Core Activity 1 • Cool-Down

	Day 1 (30 minutes) Wednesday	Day 2 (30 minutes) Friday	Home Activities Friday
Week 22 **Date:**	Lesson 3 • Warm-Up • Core Activities 1, 2, and 3 • Video 1 • Cool-Down	Review Day • Address motor skills that are challenging for the group OR work with individual children. • Read interactive motor books or play video.	• Warm-Up • Core Activity 2 • Cool-Down
Week 23 **Date:**	Lesson 4 • Warm-Up • Core Activities 1, 2, and 3 • Video 2 • Cool-Down	Lesson 5 • Warm-Up • Core Activities 1, 2, and 3 • Videos 1 and/or 2 • Cool-Down	• Warm-Up • Core Activity 3 • Cool-Down
Week 24 **Date:**	Lesson 6 • Warm-Up • Core Activities 1, 2, and 3 • Videos 1 and/or 2 • Cool-Down	Review Day • Address motor skills that are challenging for the group OR work with individual children. • Read interactive motor books or play video.	Home Component Parents and child choose which CHAMPPS activities to do at home.
	**UNIT 7 Kicking**		
Week 25 **Date:**	Lesson 1 • Warm-Up • Core Activities 1, 2, and 3 • Cool-Down	Lesson 2 • Warm-Up • Core Activities 1, 2, and 3 • Cool-Down	• Warm-Up • Core Activity 1 • Cool-Down
Week 26 **Date:**	Lesson 3 • Warm-Up • Core Activities 1, 2, and 3 • Video 1 • Cool-Down	Review Day • Address motor skills that are challenging for the group OR work with individual children. • Read interactive motor books or play video.	• Warm-Up • Core Activity 2 • Cool-Down
Week 27 **Date:**	Lesson 4 • Warm-Up • Core Activities 1, 2, and 3 • Video 2 • Cool-Down	Lesson 5 • Warm-Up • Core Activities 1, 2, and 3 • Videos 1 and/or 2 • Cool-Down	• Warm-Up • Core Activity 3 • Cool-Down
Week 28 **Date:**	Lesson 6 • Warm-Up • Core Activities 1, 2, and 3 • Videos 1 and/or 2 • Cool-Down	Review Day • Address motor skills that are challenging for the group OR work with individual children. • Read interactive motor books or play video.	Home Component Parents and child choose which CHAMPPS activities to do at home.

Visit the Brookes Download Hub for additional sample schedules.

Foundational Skills

CHAMPPS

UNIT 1

Body Awareness, Motor Imitation, and Visual Tracking

Unit Objectives

1. **Motor Movement.** Become familiar with these movement concepts: stretching, walking, running, grasp and release, jumping, balance, and kicking.

2. **Body Awareness.** Identify and move head, shoulders, waist, arms, legs, knees, hands, feet, heels, and toes.

3. **Personal Space.** Share space with peers and stay on own floor marker.

4. **Motor Imitation.** Imitate or copy a movement modeled by teacher.

5. **Visual Tracking.** Throw, watch, and catch scarf.

6. **Sustained Physical Activity.** Engage in continuous movement during music video.

Key Vocabulary

Body Parts	**arms, feet, hands, head, hips, knees, legs, shoulders, toes**
Motor Movement	**balance, catch, fly, gallop, hold, jog, jump, kick, leap, march, run, shake, squeeze, stomp, stretch, throw, tiptoe, walk, watch**
Concepts	**cool-down, personal space, warm-up**
Pre-academic	Animals: **bird, cheetah, elephant, frog, horse, mouse**
	Habitats: **barn, desert, hut, lily pad, mouse hole, nest**
	Animal noises: **neigh, ribbit, roar, squeak, trumpet, tweet**
	Other: **heart rate**
Social-Emotional	**happy, hot, sad, sweaty, thirsty, tired**

UNIT LESSON

Time	Activity	Focus		
3–5 min	WARM-UP	Gathering	Increase Heart Rate	Warm-Up Muscles
5 min	CORE 1: **Popcorn Kernels**	Motor Movement		Visual Tracking
5 min	CORE 2: **Follow Me Home**	Motor Movement	Personal Space	Motor Imitation
5 min	CORE 3: **Simon Says**		Body Awareness	
2–4 min	PHYSICAL ACTIVITY: Music Video (Lessons 3–6 only)	Motor Imitation & Sustained Physical Activity		
3 min	COOL-DOWN	Gathering	Decrease Heart Rate	Cool-Down Muscles

PREPARATION AND MATERIALS

Activity	Materials (class of 15 children with 2 adults)
WARM-UP COOL-DOWN Whole Group	Floor markers (1 per person)
CORE 1 **Popcorn Kernels** Whole Group	Numbered floor markers Scarves (1–2 per person)
CORE 2 **Follow Me Home** Whole group	Numbered floor markers Bell Animal picture cards
CORE 3 **Simon Says** Whole group	Numbered floor markers Scarves (1–2 per person) Animal picture cards

Visual Support Cards

Used for these movements: stand, stand in circle, sit, lift your arms, stretch arms, touch toes, wave scarf, grasp scarf, shake scarf, throw scarf, watch scarf, flap wings, fly, jog in place, airplane arms, air kicks, bend and stretch, touch toes, hug knees, wave hand.

Visit the Brookes Download Hub to download and print the Visual Support Cards for Unit 1.

SETUP

1. Place floor markers in a circle or square arm's length apart.
2. Place scarves in the middle of the circle or square for easy access. See Figure U1.1.

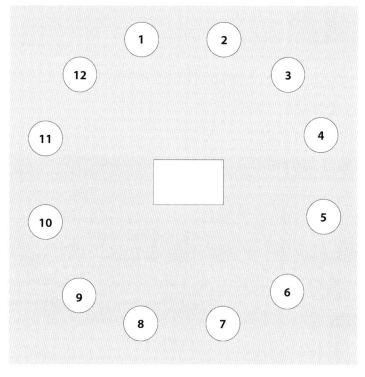

Figure U1.1. Classroom setup for Unit 1 warm-up, core activities, and cool-down.

Featured Interactive Movement Books

- *Hop, Hop, Jump!*, written by Lauren Thompson and illustrated by Jarrett J. Krosoczka. Margaret K. McElderry Books, 2012.
- *Dancing Feet!*, written by Lindsey Craig and illustrated by Marc Brown. Knopf Books for Young Readers, 2012.
- *From Head to Toe*, written and illustrated by Eric Carle. HarperFestival, 1999.

Video Content

For this unit, you will need to select two music videos, each approximately 2–4 minutes long, illustrating the following: imitating motor movements such as stretching, jumping, and twisting.

See the recommended list of video sources on Page 265 and the criteria for video selection on Page 266.

BEFORE YOU START

1. Read through the unit. In particular, read through all of the lesson activities. Visualize the space where you will have CHAMPPS and how you will implement each activity with the children with whom you work.

2. Identify the school readiness skills you will focus on in each lesson activity; school readiness skills should correspond to your core curriculum.

3. Identify universal design for learning (UDL) strategies and adaptations to use for particular activities and/or to support individual children. For example, download the visual supports for use with the lesson prior to starting.

4. Review the lesson variations to determine which you will use, if needed.

5. Plan ahead for how you will shorten the lesson, if needed (see below).

6. Complete the Planning Notes.

If you need to shorten the lesson:
Depending on the needs of the children you teach, you may choose to shorten the lesson on the first day or first two days of Unit 1 to allow children to get used to the CHAMPPS routine. For example, you could do the Warm-Up with the song, one or two core activities, and the Cool-Down with the song. Then, on the third day, you could add the third core activity.

UNIT 1 PLANNING NOTES

Motor movements to focus on:

Vocabulary to focus on:

Children who will be positioned near an adult for additional support and attention:

Children who will help with setup:

Children who will help with cleanup:

■ WARM-UP

Structure: Whole group

Get ready! Focus on:
- Gathering
- Increasing heart rate
- Warming up muscles

Total time: 3–5 minutes

Key Vocabulary:
- arms, feet, hot, jog, legs, march, personal space, stretch, sweaty, tired, walk, warm-up

1. MOVE: Motor Movements

Have children start on their floor marker, warming up their bodies while singing the "CHAMPPS Warm-Up Song" with each movement you model. Verbal prompts are provided below, if needed.

- Have children **walk** in a circle. Say: *Step one foot forward. **Heel first, then toe. Swing your arms** forward and backward.*
- Have children **march** in a circle. Say: *Step with **high knees.** Hold your arms straight in front. **Touch your knees to your hands.***
- Have children **jog** in a circle. Say: *A jog is a **slow run.** Move your legs quickly, keep your **head up,** and **pump your arms** forward and back.*
- Have children **stretch** on their floor marker. Say: *Raise your **arms up** to the ceiling. Now bend down and **touch your toes.***

2. ADAPT: UDL Strategies

Adapt the activity to meet the needs of the children with whom you work. See the suggestions in the following table; for additional ways to adapt, use the UDL Suggestions for Unit 1.

Engagement	Representation	Action & Expression
Give children choices. Ask children to choose the next warm-up movement(s).	• Use verbal prompts to encourage movement. See the Glossary of Verbal Prompts. • Use visual supports. See Visual Support Cards for stand, stand in circle, sit, lift your arms, stretch arms, touch toes.	Encourage children to sing along. Give children the option to hum or clap to the melody/rhythm.

3. SUPPORT: School Readiness

Choose one to three school readiness skills to focus on. See the suggestions in the following table; for additional ways to support school readiness, turn to Page 50.

Language	Mathematics	Approaches to Learning
• Encourage children to sing along. • Have children listen for verbal prompts. • Have children identify body parts.	• Use ordinal language (*first, second, third*) with children.	• Create a smooth transition between activities. • Have children follow directions. • Guide children to remain focused and continue moving. • Encourage whole-group engagement.

4. LESSON VARIATIONS

If children learn these activities quickly and need no further practice, or if you want to vary activities for review days, see Lesson Variations on Page 56.

■ CORE ACTIVITY 1: **Popcorn Kernels**

Structure: Whole group

Focus on these objectives:
- Motor movement: Grasp and release
- Visual tracking

Total time: 3–5 minutes

Key Vocabulary:
- catch, hands, hold, personal space, shake, squeeze, throw, watch

---

1. MOVE: Motor Movements

Have children stand on their floor marker. Have available one or two scarves per person.

Make "popping popcorn." Sing "Popcorn Kernels" as children complete the movements.

- Have children **hold** their scarves and wave scarf from side to side.
- Have children **squeeze** their scarves into a ball in front of chest.
- Have children **shake** their scarves up and down with both hands.
- Have children **throw** their scarves up, **watch** them fall, and **catch** their scarf with two **hands.** See Figure U1.2.

| wave scarf | squeeze scarf | shake scarf | throw, watch, catch |

Figure U1.2. Activities with scarves: grasp scarf, wave scarf, shake scarf, throw scarf, and watch scarf. (See also the Visual Support Cards for Unit 1.)

2. ADAPT: UDL Strategies

Adapt the activity to meet the needs of the children with whom you work. See the suggestions in the following table; for additional ways to adapt, use the UDL Suggestions for Unit 1.

Engagement	Representation	Action & Expression
• Challenge children by varying complexity. Have them catch with one hand, knee, foot, or elbow or on their head. • Provide children choices, praise, and encouragement.	• Use verbal prompts to encourage movement. See the Glossary of Verbal Prompts. • Use visual supports. See Visual Support Cards for stand, stand in circle, sit, wave scarf, grasp scarf, shake scarf, throw scarf, and watch scarf. • Define or model vocabulary as needed.	Have children raise the scarf in the air and then touch the scarf to a body part instead of throwing and catching it.

3. SUPPORT: School Readiness

Choose one to three school readiness skills to focus on. See the suggestions in the following table; for additional ways to support school readiness, turn to Page 50.

Language	Mathematics	Approaches to Learning
• Encourage sing-along. • Have children listen for verbal prompts. • Have children identify body parts. • Encourage active discussion about favorite movement or identifying objects in the room that match the color of their scarf.	• Use positional words (*up, down, above, below, side to side*) with children. • Use ordinal language (*first, second, third*) with children. • Counting: Have children count while moving. • Recognize numbers: Boys hop to 3, girls hop to 7.	• Have children follow directions. • Guide children to remain focused and continue moving. • Encourage whole-group engagement.

4. LESSON VARIATIONS

If children learn these activities quickly and need no further practice, or if you want to vary activities for review days, see Lesson Variations on Page 56.

■ CORE ACTIVITY 2: **Follow Me Home**

Structure: Whole group

Focus on these objectives:
• Motor movement: Locomotion
• Personal space
• Motor imitation

Total time: 3-5 minutes

Key Vocabulary:
• **arms, feet, knees, legs**
• **bird, cheetah, elephant, frog, horse, mouse**
• **fly, gallop, leap, run, stomp, tiptoe**
• **barn, desert, hut, lily pad, mouse hole, nest**
• **neigh, ribbit, roar, squeak, trumpet, tweet**

1. MOVE: Motor Movements

Have children stand on their floor marker. Show an animal picture card. Ask: *What animal is this? What sound does it make? How does it move? Where is the animal's habitat?*

Model the animal's sound and movement and have children imitate as they move around the circle. After each animal, ring the bell and say: *Dinner time!* Then have children return to their floor marker.

• Mouse: Say: *Tiptoe in a circle. **Squeak.** Return to the* **mouse hole.**
• Elephant: Say: *Stomp with giant steps in a circle. **Trumpet.** Return to the* **hut.**
• Horse: Say: *Gallop in a circle. **Neigh.** Return to the* **barn.**
• Frog: Say: *Leap in a circle. **Ribbit.** Return to the* **lily pad.**
• Bird: Say: *Fly by walking and flapping your arms. **Tweet.** Return to the* **nest.**
• Cheetah: Say: *Run in a circle. **Roar.** Return to the* **desert.**

2. ADAPT: UDL Strategies

Adapt the activity to meet the needs of the children with whom you work. See the suggestions in the following table; for additional ways to adapt, use the UDL Suggestions for Unit 1.

Engagement	Representation	Action & Expression
Give children choices. Ask children to 1) choose a unique animal and 2) model and imitate the animal's movement and sound.	Use visual supports. See Visual Support Cards for stand, stand in circle, sit, flap wings, and fly.	• Provide option for children to move in place instead of moving around the circle. • Provide option for doing sound or movement only, partial movement, or one animal at a time.

3. SUPPORT: School Readiness

Choose one to three school readiness skills to focus on. See the suggestions in the following table; for additional ways to support school readiness, turn to Page 50.

Language	Mathematics	Science	Approaches to Learning
Ask questions about animals: *What is your favorite animal, animal movement, or animal sound?* *Can you imitate the sounds made by a horse? Frog? Bird? Mouse?*	• Have children categorize and sort animals: *Which animals live in water? Live on land? Fly? Have four legs? Have two legs?* • Have children count when they gallop like a horse, when they leap like a frog, or when they flap their wings (arms) like a bird.	• Have children imitate animal sounds and movements. • Have children identify foods different animals eat. • Have children match animal to their habitat.	• Create a smooth transition and focused attention by using signals (clap, blink lights, ring bell). • Provide prompt/praise to encourage children to listen and follow directions during whole-group activity.

4. LESSON VARIATIONS

If children learn these activities quickly and need no further practice, or if you want to vary activities for review days, see Lesson Variations on Page 56.

■ CORE ACTIVITY 3: **Simon Says**

Structure: Whole group
Focus on these objectives:
- Body movement
- Body awareness
- Motor imitation

Total time: 3–5 minutes
Key Vocabulary:
- balance, jog, jump, kick, march, walk
- hands, head, hips, knees, legs, shoulders

1. MOVE: Motor Movements

Have children stand on their floor marker. Play Simon Says. Say: *Simon says _____.* Model the action. Have children imitate and repeat what you said (echo).

Use the following actions to focus on body movement and/or body awareness.

Body Movement

- Say: *Let's **walk** (in place). Alternate steps. **Swing arms.***
- Say: *Let's **march** (in place). Step with **high knees. Swing arms.***
- Say: *Let's **jog** (in place). Quick feet. **Pump arms.***
- Say: *Let's **jump** (up and down). **Bend** knees. **Feet together. Push up.***
- Say: *Let's **balance** (on one foot). Lift one foot. Hold **airplane arms** out to balance. Count to five.*
- Say: *Let's **kick.** Lift one foot. **Kick** out. Feet together. Repeat with other foot.*

Body Awareness

- **Hands:** Wave, clap.
- **Head:** Touch, shake head.
- **Shoulders:** Touch, shrug shoulders up/down.
- **Knees:** Touch, bend, wiggle.
- **Legs:** Touch, shake.
- **Hips:** Touch, shake side to side.

2. ADAPT: UDL Strategies

Adapt the activity to meet the needs of the children with whom you work. See the suggestions in the following table; for additional ways to adapt, use the UDL Suggestions for Unit 1.

Engagement	Representation	Action & Expression
Vary setup to allow child leadership. Choose a child to be "Simon."	• Use verbal prompts to describe movement. See the Glossary of Verbal Prompts. • Use visual supports. See Visual Support Cards for stand, stand in circle, sit, jog in place, airplane arms, and air kicks.	Have children verbally repeat (echo) what "Simon" says.

3. SUPPORT: School Readiness

Choose one to three school readiness skills to focus on. See the suggestions in the following table; for additional ways to support school readiness, turn to Page 50.

Language	Approaches to Learning	Mathematics
• Have children repeat (echo). • Have children identify body parts.	• Provide prompts and praise to encourage children to listen and follow directions. • Create a smooth transition and focused attention by using signals (*clap, blink lights, ring bell*).	• Use ordinal numbers: Add up to three consecutive moves (e.g., *first clap, second jump*). • Create a movement pattern (*walk backward five steps, forward five steps*).

4. LESSON VARIATIONS

If children learn these activities quickly and need no further practice, or if you want to vary activities for review days, see Lesson Variations on Page 56.

■ PHYSICAL ACTIVITY: **Music Video**

Structure: Whole group

Focus on this objective:
Sustained physical activity

Total time: 2-4 minutes

Key Vocabulary:
• **heart rate, hot, sweaty, thirsty, tired**

1. MOVE: Motor Movements

Have children stand on their floor marker. Spread out for enough space for floor movement. Say: ***Arms out. Make wide, airplane arms. Make sure you are not touching a friend.***

Have children move to the music video you selected.

Lesson	Video	Total Time
3	Video 1: Shaking and moving	2 minutes
4	Video 2: Standing up and sitting down	3 minutes
5	Video 1 and/or Video 2	4 minutes
6		

2. ADAPT: UDL Strategies

Adapt the activity to meet the needs of the children with whom you work. See the suggestions in the following table; for additional ideas to adapt, use the UDL Suggestions for Unit 1.

Engagement	Representation	Action & Expression
Provide specific praise and encouragement (e.g., *I love your dance moves!* Or *Excellent job, keep moving!*) • Provide children with choices, e.g., *Which music video do you want today?* • Vary the setup or complexity for additional challenge.	• Use verbal prompts to describe movement. See the Glossary of Verbal Prompts. • Use visual supports. See Visual Support Cards for stand, stand in circle, sit, and airplane arms. • Add bells or pompom shakers to the activity to increase interest.	• Stand in close proximity to children and model modified movements (e.g., bend knees instead of sit). • Encourage partial movements or alternative responses such as singing, humming, or clapping.

3. SUPPORT: School Readiness

During the music video, the primary goal is to have all children maintain sustained/increased physical activity levels. To achieve this goal, teachers can provide models/prompts for motor imitation (imitate actions/songs from video, maintain personal space) and approaches to learning (active engagement, following instructions from video).

4. LESSON VARIATIONS

If children learn these activities quickly and need no further practice, or if you want to vary activities for review days, see Lesson Variations on Page 56.

■ COOL-DOWN

Structure: Whole group

Wrap up: Focus on
• Gathering
• Decreasing heart rate
• Cooling down muscles

Total time: 3-5 minutes

Key Vocabulary:
• arms, cool-down, hands, happy, heart rate, legs, sad, sweaty, tired, toes

1. MOVE: Motor Movements

Have children sit on their floor marker and cool-down their bodies with the following movements. Once you have modeled each movement listed below, sing the "CHAMPPS Cool-Down Song" while doing the movements (see "CHAMPPS Cool-Down Song," Page 46).

• Bend and stretch. Say: *Sit with a straight back. Legs straight. Raise your* **arms up.** *Slowly sway your arms* **side to side** *to bend and stretch.*

• Touch toes. Say: *Sit with a straight back.* **Arms up.** *Slowly bend forward and reach to* **touch your toes.**

• Stretch arms. Use one beanbag per child. Say: *Arms straight in front of you.* **Make an X** *or a butterfly. Touch the beanbag to your shoulder.* **Hold.** *Switch sides. (Beanbag in right hand touches left shoulder. Beanbag in left hand touches right shoulder.)*

• Wave goodbye. Say: *Look at your friends. Hold out your hand and* **wave** *goodbye.*

Optional: Consider doing the following yoga poses as a way to calm children prior to the "CHAMPPS Cool-Down Song"/movements.

• Boat Pose. (See Figure U1.3.) Say: *Now, place your feet on the ground. Grab a pretend paddle. Row to one side. Row to the other side.* Ask: *What animals do you see?*

• Otter Roll. (See Figure U1.4.) Say: *Now, lie down. Hug your knees to your chest. Rock side to side like an otter.*

Figure U1.3. Boat Pose.

Figure U1.4. Otter Roll.

2. ADAPT: UDL Strategies

Adapt the activity to meet the needs of the children with whom you work. See the suggestions in the following table, along with additional ideas to adapt using the UDL strategies on Page 48.

Engagement	Representation	Action & Expression
• Vary volume of voice to match movement (soft for tiptoe, loud for stomp). • Match speed of speech with pace of movement.	• Use verbal prompts to describe movement. See the Glossary of Verbal Prompts. • Use visual supports. See Visual Support Cards for sit, bend and stretch, lift your arms, stretch arms, touch toes, hug knees, and wave hand.	Begin with simple movements and no singing.

3. SUPPORT: School Readiness

Choose one to three school readiness skills to focus on. See the suggestions in the following table, along with additional ideas to support school readiness on Page 50.

Language	Mathematics	Approaches to Learning
• Encourage sing-along. • Have children listen for verbal prompts.	Use ordinal language (*first, second, third*).	• Create a smooth transition between movements. • Have children follow directions. • Encourage whole-group engagement.

4. LESSON VARIATIONS

If children learn these activities quickly and need no further practice, or if you want to vary activities for review days, see Lesson Variations on Page 56.

Walk-Around Card

1	**Warm-Up**		
	Gathering, increase heart rate, warm up muscles		
	MATERIALS	• 1 floor marker per child • 2 scarves per child (1 in each hand)	
	ACTIVITIES	Sing "CHAMPPS Warm-Up Song." Walk, march, jog, and stretch.	
2	**Core Activity 1: Popcorn Kernels**		
	Grasp and release, visual tracking		
	MATERIALS	• 1 floor marker per child • 1 scarf per child	
	ACTIVITIES	Sing "Popcorn Kernels." First: Wave, squeeze, and shake scarf. Then: Throw, watch, and catch scarf.	
3	**Core Activity 2: Follow Me Home**		
	Physical movement, personal space, motor imitation		
	MATERIALS	• 1 floor marker per child	
	ACTIVITIES	First: Model animal sound/movement and have children imitate. Then: Ring bell and have children return to floor marker. Repeat.	
4	**Core Activity 3: Simon Says**		
	Physical movement, personal space, motor imitation		
	MATERIALS	• 1 floor marker per child	
	ACTIVITIES	First: Choose body movement and/or body awareness. Then: Play Simon Says. Children imitate action and repeat (echo). Repeat.	
5	**Physical Activity: Music Video**		
	Sustained physical activity		
	MATERIALS	Video, video player, wall or screen for viewing	
	Lesson 3 Video 1 (2 min.)	**Lesson 4** Video 2 (3 min.)	**Lessons 5 and 6** Videos 1 and/or 2 (4 min.)
6	**Cool-Down**		
	Gathering, lower heart rate, cool down muscles		
	MATERIALS	• 1 floor marker per child	
	ACTIVITIES	First (optional): Do yoga poses: Boat Pose and Otter Roll. Then: Sing "CHAMPPS Cool-Down Song." Bend and stretch, touch toes, stretch arms, and wave goodbye.	

Walk-Around Card

CHAMPPS Warm-Up Song

(Sung to the tune of "The Ants Go Marching")

The CHAMPPS go **walking** one by one
Hurrah! Hurrah!
The CHAMPPS go **walking** one by one
Hurrah! Hurrah!
The CHAMPPS go **walking** one by one
This is the way we have some fun
And we all go **walking** on, and on, and on

(Repeat with **marching, jogging,** and **stretching**)

Popcorn Kernels

(Sung to the tune of "Frère Jacques/Are You Sleeping?")

(Movement 1 - wave scarf)
Popcorn kernels, popcorn kernels
(Movement 2 – squeeze scarf)
In the pot, in the pot
(Movement 3 – shake scarf)
Shake them, **shake** them, **shake** them
Shake them, **shake** them, **shake** them
(Movement 4 - throw scarf, watch, and catch it)
'Til they pop! 'Til they pop!

CHAMPPS Cool-Down Song

(Sung to the tune of "Here We Go 'Round the Mulberry Bush")

This is the way we **bend** and **stretch**
Bend and **stretch, bend** and **stretch**
This is the way we **bend** and **stretch**
At the end of CHAMPPS

(Repeat with "**touch** our **toes**," "**stretch** our **arms**," and "**wave** goodbye.")

Foundational Skills | 47

GLOSSARY OF VERBAL PROMPTS

Do (Movement)	Say (Verbal Prompt)	Use
Balance	Airplane arms	Use **airplane arms** to hold yourself steady. Keep your balance.
Bend and stretch	Reach, bend, hold	Arms up. Reach up high. Bend to the side. **Hold.** Other side now. **Reach, bend, hold.**
Fly	Arms out, up/down	We're going to fly like birds. Put your **arms out** like an airplane and move them **up and down.**
Gallop	Click-clock, click-clock (for rhythmic movement)	Rock back and forward hop. **Click-clock, click-clock.** Gallop, horses!
	Step, together behind or Step, toe to heel	Let's gallop. Put one foot forward. **Step.** Now place your other foot a little behind. **Together behind.** Watch me. **Step, together behind.** Now next foot. **Step, together behind.**
Jog	Slow run	Show me how you run. See how your feet move very fast. Now let's move our feet a little slower. We are doing a **slow run.** We are jogging.
Jump	Bend knees, push up, land feet together	Let's jump. **Bend** your knees. Look up. **Push up** off the ground! **Land** with your **feet together.**
Kick	Leg up, point toe, kick	Let's kick like we are kicking a soccer ball. Stay on your floor marker. **One leg up, point your toe, and kick!**
Leap	Feet together, hands at your side, jump up	Get ready. **Feet and hands** on the ground. **Jump up** and forward!
March	High knees	Let's march! Marching is like walking, except with **high knees!** Keep those **knees up high!**
Pump (arms)	Pump your arms	**Pump your arms! Make a fist with each hand** then swing the opposite arm as you step to keep your body balanced.
Run	Fast/Slow	When we run, we move really fast. Use **fast feet** to run. Good! Let's **slow** down as we get ready to stop.
Shake (grasp)	Hold tight, don't let go	**Hold your scarf tight. Don't let go.** Squeeze that scarf. Shake it up and down.
Stomp	Giant steps	Is an elephant big or little? An elephant is big! So, are an elephant's steps big or little? Elephants take big, **giant steps.** Show me big, **giant steps** like an elephant.
Stretch	Touch toes	Stand tall. Let's bend down and **touch our toes.**
	Arms up	Stand tall again. Reach up to the sky. **Arms up.** Make a "V" above your head.
Stretch arms	Make an X	Place your arms straight in front of you like this. Now cross arms. **Make an X** with your arms.
Throw and catch (release)	Kiss your shoulder	We have our X. Now take your hand and **kiss your shoulder.** Watch me. My arm is bent, and my hand is touching my shoulder.
	Hold tight, let go	**Hold your popcorn tight.** Is it ready to pop? **Let go!** Pop it high in the air!
Tiptoe	Baby steps	We are going to tiptoe like a little mouse. This means use quiet feet. Take **baby steps** like a little mouse.
Touch toes	Touch toes, hold	Stand or sit up tall. Arms up. Bend down. **Touch toes. Hold.**
Walk	Heel down, then toe	Step, **heel down, then toe.**
	Swing arms	Walk and **swing arms** backward and forward.
Wave	Wave to a friend	Let's wave our scarves up high in the air like we are **waving to a faraway friend.**

UDL SUGGESTIONS

Engagement

Means of Engagement	Warm-Up	Core Activity 1: Popcorn Kernels	Core Activity 2: Follow Me Home	Core Activity 3: Simon Says	Video 1	Video 2	Cool-Down
Recruit Interest							
Child choice	Warm-up moves	Fast versus slow How to wave scarf (overhead, in front of body)	Animal sound, movement, and habitat	Child leads.	Say: *Which video do you want to see today?*	Say: *Which video do you want to see today?*	Cool-down movements
Novel/familiar	Familiar moves (wave hands)	Ask: *If you made popcorn, would you put salt, sugar, cheese, or syrup on your popcorn?*	Familiar materials (floor marker)	Familiar materials Familiar moves (leap, run)	Repeat video.	Repeat video.	Familiar materials (floor marker)
Sustain Effort and Persistence							
Praise/ encourage	Say: *You sang every word; good job! You ran slowly when you jogged; great listening!*	Say: *Good job watching your scarf! You caught the scarf before it touched the ground.*	Say: *Nice giant steps. You move just like an elephant!*	Say: *Great listening! You did exactly what I said!*	Say: *I love your shaking!*	Say: *You're following directions so well!*	Say: *Nice calm bodies. I like how you are moving slowly during the cool-down.*
Vary complexity	Increase/ decrease number of moves.	Vary speed. Vary how to catch (with head, knee).	Have boys do one animal movement (hop/swim/ stomp) while girls do another animal movement (gallop/fly/ leap).	Include more than one move (touch head and jump).	Vary length of video.	Vary length of video.	Increase/ decrease number of moves.
Vary setup, directions	Sing softly/ loudly.	Vary number of scarves.	Vary animals.	Child leads.	Vary materials (give instruments, scarves).	Vary materials (give pom poms, cloth napkins, scarves, bells).	Sing softly/ loudly.

Representation

Means of Representation	Warm-Up	Core Activity 1: Popcorn Kernels	Core Activity 2: Follow Me Home	Core Activity 3: Simon Says	Video 1	Video 2	Cool-Down
Forms of Communication							
Auditory	Glossary of Verbal Prompts						→
Visual	Visual Support Cards						→
Tactile	Hold scarves.	Hold scarves.	Use egg shakers or musical instruments.				→
Multiple Levels of Complexity							
Key vocabulary: define/model	walk march jog stretch	hold wave squeeze into ball throw watch catch	tiptoe stomp gallop leap fly run	walk jog jump balance kick			bend and stretch touch toes stretch arms wave goodbye

Action & Expression

Means of Expression	Warm-Up	Core Activity 1: Popcorn Kernels	Core Activity 2: Follow Me Home	Core Activity 3: Simon Says	Video 1	Video 2	Cool-Down
Variety of responses	Sing, clap, or hum song.	Sing, clap, or hum song. Drop scarf instead of throwing it. Use two hands.	Only make animal sound or only do animal movement.	Verbally repeat (echo). Identify body parts only.	Hum or clap along to song.	Hum or clap along to song.	Sit and breathe slowly. Sing, clap, or hum song. Only do movements, no singing.
Complexity of responses	Partial movement (walk instead of jogging, stomp feet instead of marching)	Partial movement (only wave scarf)	Partial movement (walk instead of galloping) One animal at a time	Partial movement (jump instead of leaping)	Partial movement (nod head instead of shaking)	Partial movement (bend knees instead of sitting)	Partial movement (touch knees instead of toes)

SUPPORT SCHOOL READINESS SKILLS

LANGUAGE AND LITERACY	Warm-Up	Core Activity 1: Popcorn Kernels	Core Activity 2: Follow Me Home	Core Activity 3: Simon Says	Cool-Down
Expresses feelings (hot, thirsty, tired, hungry, sleepy, sweaty)	Ask how children feel after warm-up.	Ask: *Who gets thirsty when eating popcorn? What do you drink when you get thirsty?*	Ask: *How do you feel when you purr like a cheetah? fly like a bird? stomp like an elephant?*	Say: *Simon Says if you are hungry hop up and down. Simon Says if you are cold, do a little wiggle.*	Ask how children feel after CHAMPPS is over.
Engages in active discussion (shares ideas, asks and answers questions)	Say: *Show us your idea for a new warm-up movement.*	Ask questions about popcorn: *Where do we eat popcorn?*	Have children ask and answer questions about animals.	Ask: *Why do we say, "Simon Says"? What else could we call this game?*	Say: *Show us your idea for a new cool-down movement.*
Communicates personal experiences and interests	Ask children about favorite warm-up move.	Ask: *Which color scarf is your favorite?*	Ask: *What is your favorite animal? Do you have any pets?*	Ask children about Simon Says movements: *Which move is hardest? Easiest? Your favorite?*	Ask: *What was your favorite activity?*
Listens to/uses formal and informal language (listens to/sings songs, uses different voices)	Have children listen and sing along.	Have children listen and sing along.	Have children make animal noises.	Have children repeat (echo) the leader.	Have children listen and sing along.
Recognizes shapes (circle, square, triangle, rectangle)	Have children move in a circle.	Have children wave scarves in a particular shape (circle, square, triangle).	Have children move in a circle.	Say: *Simon Says, point to a circle/square/triangle in the room.*	Have children sit in a circle.
Recognizes letters	Say: *Name beginning letter sound for* feet, legs, jog, march, walk.	Ask: *What letter does popcorn begin with? What other words start with P?*	Ask: *What beginning letter sound do you hear for* bird, frog, horse?	Ask: *What letter does Simon begin with? Whose name(s) has/have an S in it?*	Say: *Name the beginning letter sound for* touch, wave, bend, goodbye.

MATHEMATICS	Warm-Up	Core Activity 1: Popcorn Kernels	Core Activity 2: Follow Me Home	Core Activity 3: Simon Says	Cool-Down
Number recognition (count, one–one correspondence)	Have children count moves instead of singing.	Have children count number of throws, catches.	Have children count number of steps.	Have children do a specific number of moves.	Have children stretch for a specific number of seconds.
Positional words (*above, side to side*)		Above, side to side	Say: *Hold a friend's hand and stomp three times together, standing side by side.*	Have children follow Simon as they are told to put their hands **above** their head, on the **side** of their face	Bend side to side

MATHEMATICS	Warm-Up	Core Activity 1: Popcorn Kernels	Core Activity 2: Follow Me Home	Core Activity 3: Simon Says	Cool-Down
Ordinal language (*first, second,* etc.)	Use ordinal words to describe order of moves (*first walk, second jog,* etc.).	Use ordinal words to describe order of moves (*first wave, second squeeze,* etc.).	Ask: *Who got home first? Last?*	Add up to three consecutive moves (*first clap, second jump,* etc.).	Use ordinal words to describe order of moves.
Categorizing and sorting objects (animals, habitats)	Ask: *What animals live in water? trees? ground?*	Have children sort picture objects into SNACKS and NOT SNACKS (popcorn, chips, blocks, cars, candy, carrots, flowers, candles, pretzels, granola bars)	Have children match animals to their habitat.		Ask: *If you were a bird/frog/elephant, how would you cool down after flying/leaping/stomping?*
Patterns (recognize, describe, reproduce)	Create a movement pattern (walk backward five steps, forward five steps).	Say: *Make yourself as small as a popcorn kernel and then pop up!*	Say: *Name animals that are pets, animals that have feet, animals that swim.*	Create a movement pattern (walk backward five steps, forward five steps).	Follow patterns such as stretch, stretch, bend or bend, stretch, bend.

SCIENCE	Warm-Up	Core Activity 1: Popcorn Kernels	Core Activity 2: Follow Me Home	Core Activity 3: Simon Says	Cool-Down
Ask/answer questions together (*Who? What? Where? How?*).	Ask: *Is anybody feeling hot? Sweaty? Why do you think you feel that way?*	Ask: *When do you eat popcorn? Who makes your popcorn? Who eats popcorn with you?*	Ask questions about animals.	Ask: *Who can lead Simon Says? Who goes next? Describe how Simon Says works.*	Ask: *Who is tired? thirsty? sweaty?*
Make predictions together (*What if?*).	Ask: *What happens if we do not warm up?*	Ask: *What if we throw the scarf higher? Will it be harder or easier to catch?*	Answer questions about animals.		Discuss slowed breathing, hearts.
Discuss characteristics of living things (*humans, animals, plants*).	Say: *I feel my heart pumping! Do you? Animals have hearts, too! Plants don't!*		Ask: *What are things that all animals, people, and plants need?*	Say: *Simon says droop like a plant that needs water. Simon says take a deep breath like an elephant.*	Discuss breathing of running children, dolphins, crying babies, sleeping daddies
Use sensory vocabulary (e.g., characteristics of scarf).	Say: *Touch your heart. What do you feel? Do you feel it pumping? Beating?*	Wave, squeeze, shake, feel, watch scarf.	Discuss what some animal habitats might look, feel, and smell like: eagle's nest, bear's den, doghouse, etc.	Say: *Simon Says shiver like you are cold. Simon Says fan your face like you are hot.*	Have children place hand on their heart at the beginning and end of cool-down. Ask them to describe if their heart is beating fast of slow and why.

SUPPORT SCHOOL READINESS SKILLS *(continued)*

MOTOR	Warm-Up	Core Activity 1: Popcorn Kernels	Core Activity 2: Follow Me Home	Core Activity 3: Simon Says	Cool-Down
Balance	Bend and then stretch to touch the ceiling.	Toss and catch scarf while balancing on one foot.		Balance on one foot.	Bend and stretch.
Visual tracking	Have children use scarves during warm-up and follow scarf movement with their eyes.	Have children watch and catch scarf.	Select one child to move around the circle. Have children watch the child (follow with your eyes) as the child moves like a frog, cheetah, bird.	Say: Simon stand still and follow my pointed finger using only your eyes (watching). [Teacher moves outstretched arm and pointer finger up, left, right, down.]	Have children follow with their eye, their hands as they stretch up/down, left/right.
Motor imitation	Have children imitate leader/ peers.	→			→
Body awareness	Have children recognize which body parts to use.	→		Have children identify body parts.	Have children identify body parts.
Body movement (touch toes, raise arms, catch, throw, bend knees)	Have children touch toes, raise arms.	Have children throw, wave, catch, squeeze.	Have children flap arms (fly).	Have children shrug shoulders, wiggle foot, etc.	Have children bend and stretch, touch toes, stretch arms.
Strength/speed/ duration	Say: Let's add extra movements to our warm-up today!	Have children do Popcorn Kernels fast and slow.	Say: Let's imitate two animals quickly when I say the animal name (bird, frog). Now let's do three animals slowly (horse, elephant, rabbit).		Have children move slowly.
Coordination (eye/hand; eye/foot)		Have children throw and catch.	Have children hop/gallop to buckets and pick up bean bags (representing animal foods such as carrots, hay) and then go back to floor marker.	Add scarf to Simon Says. Say: Simon says move your scarf from one hand to another. Simon says place scarf on left foot/right foot.	Have children stretch right/ left hand across midline, to squeeze opposite shoulder. Stretch right/left hands to touch opposite foot while seated and while standing.
Locomotion (walk, run, jump, hop, kick, strike)	Have children walk, march, jog.	Have children walk or march as they catch their popcorn kernels.	Have children tiptoe, gallop, leap, run.	Have children walk, jog, jump, march.	Have children walk slowly in place, slowly pedal bicycle while seated or lying down.

MOTOR	Warm-Up	Core Activity 1: Popcorn Kernels	Core Activity 2: Follow Me Home	Core Activity 3: Simon Says	Cool-Down
Directionality (forward, backward, sidesteps)	Have children switch direction (*walk backward, sidestep*).	Practice throwing scarf up/down, left/right.	*Change the direction of movement around the circle for each animal movement, going in opposite direction each time.*	Say: *Simon says take two steps forward/backward.*	Have children lean forward/backward while seated or standing.
Personal space	Have children use own floor marker. ———————————————————————————————————————→				
Cross midline reach	Have children stretch across midline with left/right hand to opposite shoulder, knee, foot, elbow, ankle, hip.	Have children wave scarf.	Say: *Let's flutter like a butterfly, wiggling fingers up and down, with arms crossed at the wrist in the front of your body.*	Say: *Simon says touch your left/right ear with your right/left hand. Simon says touch your left/right foot with your right/left hand.*	Have children stretch right/left hand across midline, to squeeze opposite shoulder. Stretch right/left hand to touch opposite foot while seated and while standing.
Grasp and release	Have children grasp and release scarves held above their head, held below their waist, held in front/back of them.	Have children hold scarf and let go.		Include scarf or bean bag with Simon Says, adding commands for grasp and release objects in front/back/beside them.	Say: *Grasp and release your toes. Give yourself three hugs by grasping and releasing both shoulders three times.*
Motor regulation (go slow, go fast, stop)	Have children follow directions (go slow/stop) with warm-up movements.	Have children walk fast then stop, jump slowly then stop, march slowly then stop as they catch their popcorn kernels.	Have children change speed based on animal.	Say: *Simon says jog/hop/wiggle fast/slow! Simon says stop!*	Have children move slowly.
Music and dance	Have children sing. ——————————→				Have children sing.

SOCIAL-EMOTIONAL	Warm-Up	Core Activity 1: Popcorn Kernels	Core Activity 2: Follow Me Home	Core Activity 3: Simon Says	Cool-Down
Recognizes, describes, and regulates emotions	Ask: *How do you feel when it is a CHAMPPS day?*	Ask: *Popcorn pops up and down. How do you feel when you pop (hop) up and down?*	Ask: *How do you feel when you are stomping? Flying?*	Recognizes and describes facial expressions (happy, sad, etc.).	Transitions calmly into next activity.
Solves/prevents problems	Ask: *Why do we warm up before we do our motor games?*	Ask: *Should we eat popcorn that has fallen on floor? Why/why not? Should we throw popcorn? Why/why not?*	Say: *What could happen if you run into a friend? What should you do if you run into a friend?*	Ask: *Should we whisper or talk very very softly when we are the leader for Simon Says? Why/why not?*	Say: *Cool-down helps us slow down and calm down. What could happen if we cannot slow down after CHAMPPS?*

SUPPORT SCHOOL READINESS SKILLS *(continued)*

SOCIAL-EMOTIONAL	Warm-Up	Core Activity 1: Popcorn Kernels	Core Activity 2: Follow Me Home	Core Activity 3: Simon Says	Cool-Down
Learns independence/self-help	Say: *Let's see who can find a floor marker all by yourself!*	Gathers, puts away scarves.		Child leads.	Say: *Let's see who can slowly get in line, keeping hands by your side.*
Takes turns/waits turn	Have children take turns leading or modeling which warm-up movement to do next.	Say: *Let's take turns getting scarves from the bucket.*	Say: *Let's have girls/boys go first then boys/girls go next.*	Say: *Simon says if you have a blue shirt, clap your hands. If you have red shoes, stomp your feet.*	Say: *Those with green pants may line up. Those with bows in their hair may line up.*
Helps/supports peers	Moves hand in hand with partner.	Hands out/Collects scarves (Choose a child to do this.)	Moves hand in hand with partner.	Say: *Simon says put your arm around the shoulder of a friend and give a compliment/smile/wink to one another.*	Have children help one another pick up scarves and floor markers.
Plays cooperatively		Have children trade scarves with a friend.	Have children hold a friend's hand to do the movements in pairs.	Say: *Simon says shake a friend's hand. Simon says wink at a friend.*	
Shares materials	Encourage children to go to a different floor marker if the one they wanted is already taken.	Have children toss scarves in pairs, taking turns on scarf retrieval.	Have children use hula hoops to share their "animal habitat" with partner. When they go "home," two children stand in one large hula hoop.	Encourage children to go to a different floor marker if the one they wanted is already taken.	Use scarves during cool-down, encouraging children to pick another scarf if someone took the scarf they wanted.
Socializes with peers	Add a greeting to children's warm-up.	Have children wave at peers.	Partner children and have them come up with an animal movement for the group to imitate.	Say: *Simon says hold a friend's hand and wiggle together. Simon says greet a friend (handshake, say hello, give gentle high-five or gentle pat on back).*	Have children wave at peers.

APPROACHES TO LEARNING	Warm-Up	Core Activity 1: Popcorn Kernels	Core Activity 2: Follow Me Home	Core Activity 3: Simon Says	Cool-Down
Transitions into/ out of activities	Have children return to floor marker.			Have children transition smoothly from one individual being "Simon" to the next person	Say: *I spy with my little eye, someone tiptoeing quietly to a floor marker/to line up at the door.*
Listens to/follows directions	Have children listen and imitate movement.				
Demonstrates focused attention	Have children listen for next movement.				
Demonstrates sustained attention	Have children stay with whole group.				
Demonstrates active engagement in small/large group	Have children move around room with whole class.	Encourage children to sing and imitate movements to Popcorn Kernels song.	Take turns having a child do an animal movement and other children guess which animal they are imitating.	Say: *Simon says point to someone who is good at hopping, flying, galloping.*	Have children move around room with whole class.
Demonstrates active engagement in independent task		Have children toss and catch scarves independently.	Encourage children to move around circle without bumping into friends.	Have children take turns giving the Simon Says command while peers follow their instructions.	

Lesson Variations

▣ WARM-UP VARIATIONS

Music/Rhythm/Dance

Variation 1: Head, Shoulders, Knees, and Toes

Structure	Materials	Instructions
Whole group	• Floor markers • Projector with Internet access	1. Have children stand on their floor markers in warm-up circle. 2. Play a YouTube video for the song "Head, Shoulders, Knees, and Toes." (See the video selection criteria on Page 266.) 3. Have children imitate the music video for their warm-up.

Variation 2: Rhythm Bottles

Structure	Materials	Instructions
Whole group	• Recycled plastic bottles • Pebbles, buttons, beads, and/or rice	1. Add pebbles, buttons, beads, and/or rice to recycled plastic bottles to make rhythm bottles. 2. Use rhythm bottles during warm-up, cool-down, music videos, and dance.

Variation 3: Rhythm Sticks

Structure	Materials	Instructions
Whole group	• Multicolored ribbons of remnant fabric • Rulers or paint sticks (two per child)	1. Tie or glue multicolored ribbons of remnant fabric to rulers or paint sticks. (Make two per child.) 2. Use rhythm sticks during warm-up and music videos.

▣ CORE ACTIVITY 2: **Follow Me Home** VARIATIONS

Music/Rhythm/Dance

Variation 1: Animal Freeze Dance

Structure	Materials	Instructions
Whole group	• Floor markers • Projector with Internet access • Music from around the world	1. Select children's music from different regions of the world. 2. Before starting the music, say an animal's name. Then have children dance to the music as that animal. 3. When the music stops, the "animal" freezes. 4. Call out another animal's name, restart the music, and repeat the activity.

Sports/Games

Variation 2: Guess the Animal

Structure	Materials	Instructions
Whole group	• Floor markers • Animal visual supports (picture cards)	1. Place animal visual supports (cards) in the center of the circle. 2. In turns, have each child draw an animal card and move like the animal. 3. At each turn, all children guess the animal and then imitate the animal move (horse, frog, rabbit, cheetah, mouse, bird, fish, elephant, crab, or penguin).

Variation 3: Animal Relay

Structure	Materials	Instructions
Whole group	• Floor markers • Animal visual supports (picture cards)	1. Place children in two lines with visual supports (animal cards) in the middle. Mark a finish line for children to move toward. 2. Have the first child in each line select an animal card. 3. Have the child move like that animal. Have other children cheer (Go, horsey, go! Go, bunny, go!) as the child moves like that animal toward the finish line. 4. When a child reaches the finish line, his or her turn is over. The child then joins in the cheering for the next child.

■ CORE ACTIVITY 3: **Simon Says** VARIATIONS

Music/Rhythm/Dance

Variation 1: Dance Moves

Structure	Materials	Instructions
Whole group	• Floor markers	1. Teach three to five dance moves. 2. Have the leader call out dance moves for children to do.

Arts and Crafts

Variation 2: Body Art

Structure	Materials	Instructions
Whole group	• Butcher paper • Markers • Laminator	1. Trace the outline of each child's body on a large piece of butcher paper. 2. Label body parts (arms, hands, fingers, legs, feet, toes, hips, head, neck, shoulders). 3. Laminate each paper and label with the child's name. 4. Place the papers on the floor and have each child find their picture. 5. Play Simon Says using different movements and different body parts. For example, say: *Walk around your picture! Stand on your shoulders! Hop on your hands! Twist on your feet!*

■ MUSIC VIDEO VARIATIONS

Music/Rhythm/Dance

Variation 1: Following Directions

Structure	Materials	Instructions
Whole group	• Floor markers • Projector with Internet access	1. Have children stand on their floor markers in the cool-down circle. 2. Play a YouTube video that requires children to follow simple movement directions. (See the video selection criteria on Page 266.)

Variation 2: Goodbye Wiggles

Structure	Materials	Instructions
Whole group	• Floor markers • Projector with Internet access	1. Have children stand on their floor markers. 2. Play a YouTube video that requires children to follow shaking/wiggling motions. (See the video selection criteria on Page 266.) 3. Have children imitate the music video.

Variation 3: If I Were an Animal

Structure	Materials	Instructions
Whole group	• Floor markers • Access to music	1. Have children stand on their floor markers. 2. Play the game "If I Were an Animal." The teacher or children name an animal and others imitate animal movement with music playing in the background.

■ COOL-DOWN VARIATIONS

Variation 1: Animal Safari

Structure	Materials	Instructions
Whole group	• Floor markers	1. Have children start in seated position. 2. Say: *Bend knees and rock back slightly so you are making a little boat.* 3. Say: *Put your hands together in a fist, pump your arms, and move your hands side to side like you are rowing a boat.* 4. Discuss with children the different animals you "see." Ask: *What are they doing? Are they eating anything?* (Lesson variation reinforces Core Activity 2: Follow Me Home and extends the cool-down.)

Home Activities Record

CHAMPPS

Child: _____   Teacher: _____
Unit: _____   Week: _____
Please return by: _____

Thank you for playing with me! Please tell my teachers if we did CHAMPPS activities this week at home. Write a check (✓) if we practiced CHAMPPS at home this week. You can also write comments to tell my teachers how I did when we practiced CHAMPPS at home! Please give this form to my teacher each week.

Check (✓) if you did CHAMPPS practice.	Parent/Child Comments

CHAMPPS: CHildren in Action Motor Program for PreschoolerS by Paddy C. Favazza and Michaelene M. Ostrosky with Melissa Stalega, Hsiu-Wen Yang, Katherine Aronson-Ensign, Martin Block, W. Catherine Cheung, and Yusuf Akemoglu. Copyright © 2023 by Paul H. Brookes Publishing Co., Inc. All rights reserved.

Home Activities Record

CHAMPPS

Child: _____   Teacher: _____
Unit: _____   Week: _____
Please return by: _____

Thank you for playing with me! Please tell my teachers if we did CHAMPPS activities this week at home. Write a check (✓) if we practiced CHAMPPS at home this week. You can also write comments to tell my teachers how I did when we practiced CHAMPPS at home! Please give this form to my teacher each week.

Check (✓) if you did CHAMPPS practice.	Parent/Child Comments

CHAMPPS: CHildren in Action Motor Program for PreschoolerS by Paddy C. Favazza and Michaelene M. Ostrosky with Melissa Stalega, Hsiu-Wen Yang, Katherine Aronson-Ensign, Martin Block, W. Catherine Cheung, and Yusuf Akemoglu. Copyright © 2023 by Paul H. Brookes Publishing Co., Inc. All rights reserved.

CHAMPPS Home Activities

Hi, Family and Friends!

I am beginning CHAMPPS at school! I am learning all about my body and how it moves. Now I want to play CHAMPPS with you! It only takes 10–20 minutes. Thank you for playing with me!

Love, Your Little CHAMP

■ ACTIVITY 1: **Warm-Up**

Materials None
Directions Move and sing with me.
CHAMPPS Warm-Up Song
(Tune: "The Ants Go Marching")

The CHAMPPS go walking one by one
Hurrah, hurrah!
The CHAMPPS go walking one by one
Hurrah, hurrah!
The CHAMPPS go walking one by one
This is the way we have some fun
And we all go walking on, and on, and on!

Repeat with: marching, jogging.

■ ACTIVITY 2: **Popcorn Kernels**

Materials Scarf, napkin, or kitchen towel
Directions Hold a scarf and sing with me.
Popcorn Kernels
(Tune: "Frère Jacques/Are You Sleeping?")

Popcorn kernels, popcorn kernels [wave scarf]
In the pot, in the pot [squeeze scarf]
Shake them, shake them, shake them [shake scarf]
Shake them, shake them, shake them
'Til they pop! 'Til they pop! [throw and catch scarf]

Sing again. Catch scarf with one hand, two hands, head, knee, or foot.

| wave scarf | squeeze scarf | shake scarf | throw, watch, catch |

■ ACTIVITY 3: **Cool-Down**

Materials None
Directions Stretch and sing with me.
CHAMPSS Cool-Down Song
(Tune: "Here We Go 'Round the Mulberry Bush")

This is the way we touch our toes
Touch our toes, touch our toes
This is the way we touch our toes
At the end of CHAMPPS

Repeat with: bend and stretch, wave goodbye.

| sit | touch toes | bend and stretch | wave hand |

Read and move together!
Look for this book at your local library: *Hop, Hop, Jump!* by Lauren Thompson.
Dance to this YouTube video: _____

Thank you for playing with me!

CHAMPPS Home Activities

Hi, Family and Friends!

I am doing CHAMPPS at school! I am learning all about my body and how it moves. Now I want to play CHAMPPS with you! It only takes 10–20 minutes. Thank you for playing with me!

Love, Your Little CHAMP

■ ACTIVITY 1: **Warm-Up**

Materials No materials needed.
Directions Move and sing with me.

CHAMPPS Warm-Up Song

(Tune: "The Ants Go Marching")

The CHAMPPS go walking one by one
Hurrah, hurrah!
The CHAMPPS go walking one by one
Hurrah, hurrah!
The CHAMPPS go walking one by one
This is the way we have some fun
And we all go walking on, and on, and on!

Repeat with: marching, jogging.

■ ACTIVITY 2: **Follow Me Home**

Materials

Bell: A spoon and pot lid to tap, a whistle, or bell

Home: A carpet square, placemat, or towel

Directions

1. Start at home.
2. Choose an animal. Move and make noise.
3. Ring the bell, whistle, etc.
4. Choose a new animal.

Animal	Move/Sound	Home
Mouse	Tiptoe and squeak	Mouse hole
Horse	Gallop and whinny (neigh)	Barn
Frog	Leap and ribbit	Lily pad
Lion	Stomp and roar	Den
Bird	Fly and tweet	Nest

■ ACTIVITY 3: **Cool-Down**

Materials None
Directions Stretch and sing with me.

CHAMPPS Cool-Down Song

(Tune: "Here We Go 'Round the Mulberry Bush")

This is the way we touch our toes
Touch our toes, touch our toes
This is the way we touch our toes
At the end of CHAMPPS

Repeat with: bend and stretch, wave goodbye.

sit

touch toes

bend and stretch

wave hand

Read and move together!

Look for this book at your local library: *Dancing Feet!* by Lindsey Craig.

Dance to this YouTube video: _____

Thank you for playing with me!

CHAMPPS Home Activities

CHAMPPS

Hi, Family and Friends!

I am finishing up Unit 1 of CHAMPPS at school! I am learning all about my body and how it moves. Now I want to play CHAMPPS with you! It only takes 10–20 minutes. Thank you for playing with me!

Love, Your Little CHAMP

■ ACTIVITY 1: **Warm-Up**

Materials None
Directions Move and sing with me.

CHAMPPS Warm-Up Song

(Tune: "The Ants Go Marching")

The CHAMPPS go walking one by one
Hurrah, hurrah!
The CHAMPPS go walking one by one
Hurrah, hurrah!
The CHAMPPS go walking one by one
This is the way we have some fun
And we all go walking on, and on, and on!

Repeat with: marching, jogging.

■ ACTIVITY 2: **Simon Says**

Materials None
Directions

1. You move. I will copy you.
2. Say: "Simon says, _____."
3. Show me the move or touch. I will copy you.
4. Repeat!

Move in Place	Touch
Walk	Hands
March	Head
Jog	Shoulders
Balance on one foot	Knees
Kick in the air	Legs

■ ACTIVITY 3: **Cool-Down**

Materials None
Directions Stretch and sing with me.

CHAMPPS Cool-Down Song

(Tune: "Here We Go 'Round the Mulberry Bush")

This is the way we touch our toes
Touch our toes, touch our toes
This is the way we touch our toes
At the end of CHAMPPS

Repeat with: bend and stretch, wave goodbye.

sit

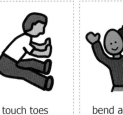
touch toes   bend and stretch

wave hand

Read and move together!
Look for this book at your local library: *From Head to Toe* by Eric Carle.

Dance to this YouTube video: _____

Thank you for playing with me!

Get Moving: CHAMPPS Motor Skills Units

Walking and Running

Unit Objectives

1. **Motor Movement.** Focus on walking (speed walk, march, tiptoe, lunge, step over/side). Focus on running. Reinforce previously learned skills such as stretching, touching toes, and touching arms.

2. **Body Awareness.** Identify and move head, arms, shoulders, hands, knees, feet, heels, and toes.

3. **Personal Space.** Share space with peers and stay on own floor marker.

4. **Motor Control.** Listen for and initiate: fast versus slow, stop versus go.

5. **Sustained Physical Activity.** Engage in continuous movement during music video.

Key Vocabulary

Body Parts	**arms, feet, knees, legs, toes**
Motor Movement	**jog, lunge, march, run, sidestep, speed walk, step (over), stretch, tiptoe, walk**
Concepts	**big/small, fast/slow, forward/backward, over, stop/go**
Pre-academic	Weather: **snow, winter**
	Transportation and colors: **red/yellow/green light**
Social-Emotional	**cheer, team**

UNIT LESSON

Time	Activity	Focus		
3 min	WARM-UP	Gathering	Increase Heart Rate	Warm-Up Muscles
5 min	CORE 1: **Snowflake, Snowflake**	Motor Movement	Personal Space	Motor Control
5 min	CORE 2*: **Obstacle Course**	Motor Movement		
5 min	CORE 3*: **Red Light, Green Light**	Motor Movement	Personal Space	Motor Control
2-4 min	PHYSICAL ACTIVITY: Music Video (Lessons 3-6 only)	Motor Imitation & Sustained Physical Activity		
3 min	COOL-DOWN	Gathering	Decrease Heart Rate	Cool-Down Muscles

*Core 2 and Core 3 occur simultaneously with the class divided into two small groups. After both small groups complete one activity, children remain with their group and the small groups switch locations/activities.

PREPARATION AND MATERIALS

Activity	Materials (class of 15 children with 2 adults)
WARM-UP COOL-DOWN Whole Group	Numbered floor markers (1 per person)
CORE 1 **Snowflake, Snowflake** Whole Group	Numbered floor markers Scarves (1-2 per person)
CORE 2 **Obstacle Course** Small Group*	Stars (10-12) Hurdles (3, of various heights) Egg shakers (1 per person for cheering)
CORE 3 **Red Light, Green Light** Small Group*	Tape - to make lanes Cones (8 - one for each lane) Stars (8 - one per lane; used to designate starting place in each lane) Number cards (can use 1-8 or choose other numerals corresponding to ones being taught in pre-kindergarten curriculum)
Visual Support Cards	
Used for these movements: stand, stand in circle, sit, lift your arms, stretch arms, touch toes, stop/freeze, go, slow down, melt/lie down, airplane arms, bend and stretch, wave hand, walk, speed walk, tiptoe, march, jog, run, lunge, sidestep, walk backward. Visit the Brookes Download Hub to download and print the Visual Support Cards for Unit 2.	

*Because Core 2 and Core 3 Activities occur simultaneously, use the Planning Notes form before starting to preassign children to Small Group 1 or Small Group 2. Once children complete the Core 2 or Core 3 activity, they switch to the other activity. For smooth transitions to the next activity, small groups can remain relatively stable once set, unless a teacher determines that a child needs to be placed in a different group.

SETUP

Warm-Up and Cool-Down

Place floor markers in numerical order in a square, with Numbers 1-8 on each side. Each numbered floor marker should match the floor marker that is parallel (i.e., #1 aligns with #1, #2 aligns with #2, etc.). See Figure U2.1.

Obstacle Course (Beginner's Course)

1. Line up five to six stars in a straight line. Line up five to six floor markers *after* the stars, followed by three or four more stars forming a horseshoe.

2. Place three low or medium-height hurdles in between the floor markers, making sure hurdles are far enough apart from one another so children can take two to three steps between hurdles. Use additional floor markers as needed. See Figure U2.2.

Red Light, Green Light

1. Place tape on the floor to create eight lanes.

2. Place stars to show the "Start."

3. Place eight cones of various colors to show the "Finish."

4. Place a number (1-8) on top of each cone. See Figure U2.3.

Sample Classroom Setups

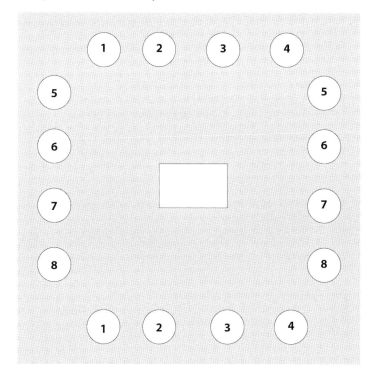

Figure U2.1. Classroom setup for Unit 2 warm-up and cool-down.

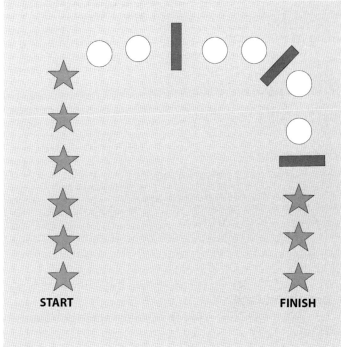

Figure U2.2. Classroom setup for Obstacle Course.

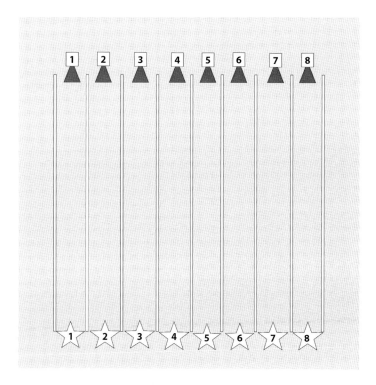

Figure U2.3. Classroom setup for lanes for Red Light, Green Light.

Featured Interactive Movement Books

- *Dance with Me*, written by Charles R. Smith, Jr. and illustrated by Noah Z. Jones. Candlewick, 2008.
- *Wiggle! Like an Octopus*, written by Harriet Ziefert and illustrated by Simms Taback. Blue Apple Books, 2011.
- *We're Going on a Picnic!*, written and illustrated by Pat Hutchins. Greenwillow Books, 2002.
- *The Snowy Day*, written and illustrated by Ezra Jack Keats. Viking, 1962.

Video Content

Note: For this unit, you will need to select one or two music videos, each approximately 2-4 minutes long, illustrating motor movements such as the following: marching or running in place, stepping forward and backward, sidestepping left and right, and jumping up and down or side to side. Note, you can select a longer (4-minute) music video and use 2 minutes of it for Lesson 3, 3 minutes for Lesson 4, and the entire 4 minutes for Lessons 5 and 6.

See the recommended list of video sources on Page 265 and the criteria for video selection on Page 267.

BEFORE YOU START

1. Read through the unit. In particular, read through all of the lesson activities. Visualize the space where you will have CHAMPPS and how you will implement each activity with the children with whom you work.
2. Identify the school readiness skills you will focus on in each lesson activity; school readiness skills should correspond to your core curriculum.
3. Identify universal design for learning (UDL) strategies and adaptations to use for particular activities and/or to support individual children. For example, download the visual supports for use with the lesson prior to starting.
4. Review the lesson variations to determine which you will use, if needed.
5. Plan ahead for how you will shorten the lesson, if needed (see below).
6. Complete the Planning Notes.

If you need to shorten the lesson:
Depending on the needs of the children you teach, you may choose to shorten the lesson on the first day or first two days of Unit 2 to allow children to get used to the CHAMPPS routine. For example, you could do the Warm-Up with the song, one or two core activities, and the Cool-Down with the song. Then, on the third day, you could add the third core activity.

UNIT 2 PLANNING NOTES
Motor movements to focus on:
Vocabulary to focus on:
Children who will be positioned near an adult for additional support and attention:
Children who will help with setup:
Children who will help with cleanup:
Children in Small Group 1:
Children in Small Group 2:

■ WARM-UP

Structure: Whole group

Get ready! Focus on:
- Gathering
- Increasing heart rate
- Warming up muscles

Total time: 3–5 minutes

Key Vocabulary:
- arms, feet, legs, toes
- jog, march, walk

1. MOVE: Motor Movements

Have children start on their floor marker, warming up their bodies while singing the "CHAMPPS Warm-Up Song" with each movement you model. Verbal prompts are provided below, if needed.

- Children **walk** in a circle. Say: *Step one foot forward.* ***Heel down** first,* ***then toe. Swing your arms** forward and backward.*
- Children **march** in a circle. Say: *March with **high knees**. Hold your hands in front, palms down. **Touch your knees to your hands.***
- Children **jog** in a circle. Say: *A jog is a **slow run**. Move your legs quickly, keep your **head up**, and **pump your arms** forward and back.*
- Children **stretch** on their floor marker. Say: *Raise your **arms up** to the ceiling. Now slowly bend down and **touch your toes.***

2. ADAPT: UDL Strategies

Adapt the activity to meet the needs of the children with whom you work. See the suggestions in the following table; for additional ways to adapt, use the UDL Suggestions for Unit 2.

Engagement	Representation	Action & Expression
Give children choices. Ask children to choose the next warm-up movement(s).	• Use verbal prompts to describe movements. See the Glossary of Verbal Prompts. • Use visual supports. See Visual Support Cards for stand, stand in circle, sit, lift your arms, stretch arms, touch toes, walk, march, and jog.	Encourage children to sing along. Give children the option to hum or clap to the melody/rhythm.

3. SUPPORT: School Readiness

Choose one to three school readiness skills to focus on. See the suggestions in the following table; for additional ways to support school readiness, turn to Page 79.

Language	Mathematics	Approaches to Learning
• Encourage children to sing along. • Have children listen for verbal prompts. • Have children identify body parts. • Have children describe body movements.	• Use ordinal language (*first, second, third*) with children.	• Create a smooth transition between movements. • Have children follow directions. • Guide children to remain focused and continue moving. • Encourage whole-group engagement.

4. LESSON VARIATIONS

If children learn these activities quickly and need no further practice, or if you want to vary activities for review days, see Lesson Variations on Page 85.

■ CORE ACTIVITY 1: **Snowflake, Snowflake**

Structure: Whole group

Focus on these objectives:
- Following directions
- Personal space
- Walking: speed walk, lunge, sidestep, tiptoe
- Jogging: slow run

Total time: 3-5 minutes

Key Vocabulary:
- **arms, feet, knees, legs, toes**
- **lunge, march, speed walk, tiptoe, walk**
- **big/small, fast/slow, stop/go**
- **snow, water**

1. MOVE: Motor Movements

- Children pick one or two scarves from the middle of the square and then stand on floor marker that was used for Warm-Up.
- Children sing "Snowflake, Snowflake" as they wave scarves and move freely around the room using one of these movements: **walk, speed walk, tiptoe, march,** or **lunge.**
- At end of the song, children melt by lying down on the floor.
- Repeat with a new movement.

2. ADAPT: UDL Strategies

Adapt the activity to meet the needs of the children with whom you work. See the suggestions in the following table; for additional ways to adapt, use the UDL Suggestions for Unit 2.

Engagement	Representation	Action & Expression
Sustain attention by changing volume of voice with each movement (e.g., whisper for "tiptoe").	• Use verbal prompts to describe movement. See the Glossary of Verbal Prompts. • Use Visual Support Cards: stand, stand in circle, sit, melt/lie down, walk, speed walk, tiptoe, march, and lunge.	Accept partial movements and allow children to stand and bend their knees instead of lying on floor to melt.

3. SUPPORT: School Readiness

Choose one to three school readiness skills to focus on. See the suggestions in the following table; for additional ways to support school readiness, turn to Page 79.

Language	Science	Approaches to Learning
• Discuss weather. • Have children sing along. • Encourage children to sing along.	• Ask children about what happens to snow when it gets warmer. • Make predictions about the weather with children.	• Have children follow directions. • Guide children to maintain sustained attention throughout. • Encourage whole-group engagement.

4. LESSON VARIATIONS

If children learn these activities quickly and need no further practice, or if you want to vary activities for review days, see Lesson Variations on Page 85.

■ CORE ACTIVITY 2: **Obstacle Course**

Structure: Small group

Focus on these objectives:
- Walking: lunge, sidestep, tiptoe, step (over)
- Jogging: slow run
- Motor control

Total time: 3-5 minutes

Key Vocabulary:
- **jog, lunge, march, sidestep, step (over), tiptoe, walk**
- **fast/slow, stop/go**
- **cheer, team**

1. MOVE: Motor Movements

- Place children in two small groups (three to four children in each group). One group cheers for the other group as they go through the obstacle course.
- The cheering group uses egg shakers to cheer on friends (*Go, Nick, go! Go, Mary, go!*); alternatively, they may ring small bells or wave scarves. They can also run or march in place while cheering.
- Meanwhile, have the other group move through the obstacle course. Choose a movement. Encourage continuous movement through the obstacle course.
  - **Walk.** Say: *Step one foot in front of the other. Step one foot on each star (or dot). Look forward, head up.*
  - **Sidestep.** Say: *Face me and take a big step to the side, and now bring your feet together and close. The other foot catches up. Okay, another step!*
  - **Lunge.** Say: *The first thing you do in a lunge is take a giant step forward! Now, bend your front knee! Feel that stretch in your back leg!*
- Have children move with one foot on each star or dot. Have children step over each hurdle. After children step over the last hurdle, have them follow the stars and jog back to the beginning.
- Repeat until all children have multiple opportunities to complete the obstacle course and to cheer for friends.

2. ADAPT: UDL Strategies

Adapt the activity to meet the needs of the children with whom you work. See the suggestions in the following table; for additional ways to adapt, use the UDL Suggestions for Unit 2.

Engagement	Representation	Action & Expression
Sustain attention by asking children to move a little faster each time while still keeping the movement controlled.	<ul><li>Show a picture of each movement. Model each movement with the children.</li><li>Use verbal prompts to describe movement. See the Glossary of Verbal Prompts.</li><li>Use visual supports. See Visual Support Cards for stand, stand in circle, sit, walk, sidestep, and lunge.</li></ul>	Accept partial movements (e.g., giant step instead of lunge).

3. SUPPORT: School Readiness

Choose one to three school readiness skills to focus on. See the suggestions in the following table, along with additional ways to support school readiness on Page 79.

Mathematics	Social
<ul><li>Use positional words (*up/down, over/under*).</li><li>Use ordinal language (*first walk, second step over*).</li></ul>	<ul><li>Have children take turns cheering and moving.</li><li>Have children socialize with peers by cheering for their friends by name.</li></ul>

4. LESSON VARIATIONS

If children learn these activities quickly and need no further practice, or if you want to vary activities for review days, see Lesson Variations on Page 85.

■ CORE ACTIVITY 3: Red Light, Green Light

Structure: Small group

Focus on these objectives:
- Motor control: stop/go, fast/slow
- Following directions
- Walking: walk, speed walk, walk backward, sidestep, lunge, tiptoe
- Running: jog, run

Total time: 3–5 minutes

Key Vocabulary:
- **jog, lunge, sidestep, speed walk, tiptoe, walk**
- **fast/slow, forward/backward, red/yellow/green light, stop/go**

1. MOVE: Motor Movements

- Children stand/start on a numbered floor marker (1–8) for lanes 1–8. At the opposite end of their lane is the finish, designated by a numbered cone, matching the number on their floor marker/lane, as shown in Figure U2.3.
- Tell children which movement they will use. *First we will walk! Now we will speed walk/tiptoe, etc.*
  - **Walk, speed walk, walk backward**
  - **Sidestep**
  - **Jog or run**
  - **Lunge**
  - **Tiptoe**
- Tell children: *When I say "Green light," you go! When I say "Red light," you stop (freeze in place)! Let's practice! Remember to stay in your lane! When you get to the cone, pick up your card and drive back home!* (Children use the number card as a steering wheel as they walk back home.) Use **stop/go** visual supports.
- Repeat with different movements.

2. ADAPT: UDL Strategies

Adapt the activity to meet the needs of the children with whom you work. See the suggestions in the following table; for additional ways to adapt, use the UDL Suggestions for Unit 2.

Engagement	Representation	Action & Expression
Create a challenge by using "yellow" for "slow down" or using very short intervals between saying "stop" and "go."	• Show a picture of green for "go," yellow for "slow down," and red for "stop." See Visual Support Cards. • Use verbal prompts to describe movements. See the Glossary of Verbal Prompts. • Use visual supports. See Visual Support Cards for stand, stand in circle, sit, freeze, walk backward, sidestep, lunge, tiptoe, jog, and run.	• Vary response options by using only "stop" and "go." • Use animal movements: Tiptoe like mouse, stomp like elephant.

3. SUPPORT: School Readiness

Choose one to three school readiness skills to focus on. See the suggestions in the following table; for additional ways to support school readiness, turn to Page 79.

Language	Science	Social	Approaches to Learning
Discuss transportation and traffic rules.	Make predictions with children (e.g., how many steps from start to finish line?).	• Have children play cooperatively. • Have children share space.	Have children follow directions and listen for "stop," "go," and "slow down."

4. LESSON VARIATIONS

If children learn these activities quickly and need no further practice, or if you want to vary activities for review days, see Lesson Variations on Page 85.

■ PHYSICAL ACTIVITY: **Music Video**

Structure: Whole group   **Total time:** 2–4 minutes

Focus on this objective:
Sustained physical activity

1. MOVE: Motor Movements

- Children stand on their floor markers, which are spread out for enough space for floor movement. Say: *Arms out. Make wide, airplane arms without touching a friend.*
- Children move to the selected music video.

Lesson	Video	Total Time
3	Video 1: Marching and/or running in place, sidestepping, jumping, waving arms overhead	2 minutes
4	Video 2: Running in place, jumping from side to side, stepping forward and backward	
5	Videos 1 and/or 2	4 minutes
6		

2. ADAPT: UDL Strategies

Adapt the activity to meet the needs of the children with whom you work. See the suggestions in the following table; for additional ways to adapt, use the UDL Suggestions for Unit 2.

Engagement	Representation	Action & Expression
Provide specific praise and encouragement (e.g., *I love how you're swinging your arms! Excellent job, keep moving!*)	• Use verbal prompts to describe movement. See the Glossary of Verbal Prompts. • Use visual supports. See Visual Support Cards for stand, stand in circle, sit, and airplane arms.	Stand in close proximity to children and model modified movements (e.g., rise up on tiptoes or sway side to side instead of jumping).

3. SUPPORT: School Readiness

During the music video, the primary goal is to have all children maintain sustained/increased physical activity levels. To achieve this goal, teachers can provide models/prompts for motor imitation (imitate actions/songs from video, maintain personal space) and approaches to learning (active engagement, following instructions from video).

4. LESSON VARIATIONS

If children learn these activities quickly and need no further practice, or if you want to vary activities for review days, see Lesson Variations on Page 85.

■ COOL-DOWN

Structure: Whole group   **Total time:** 3–5 minutes

Wrap up: Focus on
- Gathering
- Decreasing heart rate
- Cooling down muscles

Key Vocabulary:
- **legs, feet, arms, toes, stretch**

1. MOVE: Motor Movements

Have children sit on their floor marker. Have children cool-down their bodies with the movements described below. Sing "CHAMPPS Cool-Down Song" with each movement.

- Have children bend and stretch. Say: *Sit with a straight back. Legs straight.* **Reach** *up high. Bend to the* **side. Hold.** *Other side now.* **Reach, side, hold.**
- Have children touch their toes. Say: *Sit with a straight back.* **Arms up.** *Bend forward and reach to* **touch your toes.**
- Have children stretch arms. Say: *Arms straight in front of you.* **Make an X** *or a butterfly. Touch your hand to your shoulder.* **Hold.** *Switch sides.*
- Have children wave goodbye. Say: *Look at your friends. Hold out your hand and wave goodbye.*

End with a yoga pose: Downward-Facing Dog. Say: *Start from a kneeling position. Place your hands on floor. Keep your hips high. Make a triangle. Wag your tail.* (See Figure U2.4.)

Figure U2.4.   Downward-Facing Dog Pose.

2. ADAPT: UDL Strategies

Adapt the activity to meet the needs of the children with whom you work. See the suggestions in the following table; for additional ways to adapt, use the UDL Suggestions for Unit 2.

Engagement	Representation	Action & Expression
Vary volume of voice to match the pace of movement.	• Use verbal prompts to describe movement. See the Glossary of Verbal Prompts. • Use visual supports. See Visual Support Cards for sit, bend and stretch, lift your arms, stretch arms, touch toes, and wave hand.	Begin with simple movements and no singing.

3. SUPPORT: School Readiness

Choose one to three school readiness skills to focus on. See the suggestions in the following table; for additional ways to support school readiness, turn to Page 79.

Language	Mathematics	Approaches to Learning
• Encourage sing-along. • Have children identify body parts.	Use ordinal language (*first, second, third*).	Create a smooth transition between movements.

4. LESSON VARIATIONS

If children learn these activities quickly and need no further practice, or if you want to vary activities for review days, see Lesson Variations on Page 85.

Walk-Around Card

CHAMPPS

1	**Warm-Up**		
	Gathering, increase heart rate, warm up muscles		
	MATERIALS	• 1 floor marker per child • 2 scarves per child (1 in each hand)	
	ACTIVITIES	Sing "CHAMPPS Warm-Up Song." Children walk, march, jog, and stretch.	
2	**Core Activity 1: Snowflake, Snowflake**		
	Physical movement, personal space, motor control		
	MATERIALS	• Floor markers (1 per child) • Scarves (2 per child)	
	ACTIVITIES	Sing "Snowflake, Snowflake." Children walk, tiptoe, speed walk, lunge, and lie down.	
3	**Core Activity 2: Obstacle Course**		
	Physical movement		
	MATERIALS	• Stars (10–12 floor markers) • Hurdles (3 of various heights) • Egg shakers (1 per person for cheering)	
	ACTIVITIES	First: Have children form two small groups. Then: First group moves between stars, on top of floor markers, over hurdles. Children sidestep, lunge, step, and run. Waiting children cheer. Next: Switch groups, and repeat.	
4	**Core Activity 3: Red Light, Green Light**		
	Physical movement, personal space, motor control		
	MATERIALS	• Tape to make lanes • Cones (8, one for each lane) • Stars (8, one per lane, to designate starting place in each lane) • Number cards (can use 1–8 or choose other numerals corresponding to ones being taught in pre-kindergarten curriculum); used to identify lanes	
	ACTIVITIES	First: Choose body movement: walk, sidestep, jog, run, lunge, and/or tiptoe. Then: Say: *Green light!* Have children move from their floor markers to cones. Next: Say: *Red light!* Have children freeze. Repeat.	
5	**Physical Activity: Music Video**		
	Sustained physical activity		
	MATERIALS	Video, video player, wall or screen for viewing	
	Lesson 3 Video (2 min)	**Lesson 4** Video (3 min)	**Lessons 5 and 6** Video (4 min)
6	**Cool-Down**		
	Gathering, lower heart rate, cool down muscles		
	MATERIALS	• Floor markers (1 per child)	
	ACTIVITIES	First: Sing "CHAMPPS Cool-Down Song." Bend and stretch, touch toes, stretch arms, and wave goodbye. Then: Do yoga pose: Downward-Facing Dog.	

Walk-Around Card

CHAMPPS Warm-Up Song

(Sung to the tune of "The Ants Go Marching")

The CHAMPPS go **walking** one by one
Hurrah! Hurrah!
The CHAMPPS go **walking** one by one
Hurrah! Hurrah!
The CHAMPPS go **walking** one by one
This is the way we have some fun
And we all go **walking** on, and on, and on

(Repeat with **marching, jogging,** and **stretching**)

Snowflake, Snowflake

(Sung to the tune of "Frère Jacques/Are You Sleeping?")

Snowflake, snowflake, snowflake, snowflake
Walk around, **walk** around
Kee-eep on **walking**
Kee-eep on **walking**
'Til you melt! 'Til you melt!

(Repeat with **tiptoe, speed walk, lunge,** and **march**)

CHAMPPS Cool-Down Song

(Sung to the tune of "Here We Go 'Round the Mulberry Bush")

This is the way we **bend** and **stretch**

Bend and **stretch, bend** and **stretch**

This is the way we **bend** and **stretch**

At the end of CHAMPPS

(Repeat with "touch our **toes,**" "**stretch** our **arms,**" and "**wave** goodbye.")

CHAMPPS: CHildren in Action Motor Program for PreschoolerS by Paddy C. Favazza and
Michaelene M. Ostrosky with Melissa Stalega, Hsiu-Wen Yang, Katherine Aronson-Ensign, Martin Block,
W. Catherine Cheung, and Yusuf Akemoglu. Copyright © 2023 by Paul H. Brookes Publishing Co., Inc. All rights reserved.

GLOSSARY OF VERBAL PROMPTS

Do (Movement)	Say (Verbal Prompt)	Use
Balance	Airplane arms	Use **airplane arms** to hold yourself steady. Keep your balance.
Bend and stretch	**Reach, side, hold**	Arms up. **Reach** up high. Bend to the **side. Hold.** Other side now. **Reach, side, hold.**
Fly	Arms out, up/down	We're going to fly like birds. Put your **arms out** like an airplane and move them **up and down.**
Jog	Slow run	Show me how you run. See how your feet move very fast. Now let's move our feet a little slower. We are doing a **slow run.** We are jogging.
	Head up	Move your legs quickly and keep your **head up.**
Jump	Bend knees, push up, land feet together	Let's jump. **Bend** your knees. Look up. **Push up** off the ground! **Land** with your **feet together.**
Leap	Feet together, hands at your side, jump up	Get ready. **Feet and hands** on the ground. **Jump up** and forward!
Lunge	Step and bend	The first thing you do in a lunge is take a giant **step** forward! Now, **bend** your front knee! Feel that stretch in your back leg!
March	**High knees**	Let's march! Marching is like walking, except with **high knees!** Keep those **knees up high!**
	Touch your knees to your hands	March with **high knees.** Hold your arms straight in front. **Touch your knees to your hands.**
Pump (arms)	**Pump your arms**	**Pump your arms!** Swing the opposite arm as you step to keep your body balanced.
Run	**Fast/Slow**	When we run, we move really fast. Use **fast feet** to run. Good! Let's **slow** down as we get ready to stop.
Sidestep	Step, together/close	Face me, and take a big **step** to the side, and now **bring your feet together and close.** The other foot catches up. Okay, another step!
Speed walk	Fast steps	Speed walking means walking fast, but not as fast as running! **Fast steps!**
Step (over)	Foot up, over	Your **foot goes up and over** the obstacle. So, take a big step and lift your foot up high!
Stretch	**Touch toes**	Stand with straight knees, lean forward, and **touch your toes!**
	Arms up	Good job; now stand up tall, and reach up your arms. Put your **arms up** like a "V"!
Stretch arms	Arms up	Put your **arms up!** Good job!
	Make an X	Now **make an X with your arms, kiss your shoulder** with one arm and feel the stretch!
	Kiss your shoulder	
Tiptoe	**Baby steps**	Good; now take **baby steps** forward. Little **baby steps** while you tiptoe!
Touch toes	Touch toes, hold	It's time to **touch your toes** and **hold** your hands there.
Walk	Heel down, then toe	Put your **heel down** first, **then** your **toe. Heel, toe!**
	Swing arms	When you walk, keep your rhythm by **swinging your arms.**
	Green/yellow/red	When I say **"Green,"** you can go! **Yellow** means slow down! **Red** means stop!

UDL SUGGESTIONS

Engagement							
Means of Engagement	**Warm-Up**	**Core Activity 1: Snowflake, Snowflake**	**Core Activity 2: Obstacle Course**	**Core Activity 3: Red Light, Green Light**	**Video 1**	**Video 2**	**Cool-Down**
Recruit Interest							
Child choice	Warm-up moves	Motor moves	Motor moves Change direction	Motor moves	Which video to play	Which video to play	Cool-down movements
Novel/familiar	Familiar moves (wave hands)	Familiar objects (wave scarf) Familiar tune (Popcorn Kernels)	Familiar objects (floor markers) Familiar moves (walk, run)	Familiar moves (walk, run, jog)	New video Repeat video	New video Repeat video	Consistent use of floor markers
Sustain Effort and Persistence							
Praise/ encourage	Say: *You sang every word; good job!* *You ran slowly when you jogged; great listening!*	Say: *Nice job freezing right away!* *You wave those scarves beautifully!*	Say: *Good job staying on the floor markers!* *Nice, big sidesteps!*	Say: *Way to stop right away!* *What long lunges!* *Such fast running!*	Say: *Excellent energy!* *Fantastic, fast running!*	Say: *Beautiful job copying the video!* *Such high jumping!*	Say: *Nice calm bodies. I like how you are moving slowly during the cool-down.*
Vary complexity	Increase/ Decrease number of moves.	Vary speed of song, movements.	Vary movements (walk or crawl instead of jog).	Vary movements (walk slowly instead of tiptoe).	Vary volume of singing (yell or whisper).	Vary volume of singing (yell or whisper).	Increase/ Decrease number of moves.
Vary setup, directions	Sing softly/ loudly.	Sing softly/ loudly. Vary number of scarves (1 or 2).	Vary length. Beginner versus advanced/ intermediate course	Vary distance. Hold colored papers instead of giving verbal directions.	Vary materials (give scarves, instruments).	Vary materials (give scarves, instruments).	Vary materials (use instruments instead of scarves).

Representation

Means of Representation	Warm-Up	Core Activity 1: Snowflake, Snowflake	Core Activity 2: Obstacle Course	Core Activity 3: Red Light, Green Light	Video 1	Video 2	Cool-Down
Forms of Communication							
Auditory	Glossary of Verbal Prompts						→
Visual	Visual Support Cards						→
Tactile	Hold scarves.	Hold scarves.	Cheer for peers with wrist bells or small pompoms.	Add instruments, shakers, or scarves.			→
Multiple Levels of Complexity							
Key vocabulary: define/model	walk march jog stretch	walk tiptoe speed walk sidestep lunge melt	walk lunge step over tiptoe sidestep run	stop, go slow down walk backward walk speed walk sidestep jog tiptoe lunge stomp	walk sidestep run wave hands jump	walk run jump clap hands	bend and stretch touch toes stretch arms wave goodbye

Action & Expression

Means of Expression	Warm-Up	Core Activity 1: Snowflake, Snowflake	Core Activity 2: Obstacle Course	Core Activity 3: Red Light, Green Light	Video 1	Video 2	Cool-Down
Variety of responses	Sing, clap, or hum song.	Sing or hum song. Clap if not using scarves.	Walk beside the obstacle course, rather than through it. Complete only one part of the course.	Do not use "yellow light." Children repeat "Red light!" after leader. Add animal moves: Tiptoe like a mouse! Stomp like an elephant!	Say words that match movements.	Say words that match movements.	Say words that match movements. Sit and breathe slowly. Only do movements, no singing.

UDL SUGGESTIONS *(continued)*

Means of Expression	Warm-Up	Core Activity 1: Snowflake, Snowflake	Core Activity 2: Obstacle Course	Core Activity 3: Red Light, Green Light	Video 1	Video 2	Cool-Down
Complexity of responses	Partial movement (walk instead of jogging)	Partial movement (bend knees instead of lying down)	Do just one movement (walk, sidestep, tiptoe) during each repetition of the course. Have course next to wall or provide something to hold onto. Walk with a peer, holding hands for support.	Partial movement (partially stopping, big steps instead of lunges) Do the crab walk! Set up as a relay, where partner stands at cone; completes the return after partner touches hand.	Partial movement (walk instead of sidestep)	Partial movement (walk instead of run)	Partial movement (touch knees instead of toes)

SUPPORT SCHOOL READINESS SKILLS

LANGUAGE AND LITERACY	Warm-Up	Core Activity 1: Snowflake, Snowflake	Core Activity 2: Obstacle Course	Core Activity 3: Red Light, Green Light	Cool-Down
Expresses feelings (hot, thirsty, tired, hungry, sleepy, sweaty)	Ask children how they feel after warm-up.	Ask children how they feel in different types of weather.	Ask: *After finishing the obstacle course do you feel proud, tired, frustrated, happy, excited?*	Ask: *How do you feel when you are waiting to start?*	Ask: *How do you feel now that CHAMPPS is over?*
Engages in active discussion (shares ideas, asks and answers questions)	Ask: *Who can show us your favorite warm-up move?*	Have children ask/answer questions about weather/seasons.	Ask: *Which parts of the course are easy/hard for you?*	Ask: *How do we say "Stop" in sign language? In Spanish?*	Ask children for new game ideas.
Communicates personal experiences and interests	Ask children about their favorite warm-up move.	Ask about favorite seasons/holidays.	Ask which parts of the course are most difficult.	Discuss traffic lights and signs and where children have seen them before.	Ask children about their favorite CHAMPPS activity.
Listens to/uses formal and informal language (listens to/sings songs, uses different voices)	Have children listen and sing along.	Have children listen and sing along.	Have children appropriately ask for a turn on the course.	Have children repeat motor movements.	Have children sing along.
Recognizes shapes (circle, square, triangle, rectangle)	Have children move in a circle.	Have children freeze and point to a shape (circle, square, triangle) in the room.	Ask: *What shapes do you see on the course?*	Make number cards in shape of triangle, circle, square, and rectangle. Ask: *What is the shape of your number card?*	Have children sit in a circle. Hold different shape cards in each hand while doing stretches. Name your shapes!
Recognizes letters	Have children pick a letter card and hold it with two hands while doing warm-up. Ask: *What is your letter? What is a word that starts with that letter?*	Using a marker, write letters on scarves (or remnant material). Write lowercase letters on half of the scarves and uppercase letters on the other half of the scarves. Have children match upper-/lowercase letters.	Place letters along the path for children to retrieve. At the finish line, name the letters they found.	Replace number cards with letter cards. Have children name their letters. Hold signs with the words "Go" and "Stop."	Hold letter cards with two hands while doing stretches. Name your letters!

SUPPORT SCHOOL READINESS SKILLS *(continued)*

MATHEMATICS	Warm-Up	Core Activity 1: Snowflake, Snowflake	Core Activity 2: Obstacle Course	Core Activity 3: Red Light, Green Light	Cool-Down
Number recognition (count, one–one correspondence)	Have children count moves instead of singing.	Count how long (seconds) children can stay frozen without moving.	Count how many steps it takes to complete the obstacle course.	Children use one-to-one correspondence (move between numbers).	Have children stretch while counting.
Positional and directional words (*up, down, between, over, forward, backward, sideways*)	As children walk around the room, have them go forward/backward between two cones, on tiptoes, go down low, etc.	Have children wave their scarves up high, then down low.	Ask: *What do you have to step over? What do you have to walk between?*	Children walk backward, forward, sideways.	Bend side to side. Have children count while they slowly bend to left/right.
Ordinal language (*first, second, etc.*)	Use ordinal words to describe the order of moves (*first walk, second jog, etc.*).	Discuss the order of seasons: *First comes spring, second summer,* etc.	Order of moves	Ask: *Who finished first? Second? Third?*	Order of moves
Categorizing and sorting objects (height, color)	Children line up by height (shortest to tallest).	Have children with yellow and blue scarves melt while children with red and green scares float like snowflakes.	Have boys do one movement and girls do another.	Place children into lanes according to height: shortest person in lane 1 and tallest person in lane 8.	Have children in sneakers do one movement and children in sandals do another. Children wearing blue/yellow do different movements.
Patterns (recognize, describe, reproduce)	Create a movement pattern (walk backward five steps, walk forward five steps).	Have children stand in a circle in a pattern: boy, girl, boy, girl.	Ask: *What pattern do you see in the obstacle course?*	Discuss how red/green, red/green is a pattern.	Create movement pattern (touch toes then stretch, repeat).

SCIENCE	Warm-Up	Core Activity 1: Snowflake, Snowflake	Core Activity 2: Obstacle Course	Core Activity 3: Red Light, Green Light	Cool-Down
Ask/answer questions together (*Who? What? Where? How?*).	Ask: *Is anybody feeling hot? Sweaty? Why do you think you feel that way?*	Ask: *What happens to snowflakes when it gets warmer? What happens to the rain when it gets colder?*	Ask: *What part of the obstacle course is easy/hard for you?*	Ask: *Who was first, second, third? Who was last?*	Ask: *What happens to our heart when we run? When we slow down/rest?*
Make predictions together (*What if?*).		Ask: *What happens to the snowflakes if it gets hot?*	Ask: *What will happen if you go too fast through the obstacle course?*	Ask: *Is it harder to take baby steps or giant steps?*	Ask: *What would happen if you didn't stretch?*

SCIENCE	Warm-Up	Core Activity 1: Snowflake, Snowflake	Core Activity 2: Obstacle Course	Core Activity 3: Red Light, Green Light	Cool-Down
Understand weather/seasons, calendar/days of the week.	Discuss which days of the week you have CHAMPPS.	Ask: *What are the four seasons? During which season do we see snowflakes?*	Recite the days of week (or months) as you go through obstacle course.	Say: *Let's pretend it is a snowy day.* Ask: *What happens to the roads when it snows? So, what will we do in our game? (Go slow!)*	Say: *Whew! Who's hot like me? What season is the hottest?*
Discuss characteristics of living things (*humans, animals, plants*).	Discuss pumping hearts after warm-up.	Have children pretend to be animals instead of snowflakes.	Have children pretend to be riding a horse over the course or flying like a bird through the course.	Ask: *Who rides in a car? How do we keep people safe when we are in a car?*	Discuss slowing down breathing, hearts.
Use sensory vocabulary (*feel, hear, see*).	Say: *Touch your heart. What do you feel? Do you feel it pumping/beating?*	Ask: *What does snow or a snowflake feel like? Can you hear a snowflake fall?*	Ask: *How did you/ your friends feel when you finished the obstacle course?*	Ask: *Can you understand me if I use sign language? If I whisper, can you hear me?*	Have children put their hand on their chest. Ask: *Who can feel their heartbeat?*

MOTOR	Warm-Up	Core Activity 1: Snowflake, Snowflake	Core Activity 2: Obstacle Course	Core Activity 3: Red Light, Green Light	Cool-Down
Balance	Add balancing on one foot.	Ask: *Can you keep your balance while swaying like a snowflake?*	Add a balance beam to course.	Put tape on floor. Have children walk (heel/toe) on their own strip of tape.	Bend and stretch while maintaining balance.
Visual tracking	Add scarf to visually track as it falls to the ground.	Draw paper snowflakes on balloons and watch them float to the ground.	Use your eyes to follow your friend. Shake your egg/bells when your friend reaches the finish.	Use a green, yellow, or red paper to signal go, slow, or stop instead of giving verbal directions.	Use your eyes to follow your hands as you touch your toes.
Motor imitation	Have children imitate leader/peers. ⟶				
Body awareness	Have children recognize which body parts to use.	Ask: *How can you float around like snowflakes without touching your friends?*	*Show me how your hands move when you are walking.*	When children freeze, have them put their hands on their head, shoulders, etc.	Have children touch or stretch various body parts.
Body movement (touch toes, raise arms, catch, throw, bend knees)	Have children touch their toes, raise arms.	Have children throw/catch scarves.	Have children step over hurdles.	Have children shrug shoulders, wiggle foot, etc.	Have children bend and stretch, touch toes, stretch arms.

SUPPORT SCHOOL READINESS SKILLS *(continued)*

MOTOR	Warm-Up	Core Activity 1: Snowflake, Snowflake	Core Activity 2: Obstacle Course	Core Activity 3: Red Light, Green Light	Cool-Down
Strength/speed/ duration	Ask: *Who can run in place for 5 seconds (count)? 10 seconds? Longer than 10 seconds?*	Have children speed walk.	Have children jog versus run.	Call out colors/ directions at an increased speed.	Have children move slowly. Increase number of repetitions for greater duration.
Coordination (eye/ hand; eye/foot)	Add throwing/ catching scarves. Leader says, *Follow the scarf with your eyes!*	Have children float like snowflakes while placing a scarf on head, on forearm, on shoulders.	Have children go through course while moving an object (scarf, beanbag) from left to right hand.	Have children hold number card on top of head (with one hand, with two hands) while walking.	Have children stretch, touching right/left hand to opposite foot.
Locomotion (walk, run, jump, hop, kick, strike)	Have children walk, march, jog.	Have children walk, tiptoe, lunge, march.	Have children walk, sidestep, lunge, run.	Have children walk, run, jog, sidestep.	Have children walk very slowly, in place; kick in slow motion while standing and then lying on the ground.
Directionality (forward, backward, sidesteps)	Have children switch direction *(walk backward, sidestep).*	Tell "snowflakes" to walk backward, sideways.	Have children sidestep.	Have children sidestep, move forward toward leader.	Say: *Lean to the right! To the left! Forward!*
Personal space	Have children use their own floor marker.	Have children move around shared space.	Have children take turns on the obstacle course.	Have children move around shared space.	Have children sit on floor markers.
Cross midline reach	Have children use right hand to reach across body and hold left shoulder. Repeat using left hand to reach across body to hold right shoulder.	Have children hug themselves because they are "cold."	Have children go through obstacle course while giving themselves a bear hug.	Have children complete movements giving themselves a bear hug.	Have children do stretches that cross midline (e.g., stretch right/left hand to opposite foot/knee/hip).
Grasp and release	Add throwing/ tapping scarves.	Have children release scarves when they "melt."	Have children carry a beanbag through the course and drop it into a bucket.	Have children carry/squeeze nerf balls while doing red light/green light.	Have children grasp/release their foot when doing toe touches.
Self-regulation (go slow, go fast, stop)	Have children sing song slowly, move slowly.	Have children "melt" at end of song.	Have children stop at end of course.	Have children freeze on command.	Have children move slowly.
Music and dance	Encourage children to sing along, select next move.	Have children sing along, singing slow and fast while swaying (in place) slowly and quickly.	Have children dance through the obstacle course.	Have children go/ stop when music plays/stops.	Encourage children to sing along and select the next move.

SOCIAL-EMOTIONAL	Warm-Up	Core Activity 1: Snowflake, Snowflake	Core Activity 2: Obstacle Course	Core Activity 3: Red Light, Green Light	Cool-Down
Recognizes and describes emotions	Ask: *How do you feel about CHAMPPS today?*	Ask: *What are the four seasons? Which is your favorite? Why?*	Ask: *How do you feel when you hear your friends cheering for you?*	Ask: *How do you feel when you are running quickly down the course?*	Ask: *What was your favorite part of CHAMPPS today?*
Solves/prevents problems	Review personal space.	Discuss being safe in a shared space.	Discuss the importance and safety of taking turns on the course.	Have children maintain personal space.	Have children stretch out their arms to maintain personal space.
Learns independence/self-help	Have children gather their own scarves.	Have children gather their own scarves.	Have children help set up/put away the course.	Have children take turns being the leader.	Have children put away their own scarves.
Takes turns/waits turn	Have children wait to move until everyone has a scarf.	Have half of class (boys/girls) take turns floating and watching.	Have children cheer while waiting.	Have children wait until the leader says, *Green light!*	Have children wait until leader says *Girls, line up! Those wearing purple line up!*
Helps/supports peers	Have children move hand-in-hand with a partner.	Place children in groups of three, and have them hold hands and slowly float together, making sure everyone stays balanced.	Have children hold a peer's hand for balance.	Have children do this as a relay, with one partner at the start and the other partner at the cone.	Have children point to someone who is their friend. Position children next to their Cool-Down Buddy.
Plays cooperatively	Have children pass out scarves to one another.	Children share space with peers.	Have children cheer on their peers.	Have children congratulate a peer with a handshake, thumbs up or high five.	Ask: *Who was a good friend of yours today during CHAMPPS? Let's applaud our friends!*
Shares materials	Have each child hold one end of a shared scarf.	Snowflakes are "stuck together"; have each child hold one end of a partner's scarf.	Have children share materials and set up the obstacles course together.	Encourage children to pass the "steering wheel" to the next player.	Ask: *Who shared materials with you today? Let's clap for our friends!*
Socializes with peers	Add a greeting to children's warm-up.	Snowflakes are "stuck together"; have each child hold a partner's hand.	Have children call peers' names while cheering.	Have peers compliment each other, e.g., "Nice freezing!"	Have children wave at peers.

SUPPORT SCHOOL READINESS SKILLS (continued)

APPROACHES TO LEARNING	Warm-Up	Core Activity 1: Snowflake, Snowflake	Core Activity 2: Obstacle Course	Core Activity 3: Red Light, Green Light	Cool-Down
Transitions into/out of activities	Have children return to floor marker.	Have children return to floor marker.	Have children transition between being on the course and cheering on the sidelines.	Have children return to floor marker when game restarts.	Have children return to circle, sitting on floor markers.
Listens to/follows directions	Have children listen and imitate movement.	Have children listen and imitate movement.	Have children do correct movements.	⟶	
Demonstrates focused attention	Have children listen for next movement.	Have children listen for next movement.	Have children keep attention with small group.	Have children listen for next movement.	Have children listen for next movement.
Demonstrates sustained attention	Have children stay with whole group.	Have children stay with whole group.	Have children stay at obstacle course.	Have children stay with group.	Have children stay with whole group.
Demonstrates active engagement in small/large group	Have children move around room with whole class.	Have children move around room with whole class.	Have children cheer on small group.	Have children move with class.	Whole-group activity
Demonstrates active engagement in independent task	Have children take turns naming the next warm up movement.	Have children show different ways a snowflake melts.	Children walk course independently.	Children walk independently, staying in their lane.	Have children take turns naming the next cool down movement.

Lesson Variations

■ WARM-UP VARIATIONS

Music/Rhythm/Dance

Variation 1: Crab Walk

Structure	Materials	Instructions
Whole group	• Floor markers • Projector with Internet access	1. Children stand in a line, arms-length apart, facing the screen. 2. Play a YouTube video demonstrating how to crab walk. (See the video selection criteria on Page 267.) 3. Children imitate crab-walk music video for their warm-up.

Other

Variation 2: Warm-Up Yoga Poses

Structure	Materials	Instructions
Whole group	• Floor markers	1. Have children stand on their floor markers in warm-up circle. 2. Have children do the Mountain Pose. Say: *Reach your arms to the sky. Say, "Thank you, Sun."* (See Figure U2.5.) 3. Have children do the Forward Fold. Say: *Reach your fingers toward your toes and keep your knees bent slightly. Say, "Thank you, Earth."* (See Figure U2.6.) 4. Repeat steps 2–3 several times.

Figure U2.5. Mountain Pose.　**Figure U2.6.** Forward Fold.

Sports/Games

Variation 3: Tic-Tac-Toe Game

Structure	Materials	Instructions
Whole group	• Floor markers • Projector with Internet access • Small hula hoops • Scarves (one per child; half in one color and half another color)	1. To prepare for the activity, teachers watch a YouTube video to see an example of the Tic-Tac-Toe game (https://www.youtube.com/watch?v=IRDp5HcZyVA). (See recommended video listings.) 2. Place nine hula hoops together to form Tic-Tac-Toe board. 3. Use floor markers or tape to make a line parallel to the hula hoops on the other side of the classroom. 4. Have children form two lines behind the floor markers or tape. One line will use red scarves, and the other line will use blue scarves. 5. The first child in each line will start and race toward the hula hoops, placing their scarf in the middle of one. 6. Each team/line of children will try to get three scarves in a row with their red or blue scarves. 7. To modify, instead have children stand in two lines and have them race to a bucket to place the scarf in a bucket across the room.

■ CORE ACTIVITY 1: **Snowflake, Snowflake** VARIATION

Music/Rhythm/Dance

Variation 1: Instrumental "Frère Jacques"

Structure	Materials	Instructions
Whole group	• Floor markers • Projector with Internet access	1. Play an instrumental version of "Frère Jacques" during Core Activity 1, Snowflake, Snowflake. (Check YouTube for instrumental versions of the song.)

Arts and Crafts

Variation 2: Snowflake Art

Structure	Materials	Instructions
Whole group	• Paper • Printer • Crayons, colored pencils, or markers	1. Print small paper snowflake templates for all children. 2. Have children color/decorate their snowflakes. (These could be laminated with each child's name on the back for use in other games.) 3. Use the snowflakes during Core Activity 1 and the Snowflake Game.

Sports/Games

Variation 3: Snowflake Relay Game

Structure	Materials	Instructions
Whole group	• Floor markers • Paper snowflakes (see art activity above)	1. Divide class into two groups (or four, depending on class size). 2. Mark a starting line and a finish line. 3. Have half the class stand on the starting line and half on the finish line. 4. Place a paper snowflake on the first child's hands (palms up or palms down) OR have them hold it on their head (with one hand or two hands). Then have them walk toward the finish line. 5. When they reach the finish line, have them pass the snowflake to the next person. 6. Continue until all children have had a turn.

■ CORE ACTIVITY 2: **Obstacle Course** VARIATION

Music/Rhythm/Dance

Variation 1: Zorba's Dance

Structure	Materials	Instructions
Whole group	• Floor markers • Projector with Internet access	1. Play a YouTube video of the song "Zorba's Dance" during Core Activity 2, Obstacle Course. 2. The music starts off slowly, so have children start by walking. 3. As the music gets faster, have children speed walk, jog, and run.

Sports/Games

Variation 2: Running Skills

Structure	Materials	Instructions
Whole group	• Floor markers	1. Have children place their hands on the wall and learn toward it, at about a 45-degree angle. 2. Tell children to pick one foot up and bend their knee. 3. Have children switch feet. 4. Repeat several times, going faster each time.

■ CORE ACTIVITY 3: **Red Light, Green Light** VARIATIONS

Music/Rhythm/Dance

Variation 1: Songs

Structure	Materials	Instructions
Whole group	• Floor markers • Projector with Internet access	1. Select music for the activity. Two good options on YouTube are "Jambo Bwana" (a Kenyan song about saying hello) and "O Sapo não lava o pé" (a Portuguese song about frogs). 2. For "green light," play the music. 3. Stop the music for "red light."

Arts and Crafts

Variation 2: Red Light, Green Light Art

Structure	Materials	Instructions
Whole group	• Paper • Crayons, colored pencils, or markers	1. Have children make small red light, green light signs using blank paper and crayons, colored pencils, or markers. 2. Let children take turns being the leader, calling out red light (green light) and showing their red light (green light) sign at the same time.

■ MUSIC VIDEO VARIATION

Music/Rhythm/Dance

Variation 1: Stop

Structure	Materials	Instructions
Whole group	• Floor markers • Projector with Internet access	1. Have children stand on their floor markers. 2. Play a YouTube video that requires children to follow stop/go directions. (See the video selection criteria on Page 267.) 3. Have children imitate the music video.

Home Activities Record

CHAMPPS

Child: _____   Teacher: _____

Unit: _____   Week: _____

Please return by: _____

Thank you for playing with me! Please tell my teachers if we did CHAMPPS activities this week at home. Write a check (√) if we practiced CHAMPPS at home this week. You can also write comments to tell my teachers how I did when we practiced CHAMPPS at home! Please give this form to my teacher each week.

Check (√) if you did CHAMPPS practice.	Parent/Child Comments

Home Activities Record

CHAMPPS

Child: _____   Teacher: _____

Unit: _____   Week: _____

Please return by: _____

Thank you for playing with me! Please tell my teachers if we did CHAMPPS activities this week at home. Write a check (√) if we practiced CHAMPPS at home this week. You can also write comments to tell my teachers how I did when we practiced CHAMPPS at home! Please give this form to my teacher each week.

Check (√) if you did CHAMPPS practice.	Parent/Child Comments

CHAMPPS Home Activities

Hi, Family and Friends!

I am beginning Unit 2 of CHAMPPS at school! I am learning all about my body, walking, and running. Now I want to play CHAMPPS with you! It only takes 10–20 minutes. Thank you for playing with me!

Love, Your Little CHAMP

■ ACTIVITY 1: **Warm-Up**

Materials No materials needed.
Directions Move and sing with me.

CHAMPPS Warm-Up Song

(Tune: "The Ants Go Marching")

The CHAMPPS go walking one by one
Hurrah, hurrah!
The CHAMPPS go walking one by one
Hurrah, hurrah!
The CHAMPPS go walking one by one
This is the way we have some fun
And we all go walking on, and on, and on!

Repeat with: marching, jogging.

■ ACTIVITY 2: **Snowflake, Snowflake**

Materials Scarf, napkin, or kitchen towel

Directions Wave a scarf. Move and sing with me.

Snowflake, Snowflake

(Tune: "Frère Jacques/Are You Sleeping?")

Snowflake, snowflake, snowflake, snowflake
Walk around, walk around
Kee-eep on walking, kee-eep on walking
'Til you melt! 'Til you melt! [lie on floor]

Sing again. Choose: tiptoe, speed walk, lunge, jog, or march.

■ ACTIVITY 3: **Cool-Down**

Materials None

Directions Stretch and sing with me.

CHAMPPS Cool-Down Song

(Tune: "Here We Go 'Round the Mulberry Bush")

This is the way we touch our toes
Touch our toes, touch our toes
This is the way we touch our toes
At the end of CHAMPPS

Repeat with: bend and stretch, wave goodbye.

sit

touch toes

bend and stretch

wave hand

Read and move together!

Look for this book at your local library: *Dance with Me* by Charles R. Smith, Jr.

Dance to this YouTube video: _____

Thank you for playing with me!

CHAMPPS Home Activities

Hi, Family and Friends!

I am doing Unit 2 of CHAMPPS at school! I am learning all about my body and how to walk and run on a path. Now I want to play CHAMPPS with you! It only takes 10–20 minutes. Thank you for playing with me!

Love, Your Little CHAMP

■ ACTIVITY 1: **Warm-Up**

Materials None

Directions Move and sing with me.

CHAMPPS Warm-Up Song

(Tune: "The Ants Go Marching")

The CHAMPPS go walking one by one
Hurrah, hurrah!
The CHAMPPS go walking one by one
Hurrah, hurrah!
The CHAMPPS go walking one by one
This is the way we have some fun
And we all go walking on, and on, and on!

Repeat with: marching, jogging.

■ ACTIVITY 2: **Obstacle Course**

Materials Tape or string: Create a path.
Different-sized objects; for example, ball, pillow, stuffed animals, toys, books, blocks

Directions

1. Make a path for me! For ideas, look at the path my teacher made.
2. I can walk, speed walk, tiptoe, step over, and sidestep around many objects.

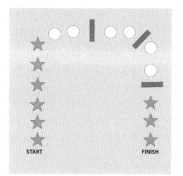

■ ACTIVITY 3: **Cool-Down**

Materials None

Directions Stretch and sing with me.

CHAMPPS Cool-Down Song

(Tune: "Here We Go 'Round the Mulberry Bush")

This is the way we touch our toes
Touch our toes, touch our toes
This is the way we touch our toes
At the end of CHAMPPS

Repeat with: bend and stretch, wave goodbye.

sit · touch toes · bend and stretch · wave hand

Read and move together!

Look for this book at your local library: *Wiggle! Like an Octopus* by Harriet Ziefert.

Dance to this YouTube video: _____

Thank you for playing with me!

CHAMPPS Home Activities

Hi, Family and Friends!

I am finishing up Unit 2 of CHAMPPS at school! I am learning all about my body and different ways to walk and run. Now I want to play CHAMPPS with you! It only takes 10–20 minutes. Thank you for playing with me!

Love, Your Little CHAMP

■ ACTIVITY 1: **Warm-Up**

Materials None
Directions Move and sing with me.

CHAMPPS Warm-Up Song

(Tune: "The Ants Go Marching")

The CHAMPPS go walking one by one
Hurrah, hurrah!
The CHAMPPS go walking one by one
Hurrah, hurrah!
The CHAMPPS go walking one by one
This is the way we have some fun
And we all go walking on, and on, and on!

Repeat with: marching, jogging.

■ ACTIVITY 3: **Red Light, Green Light**

Materials Start line and finish line: Use tape, paper, chairs, string, or pole.
Directions

1. Say "Green light" for GO. Say "Red light" for STOP.
2. Choose a movement: walk, run, lunge, tiptoe, march, or sidestep.
3. I move from START to FINISH. Look at the start and finish lines we used at school!

■ ACTIVITY 3: **Cool-Down**

Materials None
Directions Stretch and sing with me.

CHAMPPS Cool-Down Song

(Tune: "Here We Go 'Round the Mulberry Bush")

This is the way we touch our toes
Touch our toes, touch our toes
This is the way we touch our toes
At the end of CHAMPPS

Repeat with: bend and stretch, wave goodbye.

sit   touch toes   bend and stretch   wave hand

Read and move together!

Look for this book at your local library: *From Head to Toe* by Ezra Jack Keats.

Dance to this YouTube video: _____

Thank you for playing with me!

Get Moving:
CHAMPPS Motor Skills Units

CHAMPPS

UNIT 3

Balance, Jumping, and Hopping

<table>
<tr><td colspan="2">Unit Objectives</td></tr>
<tr>
<td></td>
<td>1. Motor Movement. Become familiar with these movement concepts: balance (dynamic and static), jumping (with two feet, galloping, skipping) and hopping (on one foot).</td>
</tr>
<tr>
<td></td>
<td>2. Body Awareness. Identify and move head, arms, legs, knees, feet, and toes.</td>
</tr>
<tr>
<td></td>
<td>3. Dynamic Balance. Move and balance. Walk on balance beam, step/hop onto floor markers and multilevel steps.</td>
</tr>
<tr>
<td></td>
<td>4. Static Balance. Maintain balance while standing in one spot.</td>
</tr>
<tr>
<td></td>
<td>5. Motor Planning. Think about and plan movement through obstacle course.</td>
</tr>
<tr>
<td></td>
<td>6. Sustained Physical Activity. Engage in continuous movement during music video.</td>
</tr>
</table>

Key Vocabulary

Body Parts	**arms, feet, knees, legs**
Motor Movement	**balance, gallop, hop, jog, jump, leap, skip, stretch, sway**
Concepts	**apart, around, move, on top, over, stand still, together, under**
Pre-academic	Animals: **alligator, bunny, duck/duckling, fox, frog, grasshopper, horse, kangaroo, lily pad, nest, wing** Other: **apples, eggs**
Social-Emotional	**cheer, team**

UNIT LESSON

Time	Activity	Focus		
3–5 min	WARM-UP	Gathering	Increase Heart Rate	Warm-Up Muscles
5 min	CORE 1: **Bunnies and Foxes**	Motor Movement		Static Balance
5 min	CORE 2*: **Hungry Horsey**	Motor Movement	Dynamic Balance	Motor Planning
5 min	CORE 3*: **River Jump**			
2–4 min	PHYSICAL ACTIVITY: Music Video (Lessons 3–6 only)	Motor Imitation & Sustained Physical Activity		
3 min	COOL-DOWN	Gathering	Decrease Heart Rate	Cool-Down Muscles

*Core 2 and Core 3 occur simultaneously with the class divided into two small groups. After both small groups complete one activity, children remain with their group and the small groups switch locations/activities.

PREPARATION AND MATERIALS

Activity	Materials (class of 15 children with 2 adults)
WARM-UP COOL-DOWN Whole group	Numbered floor markers (1 per person)
CORE 1 **Bunnies and Foxes** Whole group	Numbered floor markers (1 per person) Bell
CORE 2* **Hungry Horsey** Small group	Stars (5–6) Hurdles (2–3 of various heights) Low balance beam (2) Multilevel stepping-stones or blocks (2–3) Pool noodles (1–2 per child) (different lengths: full length, 1-foot, 2-foot) Pool noodle pieces (20–25) (cut several pool noodles into 2- or 3-inch pieces) Bucket (1 for pool noodle pieces)
CORE 3* **River Jump** Small group	Stars (15–20) Cones (3) Block (1) Number floor markers (6–10) Beanbags (2 per child) Egg shakers (1 per child) Buckets (2—one for egg shakers and one for beanbags)
Visual Support Cards	
Used for these movements: stand, stand in circle, sit, lift your arms, touch toes, balance, sway, jog in place, airplane arms, bend and stretch, wave hand, jump up and down, grasp, put in/take out. Visit the Brookes Download Hub to download and print the Visual Support Cards for Unit 3.	

*Because Core 2 and Core 3 activities occur simultaneously, use the Planning Notes form to preassign children to Small Group 1 or Small Group 2. Once all children complete one of the two core activities, they switch to the other activity. For smooth transitions to the next activity, consider keeping small groups relatively stable once they are set, unless a teacher determines that a child needs to be placed in a different group due to specific support or behavioral needs.

SETUP

Warm-Up and Cool-Down

Place floor markers in a circle or square in the middle of the room. Allow enough space between markers for children to be standing arm's length apart.

Hungry Horsey

In this activity, children walk through the course while balancing an "apple" (small pool noodle) on top of a long pool noodle. Once they get to the bucket, they place the "apple" in the bucket and gallop back home, using the long pool noodle as a horse. To set up:

1. Line up multilevel steps (or blocks) in a straight line. Place one or two balance beams just beyond the steps.

2. Line up hurdles of various heights in a crescent shape starting at the end of the balance beam.

3. Place bucket at end of hurdles, which is used to collect the "apples" (small pieces of pool noodles).

4. Line up stars from bucket all the way back to the beginning. The course should move in a loop. See Figure U3.1.

River Jump

In this activity, children move through the course like ducks while holding "eggs" (beanbags) under their arms ("wings") and walking between "alligators" (cones). Once they get to the "nest" (bucket), they place the beanbags in it. Then they leap along the path of "lily pads" to get back to the start. To set up:

1. Create a path using two lines of stars. Children will walk down the middle.

2. Place cones after the stars in a zigzag pattern. Place stars in between the cones so children can use the stars as a guide for where to walk.

3. Place a bucket following the cones. Place a block next to the bucket. Line up floor markers in a straight line all the way back to the beginning. See Figure U3.2.

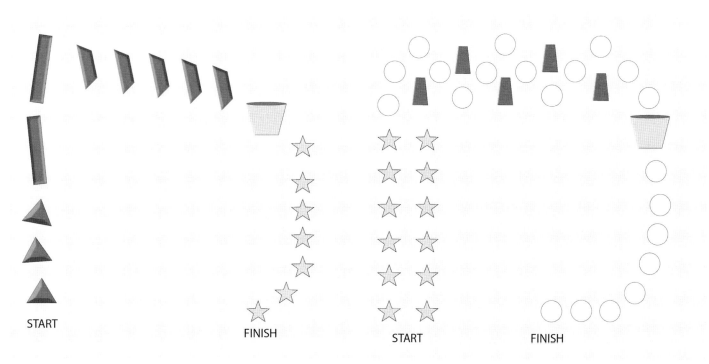

Figure U3.1. Classroom setup for Hungry Horsey.

Figure U3.2. Classroom setup for River Jump.

Featured Interactive Movement Books

- *Jump!*, written and illustrated by Steve Lavis. Dutton Juvenile, 1998.
- *Silly Sally*, written and illustrated by Audrey Wood. HMH Books for Young Readers, 1992.
- *Sometimes I Like to Curl Up in a Ball*, written and illustrated by Vicki Churchill and Charles Fuge. Sterling, 2003.

Video Content

For this unit, you will need to select one or two music videos, each approximately 2-4 minutes long, illustrating movements such as jumping, hopping on one foot and then the other, pumping arms, stepping side to side, jumping while twisting side to side (pretend "surfing" or "skiing"), and lying down to rest. Note, you can select a longer music video (4 minutes) and use 2 minutes of it for Lesson 3, 3 minutes of it for Lesson 4, and the entire 4 minutes for Lessons 5 and 6.

See the recommended list of video sources on Page 265 and the criteria for video selection on Page 268.

BEFORE YOU START

1. Read through the unit. In particular, read through all of the lesson activities. Visualize the space where you will have CHAMPPS and how you will implement each activity with the children with whom you work.
2. Identify the school readiness skills you will focus on in each lesson activity; school readiness skills should correspond to your core curriculum.
3. Identify universal design for learning (UDL) strategies and adaptations to use for particular activities and/or to support individual children. For example, download the visual supports for use with the lesson prior to starting.
4. Review the lesson variations to determine which you will complete, if needed.
5. Plan ahead for how you will shorten the lesson, if needed (see below).
6. Complete the Planning Notes.

If you need to shorten the lesson:
Depending on the needs of the children you teach, you may choose to shorten the lesson on the first day or first two days of Unit 3 to allow children to get used to the CHAMPPS routine. For example, you could do the Warm-Up with the song, one or two core activities, and the Cool-Down with the song. Then, on the third day, you could add the third core activity.

UNIT 3 PLANNING NOTES
Motor movements to focus on:
Vocabulary to focus on:
Children who will be positioned near an adult for additional support and attention:
Children who will help with setup:
Children who will help with cleanup:
Children in Small Group 1:
Children in Small Group 2:

■ WARM-UP

Structure: Whole group

Get ready! Focus on:
- Gathering
- Increasing heart rate
- Warming up muscles

Total time: 3-5 minutes

Key Vocabulary: arms, feet, knees, legs, gallop, jog, skip, sway, balance, stand still

1. MOVE: Motor Movements

Have children start on their floor marker, warming up their bodies with the following movements and singing the "CHAMPPS Warm-Up Song" with each movement you model. Verbal prompts are provided below, if needed.

- Children **jog** in a circle. Say: *A jog is **a slow run**. While we jog, we **swing our arms** for balance and speed!*
- Children **gallop** in a circle. Say: *One foot forward. **Hop forward** keeping both feet slightly apart.*
- Children **skip** in a circle. Say: *While we skip, first we **step** forward, and then we **hop** on that foot! Good! Now switch feet! **Step, hop! Step, hop!***
- Have children **sway** on their floor marker. Say: *Stand tall. When we sway, we start with **feet together** for balance. Lean side to side like a **tree blowing in the wind.***
- Children **balance** on their floor marker. Say: *Stand tall. **Hands on hips.** Standing on one foot is tricky! Let's use **airplane arms** for balance! Arms outstretched side to side like an airplane! Lift **one foot up.** Hold for 1-2-3 seconds. Now let's try the other foot.*

2. ADAPT: UDL Strategies

Adapt the activity to meet the needs of the children with whom you work. See the suggestions in the following table; for additional ways to adapt, use the UDL Suggestions for Unit 3.

Engagement	Representation	Action & Expression
Give children choices. Ask children to choose the next warm-up movement(s).	• Use verbal prompts to encourage movement. See the Glossary of Verbal Prompts. • Use visual supports. See Visual Support Cards for stand, stand in circle, sit, sway, balance, and jog in place.	Encourage children to sing along. Give children the option to hum or clap to the melody/rhythm.

3. SUPPORT: School Readiness

Choose one to three school readiness skills to focus on. See the suggestions in the following table; for additional ways to support school readiness, turn to Page 108.

Language	Mathematics	Approaches to Learning
• Encourage children to sing along. • Have children listen for verbal prompts. • Have children identify body parts.	• Use ordinal language (*first, second, third*) with children.	• Create a smooth transition between movements. • Have children follow directions. • Guide children to remain focused and continue moving. • Encourage whole-group engagement.

4. LESSON VARIATIONS

If children learn these activities quickly and need no further practice, or if you want to vary activities for review days, see Lesson Variations on Page 114.

■ CORE ACTIVITY 1: **Bunnies and Foxes**

Structure: Whole group

Total time: 3–5 minutes

Focus on these objectives:
- Following directions
- Jumping
- Balancing (one foot)
- Squatting

Key Vocabulary:
- **arms, feet, knees, legs**
- **balance, hop, jump, leap**
- **fox, frog, grasshopper, kangaroo, bunny**
- **stand still**

1. MOVE: Motor Movements

- Have children remain standing in warm-up area.
- Next, have children **jump** around the room like bunnies and sing "Jumping Bunnies." Say: *Let's jump like bunnies! First, stand steady and* **bend your knees** *down low. This is called squatting! Now let's push up and* **lift off** *like a rocket! Ready, set,* **lift off!**
- Ring bell (clap, blink lights) at the end of the song and say: *Here comes the* **fox!** Have children return to their floor marker.
- Have children **balance** on one foot for 3 seconds or for up to 10 seconds. Say: *Count how long you can* **balance.**
- Repeat with different jumping animals: **kangaroo, frog, grasshopper.**

2. ADAPT: UDL Strategies

Adapt the activity to meet the needs of the children with whom you work. See the suggestions in the following table; for additional ways to adapt, use the UDL Suggestions for Unit 3.

Engagement	Representation	Action & Expression
Encourage child leadership. Ask a child to be the fox.	• Use verbal prompts to encourage movement. See the Glossary of Verbal Prompts. • Use visual supports. See Visual Support Cards for stand, stand in circle, balance, and jump up and down.	Modify the movements by encouraging children to hold hands and balance or bend knees and squat instead of jump.

3. SUPPORT: School Readiness

Choose one to three school readiness skills to focus on. See the suggestions in the following table; for additional ways to support school readiness, turn to Page 108.

Language	Mathematics	Science	Social	Approaches to Learning
Encourage active discussion and ask questions.	• Emphasize positional words (*around, on top of*) with children. • Encourage counting when balancing.	Ask various questions about animals. (*What do they eat? How do they move? Where do they live?*)	Have children hold hands as they balance to help peers.	• Have children follow directions. • Guide children to sustain attention during the whole-group activity.

4. LESSON VARIATIONS

If children learn these activities quickly and need no further practice, or if you want to vary activities for review days, see Lesson Variations on Page 114.

■ CORE ACTIVITY 2: Hungry Horsey

Structure: Small group

Total time: 3-5 minutes

Focus on these objectives:
- Walking
- Dynamic balance
- Stepping (on, over)
- Galloping
- Motor planning

Key Vocabulary:
- apart, apples, balance, cheer, gallop, hop, horse, move, on top, over, together

1. MOVE: Motor Movements

- Have each child hold one long pool noodle (their **"horse"**) and balance one small pool noodle piece (their **"apple"**) on top of the longer pool noodle. Throughout the Hungry Horsey course, they keep their **"apple"** balanced on the **"horse"** (the top of the pool noodle).
- Have children walk on the multilevel steps and balance beam until they reach the end of the course, and then have them place their **apple** into the bucket. Say: *When you go over the balance beam, make sure you walk slowly with a steady body so you don't fall or drop your apple!*
- Next, have the children **hop** onto their **horse** and **gallop** back to the beginning of the course. Say: *Let's gallop like horses, hop forward! Keep one foot in front! Neigh!*
- Keep children moving continuously for minimal wait time. Children in groups who are waiting to use the course can **balance** beanbags on their heads.

(*Source:* GO WITH YOYO: Fitness Fun for Kids. [2010, April 13]. *Noodle balance - preschool fitness games!* [Video]. YouTube. https://www.youtube.com/watch?v=WPsUQusTWyc)

2. ADAPT: UDL Strategies

Adapt the activity to meet the needs of the children with whom you work. See the suggestions in the following table; for additional ways to adapt, use the UDL Suggestions for Unit 3.

Engagement	Representation	Action & Expression
• Create challenge by adding more apples for children to balance on their horse. • Provide pool noodles of different lengths to accommodate children's varying abilities.	Use visual supports. Place a Visual Support Card of each movement (balance, grasp, put in/take out) along the Hungry Horsey course or use the cards with individual children.	Accept partial movement and ask children to move through the Hungry Horsey course without the pool noodle.

3. SUPPORT: School Readiness

Choose one to three school readiness skills to focus on. See the suggestions in the following table, along with additional ideas to support school readiness on Page 108.

Mathematics	Science	Social	Approaches to Learning
Emphasize positional words (*beside, over, on top of*).	Discuss animals. (*What do horses eat? How do horses move?*)	Ask children to cheer on their friends while they wait their turn.	• Guide children to stay on task during small-group activity. • Have children move through activities independently.

4. LESSON VARIATIONS

If children learn these activities quickly and need no further practice, or if you want to vary activities for review days, see Lesson Variations on Page 114.

■ CORE ACTIVITY 3: **River Jump**

Structure: Small group

Total time: 3–5 minutes

Focus on these objectives:
- Waddling
- Dynamic balance
- Leaping
- Motor planning

Key Vocabulary:
- **balance, leap**
- **around, under**
- **alligator, duck/duckling, eggs, lily pad, nest, wing**
- **cheer**

1.   MOVE: Motor Movements

- Have children move through the River Jump activity. Children waiting their turn will **cheer** while **balancing** beanbags on their heads as they wait.
- Have children place one beanbag (**"egg"**) under each **arm** ("wing"). Tell children: *Hold your **arms at your sides** like a duck's wings.*
- Have children walk (or waddle) between stars. Say: *When you're on the course, you need to **watch** for obstacles and then **step** around them! **Watch, step!***
- Tell children the cones are alligators. Have them walk around the cones to protect their **eggs** from the alligators.
- At the end of the "river," children place their **eggs** in the nest (bucket).
- Have children step onto the block and **leap like a frog** onto each floor marker ("lily pad") to make their way back to the beginning. Say: *Time to **jump up!** Jump as high as you can while pushing yourself forward!*
- Model how to cheer with the children waiting their turn. For example, call out "Go, Mike, go!" while shaking a sensory egg. Include new vocabulary if desired, for example, "**Waddle**, Mike, waddle!"
- Continue having children take their turn through the River Jump as other children **cheer** them on. Repeat until all children have had multiple opportunities to move through the River Jump and **cheer.**

2.   ADAPT: UDL Strategies

Adapt the activity to meet the needs of the children with whom you work. See the suggestions in the following table; for additional ways to adapt, use the UDL Suggestions for Unit 3.

Engagement	Representation	Action & Expression
Challenge children by asking them to balance a beanbag on their head or in the palms of their hands.	• Model each movement and lead the group through the River Jump. • Use verbal prompts to describe movements. See the Glossary of Verbal Prompts. • Use visual supports. See Visual Support Cards for jump up and down, stand, stand in circle, sit, and balance.	Adapt the positioning of the beanbags as needed so children can hold the beanbags while they move. Children can carry them in the palms of their hands or balance them on the backs of their hands.

3.   SUPPORT: School Readiness

Choose one to three school readiness skills to focus on. See the suggestions in the following table; for additional ways to support school readiness, turn to Page 108.

Mathematics	Science	Social	Approaches to Learning
Emphasize positional words (*around, in between, over*).	Talk about animals. (*How do ducks move? How do frogs move?*)	Encourage children to cheer and call out their friends' names.	Guide children to stay on task during small-group activity.

4.   LESSON VARIATIONS

If children learn these activities quickly and need no further practice, or if you want to vary activities for review days, see Lesson Variations on Page 114.

■ PHYSICAL ACTIVITY: **Music Video**

Structure: Whole group

Focus on this objective:
Sustained physical activity

Total time: 2-4 minutes

Key Vocabulary:
- heart rate, hot, sweaty, thirsty, tired

1. MOVE: Motor Movements

Have children stand on their floor marker, facing the music video. Spread out for enough space for floor movement.
Say: ***Arms out.** Make wide, **airplane arms.** Make sure you are not touching a friend.*

Have children move to the music video you selected.

Lesson	Video	Total Time
3	Video 1: jumping, hopping galloping, squatting, leaping, skipping/jogging in place	2 minutes
4	Video 2: jumping, hopping galloping, squatting, leaping, skipping/jogging in place	3 minutes
5	Videos 1 and/or 2: See above.	4 minutes
6		

2. ADAPT: UDL Strategies

Adapt the activity to meet the needs of the children with whom you work. See the suggestions in the following table, along with additional ideas to adapt using UDL strategies on Page 108.

Engagement	Representation	Action & Expression
Provide descriptive praise and encouragement (e.g., *Great jumping!* Or *Excellent job jogging; keep moving!*)	• Use verbal prompts to describe movement. See the Glossary of Verbal Prompts. • Use visual supports. See Visual Support Cards for stand, stand in circle, sit, and airplane arms.	• Stand in close proximity to children and model modified movements (e.g., squatting and standing instead of jumping). • For additional support in balancing, provide chairs for children to hold onto or have them hold onto another person.

3. SUPPORT: School Readiness

During the music video, the primary goal is to maintain sustained/increased physical activity levels in all children. To achieve this goal, teachers can provide models/prompts for motor imitation (imitate actions/songs from video, maintain personal space) and approaches to learning (active engagement, following instructions from video).

4. LESSON VARIATIONS

If children learn these activities quickly and need no further practice, or if you want to vary activities for review days, see Lesson Variations on Page 114.

■ COOL-DOWN

Structure: Whole group

Wrap up: Focus on
- Gathering
- Decreasing heart rate
- Cooling down muscles

Total time: 3-5 minutes

Key Vocabulary:
- arms, knees, legs, stretch

1. MOVE: Motor Movements

Have children sit on their floor marker and cool-down their bodies with the following movements. Once you have modeled each movement listed below, sing the "CHAMPPS Cool-Down Song" while slowly doing the movements (see "CHAMPPS Cool-Down Song," Page 104).

- Touch toes. Say: *Sit with a tall, straight back.* **Arms up.** *Slowly bend forward and reach to* **touch your toes.**
- Bend and **stretch.** Say: *Sit with a tall, straight back. Legs straight. Raise your* **arms up.** *Slowly sway your arms* **side to side** *to bend and stretch.*
- Wave goodbye. Say: *Sit up slowly. Look at your friends. Hold out your hand and wave goodbye.*

Optional: Consider doing deep breathing and the following yoga poses as a way to calm children prior to the "CHAMPPS Cool-Down Song"/movements.

- Frog Pose. (See Figure U3.3.) Say: *Stand up. Point your toes out like a penguin. Squat by bending your knees. Touch the floor with hands in between knees. Breathe slowly.*
- Lie Down. (See Figure U3.4.) Say: *Lie down. Stretch your legs and arms out beside your body. Close your eyes. Pretend you're looking up into the sky. Watch the clouds float by in your mind. Breathe slowly. Eyes closed.*

Figure U3.3. Frog Pose.   **Figure U3.4.** Lie Down.

2. ADAPT: UDL Strategies

Adapt the activity to meet the needs of the children with whom you work. See the suggestions in the following table; for additional ways to adapt, use the UDL strategies for Unit 3.

Engagement	Representation	Action & Expression
Vary volume of voice to match the pace of movement. For example, use a calm, soft voice while speaking slowly to calm down children.	• Use verbal prompts to describe movement. See the Glossary of Verbal Prompts. • Use visual supports. See Visual Support Cards for sit, bend and stretch, lift your arms, touch toes, and wave hand.	Begin with simple movements and no singing.

3. SUPPORT: School Readiness

Choose one to three school readiness skills to focus on. See the suggestions in the following table, along with additional ideas to support school readiness on Page 108.

Language	Mathematics	Approaches to Learning
• Encourage the children to sing along (loudly, quietly). • Have children listen for verbal prompts. • Have children identify body parts.	Use ordinal language (*first, second, third*).	Create a smooth transition between movements.

4. LESSON VARIATIONS

If children learn these activities quickly and need no further practice, or if you want to vary activities for review days, see Lesson Variations on Page 114.

UNIT 3	**Walk-Around Card**	CHAMPPS

1	**Warm-Up**
	Gathering, increase heart rate, warm-up muscles
	MATERIALS	• 1 floor marker per child
	ACTIVITIES	Sing "CHAMPPS Warm-Up Song." Children jog, gallop, skip, sway, and balance (on one foot).

2	**Core Activity 1: Bunnies and Foxes**
	Physical movement, static balance
	MATERIALS	• 1 floor marker per child • Bell
	ACTIVITIES	First: Sing "Jumping Bunnies." Children jump and balance (on one foot). Then: Ring bell (clap, blink lights) to have children return to floor marker. Repeat.

3	**Core Activity 2: Hungry Horsey**
	Physical movement, dynamic balance, motor planning
	MATERIALS	• 2 balance beams • 3 floor markers • 1–2 pool noodles per child • 1 bucket • 2–3 hurdles • Bucket full of pool noodle pieces
	ACTIVITIES	Note: Half the class does Hungry Horsey as the other half does River Jump. Then children switch groups. For Hungry Horsey: Have children balance "apple" on "horse." Then: Children walk on floor markers and step or jump over the balance beam and hurdles to place the "apple" in the bucket. Others in this group wait and cheer. Next: Children gallop back to start. Repeat until all children have multiple turns.

4	**Core Activity 3: River Jump**
	Physical movement, dynamic balance, motor planning
	MATERIALS	• 5 stars • 6 floor markers • 1 bucket • 1 block/step • 1 hula hoop • Beanbags (2 per child) • 3 cones
	ACTIVITIES	First: Three or four children hold "eggs" (beanbags) under their "wings" (arms), moving between stars and cones ("alligators"). Others in this group wait and cheer, balancing beanbags on their heads. Then: Moving children drop the beanbags in the bucket and leap (like a frog) back to start. Next: Children who were waiting now complete River Jump as their peers cheer. Repeat until all children have had at least one turn.

5	**Physical Activity: Music Video**		
	Sustained physical activity		
	Lesson 3 Video 1	**Lesson 4** Video 2	**Lessons 5 and 6** Videos 1 and/or 2

6	**Cool-Down**
	Gathering, lower heart rate, cool-down muscles
	MATERIALS	• 1 floor marker per child
	ACTIVITIES	First (optional): Do yoga poses: Frog Pose and Lie Down. Then: Sing "CHAMPPS Cool-Down Song." Stretch legs, touch toss, bend and stretch, and wave goodbye.

Walk-Around Card

CHAMPPS Warm-Up Song

(Sung to the tune of "The Ants Go Marching")

The CHAMPPS go **jogging** one by one
Hurrah! Hurrah!
The CHAMPPS go **jogging** one by one
Hurrah! Hurrah!
The CHAMPPS go **jogging** one by one
This is the way we have some fun
And we all go **jogging** on, and on, and on

(Repeat with **galloping, skipping, swaying,** and **balancing**)

Jumping Bunnies

(Sung to the tune of "Frère Jacques/Are You Sleeping?")

Jumping bunnies, **jumping** bunnies
Hop, hop, hop! Hop, hop, hop!
Kee-eep on **jumping**
Kee-eep on **jumping**
Look out, **fox!** Look out, **fox!**

CHAMPPS Cool-Down Song

(Sung to the tune of "Here We Go 'Round the Mulberry Bush")

This is the way we **stretch our legs**
Stretch our legs, stretch our legs
This is the way we **stretch our legs**
At the end of CHAMPPS

(Repeat with "**touch** our **toes**," "**bend** and **stretch**," and "**wave** goodbye.")

GLOSSARY OF VERBAL PROMPTS

Do (Movement)	Say (Verbal Prompt)	Use
Balance	**Airplane arms**	*Standing on one foot is tricky! Let's use **airplane arms** for balance! Arms outstretched side to side like an airplane!*
Bend and stretch	**Reach, side, hold**	*Sit crisscross for bend and stretch! **Reach** one arm way above your head. Now lean to the **side** and **hold** it for as long as you can! Good stretching!*
Dynamic balance (Balance while moving such as walking on beam)	**Walk slowly with steady body**	*When you are on the balance beam, make sure you **walk slowly** with a **steady body** so you don't fall!*
Gallop	**Hop forward**	*Let's gallop like horses! One foot forward. **Hop forward** keeping both feet slightly apart. Keep one foot in front! Neigh!*
Jog	**Slow run**	*We're going to warm up by jogging! Jogging is like running, but a **slow run**.*
	Swing arms	*While we jog, we **swing our arms** for balance and speed!*
Jump	**Bend knees**	*Let's jump like bunnies! First, stand steady and **bend your knees** down low. This is called squatting!*
	Lift off	*Now let's push up and **lift off** like a rocket! Ready, set, **lift off**!*
Leap	**Bend low**	*Let's leap like frogs! First, have feet pointed out (like penguin). **Bend those knees—going low** to the ground!*
	Hands on ground	*Now put your **hands on the ground, in between knees**. Ribbit, ribbit!*
	Jump up	*Time to **jump up**! Jump as high as you can while pushing yourself forward!*
Skip	**Step, hop**	*While we skip, first we **step** forward, and then we **hop** on that foot! Good, now switch feet! **Step, hop! Step, hop!***
Static balance (Balance while standing still such as standing on one foot)	**Stand still on one leg**	*We **stand very still** on one foot. The other leg is bent with foot in the air (not touching the ground or other leg). Look straight ahead.*
Step (around)	**Watch, step**	*When you're on the course, you need to **watch** for obstacles and then **step** around them! **Watch, step**!*
Step (over)	**Foot up, over**	*Uh oh, there's something in your way! You'll need to step over it! Put your **foot up** and **over**!*
Stretch leg	**One leg out/in**	*Time to stretch! Sit on the floor and put **one leg out**, straight in front of you. Keep the other **leg in**, bent like a triangle. Now reach!*
Sway	**Feet together, side to side**	*When we sway, we start with **feet together** for balance. Now lean **side to side**!*
Tiptoe	**Baby steps**	*We are going to tiptoe like a little mouse. This means use quiet feet. Take **baby steps** like a little mouse.*
Touch toes	**Touch toes, hold**	*Now put both legs out straight in front of you, reach forward, and **touch your toes**! **Hold** it for as long as you can!*
Waddle	**Arms at sides, sway back and forth**	*Let's waddle like ducklings! Keep your **arms at your sides**, and **sway back and forth** while moving forward!*
Walk	**Heel down, then toe**	*Let's walk carefully through the obstacle course. Step with your **heel first, then toe**.*
Wave goodbye	**Arms up**	*Great work today, CHAMPPS! Put your **arms up** and wave goodbye!*

UDL SUGGESTIONS

Engagement

Means of Engagement	Warm-Up	Core Activity 1: Bunnies and Foxes	Core Activity 2: Hungry Horsey	Core Activity 3: River Jump	Video 1	Video 2	Cool-Down
Recruit Interest							
Child choice	Ask: *Which warm-up move will we do first?*	Ask: *What jumping animal could we do next?* (kangaroos, frogs)	Ask: *What snack does your horse want?* (Fruits: apples, bananas, oranges, strawberries. Vegetables: carrots, celery, peas, pumpkins.)	Ask: *Which body part do you want to use to hold a beanbag?*	Ask: *Who wants to be the leader with me today?* (Choose 2-3 children to stand in front with teacher. Rotate who is chosen each time.)	Ask: *Which do you like better? Hopping (model) or jumping (model)?*	Ask: *Which cool-down movements will we do first?*
Novel/familiar	Familiar moves (wave hands)	Familiar tune ("Frère Jacques") Familiar objects (floor markers)	Familiar activity (crossing obstacle course) Horse sounds	Familiar objects (floor markers) Familiar movements (sidestep, jump)	New video Optional: Repeat video	New video Optional: Repeat video	Familiar moves (touch toes, bend and stretch)
Sustain Effort and Persistence							
Praise/ encourage	Say: *You sang every word; fantastic job!* Say: *You moved slowly while jogging!*	Say: *I love how high you jumped!* Say: *Excellent steady balancing on one foot!*	Say: *Nice job balancing the apple!* Say: *Wow-what high hops while you gallop!*	Say: *I like how you kept your egg under your arm!* Say: *You leaped really far!*	Say: *Great jumping!* Say: *Good job lying down right away!*	Say: *Nice job hopping on one foot!* Say: *I like how you're moving side to side!*	Say: *Nice calm bodies. I like how you are moving slowly during the cool-down.*
Vary complexity	Increase/ Decrease number of moves.	"Fox" (leader) chases and tries to tag children.	Give two or three pool noodle pieces; give longer pool noodles; hold pool noodle with one hand instead of two.	Give additional beanbags.	If children are tired, let them lie down for a longer period of time.	If children are tired, let them "freeze like a statue" to rest.	Increase/ Decrease number of moves.
Vary setup, directions	Sing softly/ loudly; slowly/fast.	Sing softly/ loudly; slowly/ fast. Change signal to go home by clapping hands, blinking lights.	Vary length and complexity of course (painters' tape instead of balance beam).	Vary length and complexity of course (floor markers instead of stepping-stones).	Vary materials (give instruments, scarves).	Ask: *Show me how far we should stand from the video screen. From your friends?*	Sing softly/ loudly.

Representation

Means of Representation	Warm-Up	Core Activity 1: Bunnies and Foxes	Core Activity 2: Hungry Horsey	Core Activity 3: River Jump	Video 1	Video 2	Cool-Down
Forms of Communication							
Auditory	Glossary of Verbal Prompts						→
Visual	Visual Support Cards						→
Tactile	Give instruments/ scarves.	→	Hold noodle.	Hold beanbags.	Give instruments/ scarves.	→	
Multiple Levels of Complexity							
Key vocabulary: define/model	jog gallop skip sway	jump balance stand like a tree squat	balance gallop jump	walk waddle balance jump leap hop	jump turn around	hop slide feet ride waves ski balance	sway stretch legs touch toes bend and stretch wave goodbye

Action & Expression

Means of Expression	Warm-Up	Core Activity 1: Bunnies and Foxes	Core Activity 2: Hungry Horsey	Core Activity 3: River Jump	Video 1	Video 2	Cool-Down
Variety of responses	Sing, clap, or hum song.	Sing, clap, or hum song. Stay within bunny hole while jumping.	Hold pool noodle piece in hand. Child keeps one hand on top of pool noodle piece. Child places hands on different parts of pool noodle (top, middle, bottom).	Child carries beanbag on palm or back of hand.	Say word that matches movements.	Say word that matches movements.	Sit and breathe slowly. Sing, clap, or hum song. Only do movements, no singing.
Complexity of responses	Partial movement (balance on one foot instead of hopping)	Partial movement (squat and straighten knees instead of jumping, stand still instead of balancing) For additional support, child holds on to chair or a friend's hand when balancing.	Partial movement (walk instead of galloping) Leap halfway down the course, then walk the rest of the way.	Partial movement (shift weight from left to right without moving forward instead of waddling) Hop beside course, rather than on it.	Partial movement (bend and straighten knees instead of jumping)	Partial movement (jump rather than hop)	Partial movement (touch knees instead of toes)

SUPPORT SCHOOL READINESS SKILLS

LANGUAGE AND LITERACY	Warm-Up	Core Activity 1: Bunnies and Foxes	Core Activity 2: Hungry Horsey	Core Activity 3: River Jump	Cool-Down
Expresses feelings and preferences (hot, thirsty, tired, hungry, sleepy, sweaty)	Ask: *Are you ready to jump? What do you like to do in CHAMPPS?*	Ask: *How do you think the bunny feels when the fox is coming?*	Ask: *Would you feel excited, scared, happy, nervous riding a real horse?*	Say: *The mother duck feeds and keeps her ducklings warm. How do you feel when you are fed and kept warm?*	Ask: *How do you feel?* (thirsty, hot, tired, sweaty, etc.)
Engages in active discussion (shares ideas, asks and answers questions)		Have children ask and answer questions about bunnies and foxes.	Have children ask and answer questions about horses.	Have children ask and answer questions about frogs, ducks, and ducklings.	Ask: *What yoga pose has been your favorite so far?*
Communicates personal experiences and interests	Ask: *What was your favorite part of warm-up?*	Ask: *Does anyone have a pet bunny?*	Say: *Horses love to eat apples. Who likes apples?*	Ask: *What's your favorite thing to do in water?*	Ask: *What was your favorite activity?*
Listens to/uses formal and informal language (listens to/sings songs, uses different voices)	Have children listen and sing along.	Have children listen and sing along.	Have children make animal noises (horse, frog, duckling, etc.).	Have children repeat (imitate) the leader.	Have children listen and sing along.
Recognizes shapes (circle, square, triangle, rectangle)	Have children move in a circle.	Have children move in a circle.	Have children discuss which shapes they see.	Have children discuss which shapes they see.	Have children sit in a circle.
Recognizes letters	Label floor markers with letters. Ask: *Which letter are you standing on?*	Label floor markers with letters. Ask: *Which letter are you standing on?*	Label "apples" with letters. Prompt children to pick up certain letters.	Put letters on the floor markers. Encourage children to name the letters as they jump.	Label floor markers with letters. Ask: *What letter are you sitting on?*

MATHEMATICS	Warm-Up	Core Activity 1: Bunnies and Foxes	Core Activity 2: Hungry Horsey	Core Activity 3: River Jump	Cool-Down
Number recognition (count, one-one correspondence)	Have children count moves instead of singing.	Have children count jumps instead of singing.	Have children count the number of apples balanced.	Have children count the number of jumps.	Have children stretch for a specific number of seconds.
Positional words (*above, side to side*)	Say: *Hold your floor marker above your head. Move the floor marker side to side* (model moving it to touch left hip and right hip) *beside your body.*	Around, in, on top of	Over, on top of, beside	In between, over, around	Bend side to side

MATHEMATICS	Warm-Up	Core Activity 1: Bunnies and Foxes	Core Activity 2: Hungry Horsey	Core Activity 3: River Jump	Cool-Down
Ordinal language (*first, second,* etc.)	Use numbered bibs 1-8 to stress first through eighth. During opening, practice saying ordinal numbers (first, second, third, etc.) with matching numerals on floor markers and/or bibs.	Instead of singing, say: *Girls jump first, boys jump second, etc.* Say: *Those wearing blue jump first. Those wearing green jump second, etc.*	Use ordinal words to describe order in line (*first cheer, second course,* etc.).	Use ordinal words to describe order in line (*first cheer, second course,* etc.).	Use ordinal words to describe order of moves.
Categorizing and sorting objects (animals)	Ask: *Which animals have 4 legs? 2 legs? No legs? Name animals that fly, run, swim.*	Say: *Bunnies can be pets. What other animals can be pets?*	Say: *Name things a horse can jump over. Name things a horse can go under.*	Ask: *What other animals live in water? What animals live on land?*	Say: *Let's close our eyes and think about our favorite hopping animals. What animal did you think about?*
Patterns (recognize, describe, reproduce)	Create a movement pattern (walk back five steps, forward five steps).	*Name animals that hop/jump.* Ask: *Who can show us how to hop like a bunny, frog, kangaroo?*	Create a color pattern with the "apples." Ask: *How is a zebra like/different from a horse?*	Create a movement pattern (walk backward five steps, forward five steps).	

SCIENCE	Warm-Up	Core Activity 1: Bunnies and Foxes	Core Activity 2: Hungry Horsey	Core Activity 3: River Jump	Cool-Down
Ask/answer questions together (*Who? What? Where? How?*).	Ask: *Is anybody feeling hot? Sweaty? Why do you think you feel that way?*	Ask: *How do bunnies move? What animal likes to chase bunnies?*	Ask: *Where do you see horses? What snacks do horses like?** (*Responses will vary. See UDL Engagement chart for accurate examples.)	Ask: *Where do you see ducklings? Frogs?*	Say: *Where is your heart? Put your hand on your chest to feel your heartbeat. Imitate the beat with your hand by tapping chest fast/slow. Who has a fast/slow beating heart? What makes your heart go fast/slow?*
Make predictions together (*What if?*).	Ask: *What if we did not exercise. How would it make us feel?*	Ask: *How long can you balance on one foot? Try it and count.*	Ask: *What if I pile the apples really high? Will it be easy or hard to balance?*	Ask: *If I make a zigzag with the lily pads, will it be harder or easier to jump?*	Discuss slowed breathing, hearts.
Understand weather/seasons, calendar/days of the week.	Ask: *Who will give the weather report today? Is it sunny, cloudy, rainy, hot, or cold?*	Ask: *Where do bunnies and foxes go when it rains/snows?*	Ask: *Where does a horse go when it rains/snows?*	Ask: *Where do ducklings go when it rains/snows?*	Say: *Let's say the days of the week (months of year) while we do our stretches!*

SUPPORT SCHOOL READINESS SKILLS *(continued)*

SCIENCE	Warm-Up	Core Activity 1: Bunnies and Foxes	Core Activity 2: Hungry Horsey	Core Activity 3: River Jump	Cool-Down
Discuss characteristics of living things (*humans, animals, plants*).	Discuss hearts pumping after warm-up.	Discuss animal movements and instincts.	Talk about animals: What do they eat? How do they move? Where do they live?	Talk about animals: What do they eat? How do they move? Where do they live?	Discuss slowed breathing, hearts.
Use sensory vocabulary.	Say: *Touch your chest with your hand. What do you feel? Do you feel your heart beating? Show me how fast your heart is beating with your hand on your chest.*	Ask: *Do foxes and bunnies have hair or fur? What does fur feel like (soft, smooth, warm)?*	Ask: *How does the noodle feel?*	Ask: *How does the beanbag feel? Soft? Light?*	Ask: *How do you feel after CHAMPPS?*

MOTOR	Warm-Up	Core Activity 1: Bunnies and Foxes	Core Activity 2: Hungry Horsey	Core Activity 3: River Jump	Cool-Down
Balance	Say: *What happens when we lose our balance?* Have children balance on each foot or sway, maintaining balance.	Have children stand on one foot in bunny hole. Have children count to 3/5/10 seconds while balancing on one foot.	Have children practice dynamic balance ("apples").	Have children balance beanbags.	While seated or standing, bend and stretch while maintaining balance.
Visual tracking	Have children watch and follow leader (teacher or peer carrying scarf/flag/visual support card) as they jog/gallop/skip around circle.	Have children watch and catch object.	Have children pick up fallen "apples."	Have children pick up fallen beanbags.	Have children watch and follow movements of leader (teacher or peer holding scarf/flag/visual support card).
Motor imitation	Have children imitate leader/peers. →				
Body awareness	Have children recognize which body parts to use. →				
Body movement	Have children sway, balance.	Have children throw, wave, catch, squeeze.	Have children practice dynamic balance ("apples"), step over, gallop.	Have children balance, step over/around, jump off height, leap.	Have children bend and stretch, touch toes, stretch arms.
Strength/speed/duration	Have children jog/jump in place fast/slow.	Have children jump quickly back to bunny hole.	Have children walk fast/slow through course. Ask them which worked better.	Children sustain energy while leaping.	Have children move slowly.

MOTOR	Warm-Up	Core Activity 1: Bunnies and Foxes	Core Activity 2: Hungry Horsey	Core Activity 3: River Jump	Cool-Down
Coordination (eye/hand; eye/foot)	Say: *Let's warm up. Touch your right hand to your right foot; left hand to left foot. Now, touch right hand to left foot; left hand to right foot.*	Have children balance on one foot.	Have children hold pool noodle and balance while walking.	Say: *Jump on each floor marker using the same foot, alternating your feet.*	Say: *Let's cool down. Touch your right hand to your right foot; left hand to left foot. Now, touch right hand to left foot; left hand to right foot.*
Locomotion (walk, run, jump, hop, leap, gallop, skip, squat, sway)	Have children jog, gallop, skip, sway, balance on one foot.	Have children jump.	Have children walk, gallop.	Have children walk, leap.	Have children gallop/hop/jump to the floor marker for Cool-Down.
Directionality (forward, backward, sidesteps)	Have children switch direction (walk backward, sidestep).	Have children practice hopping forward/backward.	Have children practice sidesteps while balancing "apple" or beanbag on pool noodle or on head.	Have children walk backward through course.	Have children walk forward/ backward/take sidesteps to the floor marker for Cool-Down.
Personal space	Have children use own floor marker.	Have children use own floor marker.	Have children share course with peers.	Have children share course with peers.	Have children stay on floor markers.
Grasp and release	Have children make a fist (grasp fingers tight) and pump their arms while jogging. Then stop, release fist.	Have children hop with scarf, hop to a friend and swap scarves.	Have children hold pool noodle and drop "apple" into bucket.	Have children hold beanbags and drop them into bucket or hula hoop.	Have children make two fists, open fists, and wave goodbye with two hands.
Motor regulation (go slow, go fast, stop)	Jog/Jump/ Hop in place on command: fast/ slow/stop.	Have children jump fast in place. Have children stop at bunny hole.	Have children line up and gallop with noodle fast/slow. Have children stop at end of course.	Have children line up and leap like frogs (fast/slow). Have children stop at end of course.	Have children move slowly through cool-down moves.
Music and dance	Have children sing.	Have children sing.	Have children ring bells.	Have children ring bells.	Have children sing.

SOCIAL-EMOTIONAL	Warm-Up	Core Activity 1: Bunnies and Foxes	Core Activity 2: Hungry Horsey	Core Activity 3: River Jump	Cool-Down
Recognizes, describes, and regulates emotions	Ask: *How are you feeling today in CHAMPPS?* (happy, ready, excited)	Ask: *How would you/bunny feel if you were chased by a fox?* (scared, worried, nervous)	Ask: *How do you/ horses feel when eating?* (full, happy, hungry) *When galloping?* (free, wild, happy)	Ask: *How does a frog feel when he jumps off a lily pad into water?* (cold, wet, happy)	Ask: *How do you feel?* (tired, sweaty, hot, thirsty)
Solves/prevents problems	Ask: *Who remembers what we do first? What do we do next?*	Place child's photo on floor marker; they can use this visual to find their place.	Have children who are cheering help children whose apples fall off.	Have children who are cheering wear different-colored vests.	Ask: *Who remembers what we do first? What do we do next?*

SUPPORT SCHOOL READINESS SKILLS *(continued)*

SOCIAL-EMOTIONAL	Warm-Up	Core Activity 1: Bunnies and Foxes	Core Activity 2: Hungry Horsey	Core Activity 3: River Jump	Cool-Down
Learns independence/self-help	Ask: *Who can find a floor marker to stand on, all by yourself?*	Place child's photo on floor marker.	Have children pick up fallen "apples."	Have children pick up fallen beanbags.	Ask: *Who can find a floor marker to sit on, all by yourself?*
Takes turns/waits turn	Ask: *Whose turn is it to lead? Whose turn is it to hold the picture cards?*	Have children wait in bunny hole.	Have children cheer or practice balancing an "apple" while waiting.	Have children cheer or practice balancing a beanbag on head while waiting.	Ask: *Whose turn is it to lead? Whose turn is it to hold the picture cards?*
Helps/supports peers	Children move hand in hand with partner.	Have children hold hands to help balance. Have children partner up and hold hands while jumping like bunnies.	Have children cheer while waiting.	Have children cheer while waiting.	Say: *Wave to a friend who you want to make smile. Wave to someone who was a good friend during CHAMPPS.*
Plays cooperatively	Ask: *Who can help pass out floor markers?*	Have children hold hands with a partner and jump in place together, counting their jumps. Say: *Help someone up if they fall down. Say you are sorry if you bump into someone while hopping.*	Children wait for turn.	Children wait for turn.	Say: *Everyone help clean up!*
Shares materials	Encourage children to go to different marker if the one they want is already taken.	Say: *Ask a friend if they want to use your noodle next.*	Have children share course with peers.	Have children share course with peers.	Encourage children to go to different marker if the one they want is already taken.
Socializes with peers	Add CHAMPPS greeting to children's warm-up.	Have children talk to a peer about which size noodle they will use next.	Have children call peers' names while cheering.	Have children call peers' names while cheering.	Have children wave at peers.

APPROACHES TO LEARNING	Warm-Up	Core Activity 1: Bunnies and Foxes	Core Activity 2: Hungry Horsey	Core Activity 3: River Jump	Cool-Down
Transitions into/out of activities	Have children return to floor marker.	Have children return to floor marker.	Have children switch between course and cheering.	Have children switch between course and cheering.	Say: *Let's line up quietly to go back to class.*
Listens to/follows directions	Have children listen and imitate movements. ——→				
Demonstrates focused attention	Have children listen for next movement.	Have children listen for bell/clap or watch for blinking light.	Have children watch/cheer peers.	Have children watch/cheer peers.	Have children watch the leader (teacher/peer).
Demonstrates sustained attention	Have children stay with whole group.	Have children stay within activity space.	Have children stay with their small group.	Have children stay with their small group.	Have children stay with whole group.
Demonstrates active engagement in small/large group	Have children move around room with whole class.	Have children move around room with whole class.	Have children use the course, cheer others on, or balance pool noodles with their small group.	Have children use the course, cheer on others, or practice balancing beanbags with their small group.	Have children follow the leader, doing movements with the whole group.
Demonstrates active engagement in independent task		Have children go back to their floor marker without verbally prompting them.	Have children move through course independently or practice balancing while waiting.	Have children move through course independently or practice balancing while waiting.	Have all children pick up their floor markers and return them to the bin.

Lesson Variations

■ WARM-UP VARIATIONS

Music/Rhythm/Dance

Variation 1: Balance on One Foot

Structure	Materials	Instructions
Whole group	• Floor markers • Projector with Internet access	1. Have children stand on their floor markers facing the projection screen. 2. Play a YouTube video showing how to balance on one foot. (See the video selection criteria on Page 268.) 3. Have children imitate the music video for their warm-up.

Variation 2: Jump High

Structure	Materials	Instructions
Whole group	• Floor markers • Projector with Internet access	1. Have children stand on their floor markers facing the projection screen. 2. Play a YouTube video showing how to jump high. (See the video selection criteria on Page 268.) 3. Have children imitate the music video for their warm-up.

■ CORE ACTIVITY 1: **Bunnies and Foxes** VARIATIONS

Music/Rhythm/Dance

Variation 1: Jump Into the Hoop

Structure	Materials	Instructions
Whole group	• Four or five hula hoops • Musical selection and a means of playing it (computer or smartphone with speakers, cassette recorder, etc.)	1. Place several hula hoops on the floor. 2. Encourage children to jump from one hoop to the other in a set order. 3. Play music and stop the music at various intervals. 4. Tell the children that when the music stops they must balance on one foot until the music starts again.

Sports/Games

Variation 2: Traditional Hopscotch

Structure	Materials	Instructions
Whole group	• Painters' or masking tape • Beanbags	1. Use tape to make a hopscotch outline of eight square sections (or chalk if outside). 2. Have children go through each section as they hop on one foot, two feet, one foot, etc. 3. To make it more challenging, hand one beanbag to each child. 4. Tell children to throw their beanbag in one square, and then skip the square they threw it in when they go through the entire hopscotch game.

Variation 3: Line Jumping Game

Structure	Materials	Instructions
Whole group	• Painters' or masking tape	1. Use tape to create about six lines, a foot or so apart from each other.
		2. Children start behind the first line and see how far they can jump.
		3. Ask them to remember how far they jumped and see their progress after each class.

■ CORE ACTIVITY 3: **River Jump** VARIATIONS

Sports/Games

Variation 1: Walk With My Friends

Structure	Materials	Instructions
Whole group	• River Jump obstacle course • Beanbags and/or different-sized balls ("eggs")	1. Have children form partners.
		2. Have each pair of children use different ways or different body parts to carry the beanbag ("protect their eggs"). For example, they might "protect the egg" while walking together through the River Jump obstacle course (e.g., carry 1 egg on top of hands held together, while walking back-to-back, while facing each other holding egg palm-to-palm).
		3. After children walk through the River Jump obstacle course, they place eggs in hula hoop or bucket. Then children hold hands and jump to the end of course together.

Variation 2: Slow Motion

Structure	Materials	Instructions
Whole group	• None	1. Model a slow-motion jump for children.
		2. Ask children to do the same.
		3. After five or six slow-motion jumps, switch to slow-motion walking. Repeat five or six times.

■ MUSIC VIDEO VARIATION

Music/Rhythm/Dance

Variation 1: Bunny Hop

Structure	Materials	Instructions
Whole group	• Floor markers • Projector with Internet access	1. Have children stand on their floor markers.
		2. Play a YouTube video that requires children to hop. (See the video selection criteria on Page 268.)
		3. Have children imitate the music video.

Home Activities Record

Child: _____   Teacher: _____
Unit: _____   Week: _____
Please return by: _____

Thank you for playing with me! Please tell my teachers if we did CHAMPPS activities this week at home. Write a check (✓) if we practiced CHAMPPS at home this week. You can also write comments to tell my teachers how I did when we practiced CHAMPPS at home! Please give this form to my teacher each week.

Check (✓) if you did CHAMPPS practice.	Parent/Child Comments

Home Activities Record

Child: _____   Teacher: _____
Unit: _____   Week: _____
Please return by: _____

Thank you for playing with me! Please tell my teachers if we did CHAMPPS activities this week at home. Write a check (✓) if we practiced CHAMPPS at home this week. You can also write comments to tell my teachers how I did when we practiced CHAMPPS at home! Please give this form to my teacher each week.

Check (✓) if you did CHAMPPS practice.	Parent/Child Comments

CHAMPPS Home Activities

Hi, Family and Friends!

We are beginning Unit 3 of CHAMPPS at school! I am learning all about how to hop and jump like a bunny. Now I want to play CHAMPPS with you! It only takes 10–20 minutes. Thank you for playing with me!

Love, Your Little CHAMP

◼ ACTIVITY 1: **Warm-Up**

Materials None

Directions Move and sing with me.

CHAMPPS Warm-Up Song

(Tune: "The Ants Go Marching")

The CHAMPPS go jogging one by one
Hurrah, hurrah!
The CHAMPPS go jogging one by one
Hurrah, hurrah!
The CHAMPPS go jogging one by one
This is the way we have some fun
And we all go jogging on, and on, and on!

Repeat with: galloping, skipping, and balancing (on one foot).

◼ ACTIVITY 2: **Jumping Bunnies**

Materials For "home," use a carpet square, newspaper, placemat, or towel with floor grip to prevent slipping

Directions Jump and sing with me.

Jumping Bunnies

(Tune: "Frère Jacques/Are You Sleeping?")

Jumping bunnies, jumping bunnies
Hop, hop, hop! Hop, hop, hop!
Kee-eep on jumping
Kee-eep on jumping
Look out, fox! Look out, fox!

Say: *Bunnies jump back home! Balance on one foot for 3 seconds, 5 seconds, 10 seconds. Jump and sing again!*

◼ ACTIVITY 3: **Cool-Down**

Materials None

Directions Stretch and sing with me.

CHAMPPS Cool-Down Song

(Tune: "Here We Go 'Round the Mulberry Bush")

This is the way we stretch our legs
Stretch our legs, stretch our legs
This is the way we stretch our legs
At the end of CHAMPPS

Repeat with: touch our toes, bend and stretch, wave goodbye.

sit

touch toes

bend and stretch

wave hand

Read and move together!

Look for this book at your local library: *Jump!* by Steve Lavis.

Dance to this YouTube video: _____

Thank you for playing with me!

CHAMPPS: CHildren in Action Motor Program for PreschoolerS by Paddy C. Favazza and Michaelene M. Ostrosky with Melissa Stalega, Hsiu-Wen Yang, Katherine Aronson-Ensign, Martin Block, W. Catherine Cheung, and Yusuf Akemoglu. Copyright © 2023 by Paul H. Brookes Publishing Co., Inc. All rights reserved.

CHAMPPS Home Activities

Hi, Family and Friends!
I am still doing CHAMPPS at school! I am learning about balance and new ways to move. Now I want to play CHAMPPS with you! It only takes 10–20 minutes. Thank you for playing with me!
Love, Your Little CHAMP

■ ACTIVITY 1: **Warm-Up**

Materials None
Directions Move and sing with me.

CHAMPPS Warm-Up Song

(Tune: "The Ants Go Marching")

The CHAMPPS go jogging one by one
Hurrah, hurrah!
The CHAMPPS go jogging one by one
Hurrah, hurrah!
The CHAMPPS go jogging one by one
This is the way we have some fun
And we all go jogging on, and on, and on!

Repeat with: galloping, skipping, and balancing (on one foot).

■ ACTIVITY 2: **Hungry Horsey**

Materials

Tape: Use to create a path
Different-sized objects: Ball, sock, potholder, beanbag, or balloon filled with sand
Laundry basket, hamper, or bucket
Tennis racquet or flat book

Directions

1. Make a path for me using different objects to walk around.
2. I can walk and balance my pretend apple on my hand, tennis racquet, book, or head.
3. I can put my pretend apple in the basket.
4. Then, I gallop back.
5. Look at the path we used at school!

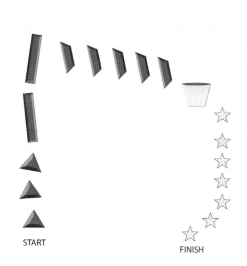

START

FINISH

■ ACTIVITY 3: **Cool-Down**

Materials None
Directions Stretch and sing with me.

CHAMPPS Cool-Down Song

(Tune: "Here We Go 'Round the Mulberry Bush")

This is the way we stretch our legs
Stretch our legs, stretch our legs
This is the way we stretch our legs
At the end of CHAMPPS

Repeat with: touch our toes, bend and stretch, wave goodbye.

| sit | touch toes | bend and stretch | wave hand |

Read and move together!
Look for this book at your local library: *Silly Sally* by Audrey Wood.

Dance to this YouTube video: _____

Thank you for playing with me!

CHAMPPS: CHildren in Action Motor Program for PreschoolerS by Paddy C. Favazza and
Michaelene M. Ostrosky with Melissa Stalega, Hsiu-Wen Yang, Katherine Aronson-Ensign, Martin Block,
W. Catherine Cheung, and Yusuf Akemoglu. Copyright © 2023 by Paul H. Brookes Publishing Co., Inc. All rights reserved.

CHAMPPS Home Activities

CHAMPPS

Hi, Family and Friends!

I am finishing up Unit 3 of CHAMPPS at school! I am learning about how to balance things, move my body, pretend, and have fun! Now I want to play CHAMPPS with you! It only takes 10–20 minutes. Thank you for playing with me!

Love, Your Little CHAMP

◼ ACTIVITY 1: **Warm-Up**

Materials None
Directions Move and sing with me.

CHAMPPS Warm-Up Song

(Tune: "The Ants Go Marching")

The CHAMPPS go jogging one by one
Hurrah, hurrah!
The CHAMPPS go jogging one by one
Hurrah, hurrah!
The CHAMPPS go jogging one by one
This is the way we have some fun
And we all go jogging on, and on, and on!

Repeat with: galloping, skipping, and balancing (on one foot).

◼ ACTIVITY 2: **River Jump**

Materials

Tape or string: Use to create a path
Pretend duck eggs: Use rolled up socks, balls of yarn, small balls such as a baseball, foam balls, etc.
Pretend alligators: Use stuffed animals, toys, pillows, blocks, etc.
Nest: Laundry basket, bucket, or large bowl
Pretend lily pads: Tape down newspaper pages, small towels, or placemats on the floor.

Directions

1. Make a path for me using different objects.
2. I am a duck walking down the river. I balance my pretend eggs on my hands OR under my arms.
3. I walk around the pretend alligators.
4. I put my pretend eggs in the nest.
5. I jump onto each lily pad.
6. I do it again!

◼ ACTIVITY 3: **Cool-Down**

Materials None
Directions Stretch and sing with me.

CHAMPPS Cool-Down Song

(Tune: "Here We Go 'Round the Mulberry Bush")

This is the way we stretch our legs
Stretch our legs, stretch our legs
This is the way we stretch our legs
At the end of CHAMPPS

Repeat with: touch our toes, bend and stretch, wave goodbye.

sit

touch toes

bend and stretch

wave hand

Read and move together!
Look for this book at your local library: *Sometimes I Like to Curl Up in a Ball* by Vicki Churchill and Charles Fuge.
Dance to this YouTube video: _____

Thank you for playing with me!

Get Moving:
CHAMPPS Motor Skills Units

UNIT 4

Catching

Unit Objectives

1. **Motor Movement.** Focus on catching objects with two hands. Reinforce previously learned skills such as jogging, walking, jumping, and stretching.

2. **Visual Tracking.** Watch and follow objects (ball, balloon, scarf) with eyes.

3. **Grasp and Release.** Hold the ball (balloon, scarf) and let it go. Pass/Roll/Throw ball.

4. **Hand–Eye Coordination.** Watch ball. Eyes guide hands to catch ball.

5. **Cooperative Play.** Focus on sharing and taking turns with friends, complimenting friends (e.g., good catch, good roll, good throw)

6. **Sustained Physical Activity.** Engage in continuous movement during music video.

Key Vocabulary

Body Parts	**arms, elbows, eyes, fingers, hands, knees**
Motor Movement	**catch, hold, jumping jacks, kneel (high-kneel, low-kneel), pass, retrieve ball, roll, roll arms, throw**
Concepts	**apart, backward, between, big, forward, hard, over, small, soft, together, under**
Pre-academic	**letters, numbers**
Social-Emotional	**friend, partner, team**

UNIT LESSON

Time	Activity	Focus			
3-5 min	WARM-UP	Gathering	Increase Heart Rate		Warm-Up Muscles
5 min	CORE 1: **Pass the Ball**	Motor Movement	Hand-Eye Coordination	Visual Tracking	Grasp and Release
5 min	CORE 2*: **Roll and Catch**				
5 min	CORE 3*: **Throw and Catch**				
2-4 min	PHYSICAL ACTIVITY: Music Video *(Lessons 3-6 only)*	Motor Imitation & Sustained Physical Activity			
3 min	COOL-DOWN	Gathering	Decrease Heart Rate		Cool-Down Muscles

*Core 2 and Core 3 occur simultaneously with the class divided into two small groups. After both small groups complete one activity, children remain with their group and the small groups switch activities.

PREPARATION AND MATERIALS

Activity	Materials (class of 15 children with 2 adults)
WARM-UP COOL-DOWN Whole Group	Numbered floor markers (1 per person)
CORE 1 **Pass the Ball** Whole Group	Numbered floor markers Stars (6-8) of various colors Masking tape Balls of various sizes
CORE 2 **Roll and Catch*** Partners	Numbered floor markers Bell Balls of various sizes
CORE 3 **Throw and Catch*** Partners	Numbered floor markers Bell Balls of various sizes

Visual Support Cards

Used for these movements: stand, stand in circle, sit, roll arms, jumping jacks, pass ball over/under, pick up ball, retrieve ball, grasp/release ball, put in/take out, roll ball, catch, throw, catch while sitting/kneeling, stretch arms, twist, airplane arms, bend and stretch, wave hand.
Visit the Brookes Download Hub to download and print the Visual Support Cards for Unit 4.

*Because Core 2 and Core 3 activities occur simultaneously, use the Planning Notes form to preassign children to Small Group 1 or Small Group 2. Once all children complete one of the two core activities, they switch to other activity. For smooth transitions to the next activity, you might keep small groups relatively stable once they are set, unless a teacher determines that a child needs to be placed in a different group due to specific support or behavioral needs.

SETUP

Warm-Up and Cool-Down
Place floor markers in a circle in the middle of the room.

Pass the Ball
Create a line of stars in a color pattern (e.g., red, blue, purple, red, blue, purple) by placing stars on masking tape line. The line of stars should go down the middle of the warm-up circle. See Figure U4.1.

Note: You may wish to plan ahead and take pictures of the classroom setup and of children engaged in the activity to send to families with the Home Activities pages.

Roll and Catch and *Throw and Catch*
1. Match pairs of numbered floor markers (i.e., 1 and 1, 2 and 2, etc.). Place half of floor markers on one side of the room (for Roll and Catch activity). Place the other half of matched floor markers on the other side of the room (for Throw and Catch). There should be 3-4 feet between the two markers in each pair. Markers could be placed closer initially; then ask children to move back as they become proficient at catching a ball. See Figure U4.2.
2. Have large bucket handy with balls of various sizes.

Featured Interactive Movement Books
- *Here Are My Hands,* written by Bill Martin, Jr., and John Archambault and illustrated by Ted Rand. Henry Holt and Company, 1987.
- *My Hands,* written and illustrated by Aliki. HarperCollins, 2000. (Original work published 1962, revised 1990.)
- *Clap Your Hands,* written and illustrated by Lorinda Bryan Cauley. G.P. Putnam's Sons Books for Young Readers, 1992.

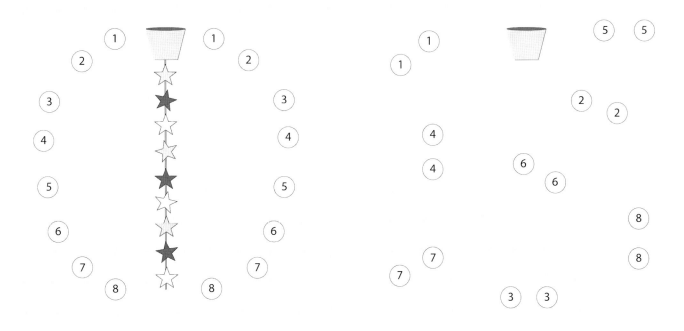

Figure U4.1. Classroom setup for Pass the Ball.

Figure U4.2. Classroom setup for Roll and Catch and Throw and Catch.

Video Content

For this unit, you will need to select one or two music videos, each approximately 2 minutes long, illustrating movements such as throwing, catching, squatting, lifting arms, and grabbing/grasping. Note, you can select a longer (4-minute) music video and use 2 minutes for Lesson 3, 3 minutes for Lesson 4, and the entire 4 minutes for Lessons 5 and 6.

See the recommended list of video sources on Page 265 and the criteria for video selection on Page 269.

BEFORE YOU START

1. Read through the unit. In particular, read through all of the lesson activities. Visualize the space where you will have CHAMPPS and how you will implement each activity with the children with whom you work.

2. Identify the school readiness skills you will focus on in each lesson activity; school readiness skills should correspond to your core curriculum.

3. Identify universal design for learning (UDL) strategies and adaptations to use for particular activities and/or to support individual children. For example, download the visual supports for use with the lesson prior to starting.

4. Review the lesson variations to determine which you will use, if needed.

5. Plan ahead for how you will shorten the lesson, if needed (see below).

6. Complete the Planning Notes.

If you need to shorten the lesson:
Depending on the needs of the children you teach, you may choose to shorten the lesson on the first day or first two days of Unit 4 to allow children to get used to the CHAMPPS routine. For example, you could do the Warm-Up with the song, one or two core activities, and the Cool-Down with the song. Then, on the third day, you could add the third core activity.

UNIT 4 PLANNING NOTES

Motor movements to focus on:

Vocabulary to focus on:

Children who will be positioned near an adult for additional support and attention:

Children who will help with setup:

Children who will help with cleanup:

Pairs of children in Small Group 1:
(e.g., 1. Delroy and Joe, 2. Cameron and Isabella)

1.

2.

3.

4.

Pairs of children in Small Group 2:

1.

2.

3.

4.

▪ WARM-UP

Structure: Whole group

Get ready! Focus on:
- Gathering
- Increasing heart rate
- Warming up muscles

Total time: 3-5 minutes

Key Vocabulary:
- **arms, elbows, knees**
- **jumping jacks, roll arms**
- **apart, forward, together**

1. MOVE: Motor Movements

Children start on their floor marker, warming up their bodies while singing the "CHAMPPS Warm-Up Song" with each movement you model. Verbal prompts are provided below, if needed.

- Children **jog** in a circle. Say: *A jog is a* **slow run.** *We are going to jog. Let's jog slowly, head up, pumping our arms forward and back.*
- Children **roll outstretched arms** using a small forward/backward circle motion. Say: *Walk in a circle. Keep arms out straight like* **airplane arms.** *Roll arms in big (or small) circles forward/backward.*
- Children do **jumping jacks** on their floor markers. Say: *Time for jumping jacks! Let's* **star jump!** *Arms up. Feet wide. We look like a star! Now feet together. Hands together. We look like a tree!* **Apart!** *We're a star!* **Together!** *We're a tree! Again!* **Apart!** *Star!* **Together!** *Tree! Let's keep going faster.* **Apart! Together!** *Star! Tree!*

2. ADAPT: UDL Strategies

Adapt the activity to meet the needs of the children with whom you work. See the suggestions in the following table; for additional ways to adapt, use the UDL Suggestions for Unit 4.

Engagement	Representation	Action & Expression
Give children choices. Ask children to choose the next warm-up movement(s).	• Use verbal prompts to encourage movement. See the Verbal Prompt Glossary. • Use visual supports. See Visual Support Cards for stand, stand in circle, sit, roll arms, and jumping jacks.	Encourage children to sing along. Give children the option to hum or clap to the melody/rhythm.

3. SUPPORT: School Readiness

Choose one to three school readiness skills to focus on. See the suggestions in the following table; for additional ways to support school readiness, turn to Page 138.

Language	Mathematics	Approaches to Learning
• Encourage children to sing along. • Children listen for verbal prompts. • Children identify body parts.	• Use ordinal language to describe movement used (*first, second, third*). • Children count jumping jacks.	• Create a smooth transition between movements. • Children follow directions. • Guide children to remain focused and continue moving. • Encourage whole-group engagement.

4. LESSON VARIATIONS

If the children you work with learn these activities quickly and need no further practice, or if you want to vary activities for review days, see Lesson Variations on Page 143.

■ CORE ACTIVITY 1: **Pass the Ball**

Structure: Whole group

Focus on these objectives:
- Roll
- Pass
- Catch
- Following directions
- Positional words **(over/between)**
- Cooperative play **(take turns, share ball, compliment partner, e.g., good catch, good roll, good throw)**

Total time: 3-5 minutes

Key Vocabulary:
- arms, elbows, eyes, fingers, hands, knees
- catch, hold, pass
- between, over, under, together, first, last
- friend, team, partner

1. MOVE: Motor Movements

- Children line up on stars positioned on taped line on the floor. They should stand close enough to touch the shoulders of the child in front of them.
- Demonstrate how to pass ball overhead and between legs using script below.
- Next, give one ball to child at front of line and one ball to child in middle of line.
- As the group sings "Pass the Ball," children **pass** the balls down the line. Ask children to hold the ball until their **friend** receives/gets the ball rather than tossing the ball. Children can pass the ball **over** their head first and then pass the ball **between** their legs.
- Overhead Pass—Say: *First we will do an overhead pass! Arms up. Hold ball over your head with two hands. Bend elbows to hand the ball to the person behind you. Next child raises hands to get ball and then passes ball overhead to next person.* Continue until the end of the line.
- Between-Legs Pass—Say: *Now we will do a between-your-legs pass! Stand with feet wide apart. Knees bent slightly. Arms down. Hold the ball with two hands. Pass the ball **between** your legs. The next child uses two hands to get the ball and then passes the ball between their legs to the next person.* Continue until the end.

Note: When the ball gets to the last child, an adult can walk the ball to the front of the line or the last child can walk it to the front of the line and begin passing the ball again.

2. ADAPT: UDL Strategies

Adapt the activity to meet the needs of the children with whom you work. See the suggestions in the following table; for additional ways to adapt, use the UDL Suggestions for Unit 4.

Engagement	Representation	Action & Expression
Engage children by encouraging them to move faster each time.	• Use verbal prompts for each movement. See the Glossary of Verbal Prompts. • Use visual supports. See Visual Support Cards for stand, pass ball overhead, pass ball between legs, and grasp.	Use hand-over-hand assistance to support children in passing the ball **overhead** and **between** their legs.

3. SUPPORT: School Readiness

Choose one to three school readiness skills to focus on. See the suggestions in the following table; for additional ways to support school readiness, turn to Page 138.

Language	Mathematics	Social	Approaches to Learning
• Encourage children to sing along. • Ask: *How else could you pass the ball? To the side? With your eyes closed?*	• Instead of singing, children say positional words (*over, under, between*) when passing the ball. • Children alternate pattern (over, under, over) when passing ball.	• Guide children to wait their turn and keep the balls moving. • Guide children in waiting their turn and keeping the balls moving.	• Children follow directions. • Guide children to stay focused during the whole-group activity and watch for the moving ball.

4. LESSON VARIATIONS

If the children you work with learn these activities quickly and need no further practice, or if you want to vary activities for review days, see Lesson Variations on Page 143.

■ CORE ACTIVITY 2: Roll and Catch

Structure: Partners

Focus on these objectives:
- Rolling ball
- Catching ball
- Visual tracking
- Cooperative play (take turns, share ball, compliment partner, e.g., good catch, good roll, good throw)

Total time: 3-5 minutes

Key Vocabulary:
- **eyes, fingers, hands, knees**
- **catch, hold, kneel (high kneel, low kneel), retrieve ball, roll**
- **hard, soft**
- **letters, numbers**
- **friend, partner**

1. MOVE: Motor Movements

- Children form pairs; assign each pair a **number** from 1 to 9. Children sit crisscross on their numbered floor marker. Have available one ball for each pair and a bell.
- **Partners roll** and **catch.**
    - **Roll and Catch, Seated Position.** Say: *Let's play "Roll and Catch"! Sit with your legs spread wide, facing your partner, feet touching. Hold the ball with two hands. Look at your partner, say their name, and ask, "Are you ready?" Then roll the ball to your partner.* (Gently push ball to partner.) *Partners, catch the ball with two hands. Look at your partner, say their name, and ask, "Are you ready?" Then roll ball back to partner.* Repeat rolling back and forth several times. Then, children move further apart, with feet not touching, and repeat rolling game. After 2 minutes, ring the bell to transition to next movement.
    - **Roll and Catch, Low-Kneel Position.** Say: *Now, let's play "Roll and Catch" in a low-kneel position. Kneel in* **low-kneel** *position, resting your bottom on the back of your heels like me.* Demonstrate the position. Continue roll and catch activity. After 2 minutes, ring the bell to transition to next movement.
    - **Roll and Catch, High-Kneel Position.** Say: *Now, let's play "Roll and Catch" in a high-kneel position. Kneel in* **high-kneel** *position—no longer resting your bottom on the back of your heels—and with a tall back, like me.* Demonstrate the position. Continue roll and catch activity.
    - **Retrieve Ball.** Demonstrate what to do if the ball rolls away. Instruct the child who rolled the ball to retrieve the ball. Say: *If your ball rolls away,* **retrieve** *it. Watch where the ball goes, walk over, pick it up, walk back to your place, and try again to roll it to your partner.* If this continues to happen, have partners practice while sitting/kneeling closer together.
- Optional: Encourage children to say letters of the alphabet with each roll/catch.

2. ADAPT: UDL Strategies

Adapt the activity to meet the needs of the children with whom you work. See the suggestions in the following table; for additional ways to adapt, use the UDL Suggestions for Unit 4.

Engagement	Representation	Action & Expression
Increase or decrease distance between pairs based on needs of each child.	• Use verbal prompts for each movement. See the Glossary of Verbal Prompts. • Use visual supports. See Visual Support Cards for sit, roll ball, catch, catch while sitting, and catch while kneeling.	Sit behind a child and use hand-over-hand guidance to assist in **roll** and **catch.**

3. SUPPORT: School Readiness

Choose one to three school readiness skills to focus on. See the suggestions in the following table; for additional ways to support school readiness, turn to Page 138.

Mathematics	Social	Approaches to Learning
Encourage **number** recognition and ask children to find their **number.**	Children participate in cooperative play with a partner with minimal guidance from adults.	Children follow directions.

4. LESSON VARIATIONS

If the children you work with learn these activities quickly and need no further practice, or if you want to vary activities for review days, see Lesson Variations on Page 143.

■ CORE ACTIVITY 3: **Throw and Catch**

Structure: Partners

Focus on these objectives:
- Throwing/tossing ball
- Catching ball
- Visual tracking
- Cooperative play (take turns, share ball, compliment partner, e.g., good catch, good roll, good throw)

Total time: 3–5 minutes

Key Vocabulary
- eyes, fingers, hands, knees
- catch, hold, high kneel, throw
- hard, soft
- letters, numbers
- friend, partner

1. MOVE: Motor Movements

- Children form pairs; assign each pair a **number** from 1 to 9. Children start in **high-kneel** position. Have available one ball for each pair and a bell.
- Have **partners throw** and **catch.** Say: *Hold the ball with two hands. Look at your partner while they hold their arms straight out in front. Ask, "Are you ready to catch?" Then toss the ball softly into your partner's open arms. Partners, catch the ball with two hands. Hug it close to your chest.* Repeat back and forth.
- After 2 minutes, ring the bell. Children stand. Continue **throw** and **catch** activity.
- **Optional:** Encourage children to say letters of the alphabet with each throw/catch.

2. ADAPT: UDL Strategies

Adapt the activity to meet the needs of the children with whom you work. See the suggestions in the following table; for additional ways to adapt, use the UDL Suggestions for Unit 4.

Engagement	Representation	Action & Expression
Increase or decrease distance between pairs based on needs of each child.	• Use verbal prompts to signal **throw** and **catch.** See the Glossary of Verbal Prompts. • Use visual supports. See Visual Support Cards for catch, throw, catch while kneeling, stand, and grasp.	Sit behind a child and use hand-over-hand guidance to assist in **throw** and **catch.**

3. SUPPORT: School Readiness

Choose one to three school readiness skills to focus on. See the suggestions in the following table; for additional ways to support school readiness, turn to Page 138.

Mathematics	Social	Approaches to Learning
Encourage **number** recognition and ask children to find their **number.**	Children participate in cooperative play (taking turns throwing) with a partner with minimal guidance from adults.	Children follow directions.

4. LESSON VARIATIONS

If the children you work with learn these activities quickly and need no further practice, or if you want to vary activities for review days, see Lesson Variations on Page 143.

■ PHYSICAL ACTIVITY: **Music Video**

Structure: Whole group   **Total time:** 2-4 minutes
Focus on this objective:
Sustained physical activity

---

1. MOVE: Motor Movements

Children stand on their floor marker. Spread out, allowing enough space for floor movement. Say: *Arms out. Make wide, airplane arms. Make sure you are not touching a friend.*

Children move to the music video you selected.

Lesson	Video	Total Time
3	Video 1: jumping jacks, kneel, pass, roll, lift arms, roll arms, grasp/release fingers	2 minutes
4	Video 2: same as above	3 minutes
5	Videos 1 and/or 2	4 minutes
6		

2. ADAPT: UDL Strategies

Adapt the activity to meet the needs of the children with whom you work. See the suggestions in the following table; for additional ways to adapt, use the UDL Suggestions for Unit 4.

Engagement	Representation	Action & Expression
Provide specific praise and encouragement (e.g., *I love your dance moves!* Or *Excellent job, keep moving!*)	• Use verbal prompts to describe movement. See the Glossary of Verbal Prompts. • Use visual supports. See Visual Support Cards for stand, stand in circle, sit, and airplane arms.	Stand in close proximity to children and model modified movements (e.g., bend knees instead of sitting).

3. SUPPORT: School Readiness

During the music video, the primary goal is to have all children maintain sustained/increased physical activity levels. To achieve this goal, teachers can model/prompt motor imitation (imitate actions/songs from video, maintain personal space) and approaches to learning (active engagement, following instructions from video).

4. LESSON VARIATIONS

If the children you work with learn these activities quickly and need no further practice, or if you want to vary activities for review days, see Lesson Variations on Page 143.

■ COOL-DOWN

Structure: Whole group

Wrap up: Focus on
• Gathering
• Decreasing heart rate
• Cooling down muscles

Total time: 3–5 minutes

Key Vocabulary
• **arms, fingers, knees**
• **hold, roll arms**
• **between, together**
• **hard, soft**

1. MOVE: Motor Movements

Have one small ball available for each child. Children sit on their floor marker and cool-down their bodies with the movements listed below. Once you have modeled each movement, sing the "CHAMPPS Cool-Down Song" while doing the movements (see "CHAMPPS Cool-Down Song," Page 133).

• Stretch **arms.** Say: *Hold ball with one hand.* **Make an X.** *Bend your arm. Touch ball to shoulder.*

• *Roll arms. Say: Sit with a straight back. Hold ball with two hands.* **Arms out straight. Roll your arms** *and* **make a circle.**

• Bend and stretch. Say: *Sit with a straight back. Legs straight. Raise your* **arms up.** *Slowly sway your arms* **side to side** *to bend and stretch.*

• Wave goodbye. Say: *Look at your friends. Hold out your hand and wave goodbye.*

Optional: End with yoga poses: Half-Moon and Seated Twist.

• Half-Moon. (See Figure U4.3.) Say: *Stand up. Hold your arms over your head with your hands together. Reach your arms to the right and your hips to the left. Switch sides.*

Note: As a variation and to give children additional practice controlling a ball, children hold a ball overhead with both hands and then do the Half-Moon Pose.

• Seated Twist. (See Figure U4.4.) Say: *Sit down, crisscross applesauce. Place one hand on each knee. Twist and look behind you. Switch sides.*

Figure U4.3. Half-Moon Pose.   **Figure U4.4.** Seated Twist.

2. ADAPT: UDL Strategies

Adapt the activity to meet the needs of the children with whom you work. See the suggestions in the following table; for additional ways to adapt, use the UDL Suggestions for Unit 4.

Engagement	Representation	Action & Expression
Vary volume of voice and pace of instructions to match the cool-down movement and pace of movement.	• Use verbal prompts to describe movement. See the Glossary of Verbal Prompts. • Use visual supports. See Visual Support Cards for sit, roll arms, stretch arms, bend and stretch, twist, and wave hand.	Begin with deep breathing, simple movements, and no singing.

3. SUPPORT: School Readiness

Choose one to three school readiness skills to focus on. See the suggestions in the following table; for additional ways to support school readiness, turn to Page 138.

Language	Mathematics	Approaches to Learning
• Encourage sing-along. • Children identify body parts.	Use ordinal language (*first, second, third*).	Create a smooth transition between movements.

4. LESSON VARIATIONS

If the children you work with learn these activities quickly and need no further practice, or if you want to vary activities for review days, see Lesson Variations on Page 143.

Walk-Around Card

CHAMPPS

1	**Warm-Up**	
	Gathering, increase heart rate, warm up muscles	
	MATERIALS	Numbered floor markers (1 per person)
	ACTIVITIES	Sing "CHAMPPS Warm-Up Song." Children jog, roll arms, and do jumping jacks.
2	**Core Activity 1: Pass the Ball**	
	Physical movement, hand-eye coordination, visual tracking, grasp and release, cooperative play	
	MATERIALS	• Numbered floor markers • Masking tape • Stars (6–8) of various colors • 3-4 balls of various sizes
	ACTIVITIES	Sing "Pass the Ball." Children pass the ball down the line and grasp it passing the ball overhead or passing ball between the legs.
3	**Core Activity 2: Roll and Catch**	
	Physical movement, hand-eye coordination, visual tracking, grasp and release, cooperative play	
	MATERIALS	• Numbered floor markers • Bell • Balls of various sizes (1 for each pair of children)
	ACTIVITIES	First: Children pair off. Then: Children roll and catch the ball with partner while sitting and kneeling.
4	**Core Activity 3: Throw and Catch**	
	Physical movement, hand-eye coordination, visual tracking, grasp and release	
	MATERIALS	• Numbered floor markers • Bell • Balls of various sizes (1 for each pair of children)
	ACTIVITIES	First: Children pair off. Then: Children roll and catch the ball with partner while kneeling and standing.
5	**Physical Activity: Music Video**	
	Sustained physical activity	
	MATERIALS	Video, video player, wall or screen for viewing

Lesson 3 Video (2 minutes)	Lesson 4 Video (3 minutes)	Lessons 5 and 6 Video (4 minutes)

6	**Cool-Down**	
	Gathering, lower heart rate, cool down muscles	
	MATERIALS	• Numbered floor markers • Small balls (1 per child)
	ACTIVITIES	First: Sing "CHAMPPS Cool-Down Song." Stretch arms, roll arms, bend and stretch, and wave goodbye. Then: Do yoga poses: Half-Moon Pose and Seated Twist Pose.

Walk-Around Card

CHAMPPS

CHAMPPS Warm-Up Song

(Sung to the tune of "The Ants Go Marching")

The CHAMPPS go **jogging** one by one
Hurrah! Hurrah!
The CHAMPPS go **jogging** one by one
Hurrah! Hurrah!
The CHAMPPS go **jogging** one by one
This is the way we have some fun
And we all go **jogging** on, and on, and on

(Repeat with **roll arms** and **jumping jacks** [star jumping])

Pass the Ball

(Sung to the tune of "Frère Jacques/Are You Sleeping?")

Pass the ball, pass the ball
Overhead, overhead
Kee-eep on **passing**
Kee-eep on **passing**
'til the end, 'til the end

(Repeat with **between your legs**)

CHAMPPS Cool-Down Song

(Sung to the tune of "Here We Go 'Round the Mulberry Bush")

This is the way we **stretch our arms**
Stretch our arms, stretch our arms
This is the way we **stretch our arms**
At the end of CHAMPPS

(Repeat with **roll our arms, bend and stretch,** and **wave goodbye**)

GLOSSARY OF VERBAL PROMPTS

Do (Movement)	Say (Verbal Prompt)	Use
Bend and stretch	Reach, side, hold	Arms up. **Reach** to the **side. Hold it** there. **Reach** to the other side now. **Hold** it there.
Catch the ball	Eyes ready	Get ready to catch. **Eyes ready;** watch for the ball.
	Hands ready	**Hands ready;** are you ready to catch the ball?
	Hands together, hug ball	**Hands together. Hug the ball** close.
Jog	Slow run	We are going to jog. A jog is a **slow run. Swing your arms** and **run slowly.**
Jumping jacks	Star jump	Time for jumping jacks! Let's **star jump!** Arms up. Feet wide. We look like a star! Now feet together. Hands together. We look like a tree! **Apart!** We're a star! **Together!** We're a tree! Again! **Apart!** Star! Together! Tree! Let's keep going faster. **Apart! Together!** Star! Tree!
	Apart, together	
Pass the ball	Arms up/down	Let's pass the ball to a friend. Hold tightly. **Arms up.**
	Overhead	Reach high **overhead.** Bend your elbows and pass backward **overhead.**
	Between legs	Let's pass the ball between our legs. Hold tightly. **Arms down.** Reach down low, feet wide. **Hands between your legs.** Pass backward to your friend.
Roll arms	Airplane arms	Now let's roll those arms! First, make **airplane arms,** stretched out wide!
	Circles	**Make little circles** with your arms. Feel the stretch!
Roll the ball	Arms out	Hold the ball close. **Arms out.**
	Push	**Push** the ball to your friend.
Stretch arms	Make an X	Arms out straight. **Make an X.**
	Kiss your shoulder	Take your ball and touch your opposite shoulder **(kiss your shoulder).** *kiss sound* Repeat with the other arm!
Throw the ball	Hold close	**Hold the ball close.**
	Look, push out, let go	**Look** at your friend. **Push out** your arms. **Let go** and throw.

UDL SUGGESTIONS

Engagement							
Means of Engagement	**Warm-Up**	**Core Activity 1: Pass the Ball**	**Core Activity 2: Roll and Catch**	**Core Activity 3: Throw and Catch**	**Video 1**	**Video 2**	**Cool-Down**
Recruit Interest							
Child choice	Warm-up moves	Overhead or between legs	Which ball to use	Which ball to use	Which video to play	Which video to play	Cool-down movements
Novel/familiar	Familiar moves (jog, walk) Structure (whole group) New moves (crab walk, elephant walk, windmill arms, backstroke arms)	Familiar tune ("Frère Jacques") Structure (whole group)	Familiar materials (balls, sitting on floor markers) New structure (partners)	Familiar materials (balls, sitting on floor markers) New structure (partners)	New video Optional: Repeat video.	New video Optional: Repeat video.	Familiar moves (stretch arms, bend and stretch) New materials (balls) Use ball as drum to call children over.
Sustain Effort and Persistence							
Praise/ encourage	Say: *I like your big circles when you roll your arms!* Say: *You walk backward so carefully!*	Say: *I like how you're watching for the ball!* Say: *Your hands are ready to catch the ball. Well done!*	Say: *Nice eyes on ball!* Say: *You are hugging that ball nice and tight to catch.*	Say: *It's great when everyone stays with their partner!* Say: *Great job keeping the ball with your partner.*	Say: *Great job doing "left" then "right"!* Say: *We are pretending to pitch like Major League Baseball players!*	Say: *You're reaching so high!* Say: *Excellent stretching arms to throw the stars!*	Say: *I like how you looked at all your friends to say goodbye!*
Vary complexity	Increase/ Decrease number of moves.	Sit down and pass ball around in circle. Increase/ Decrease number of balls.	Vary distance from partner (close/far). Vary object size.	Vary distance from partner (close/far). Vary object size.	Allow children to "freeze" like statues when tired.	If children are tired, let them "freeze like a statue" to rest. Add optional yoga moves.	Increase/ Decrease number of moves.
Vary setup, directions	Sing softly/ loudly. Move slowly/ fast.	Sing softly/ loudly. Move slowly/ fast.	Change group size (three children).	Change group size (three children).	Vary materials (give instruments, scarves).	Vary materials (give instruments, scarves).	Vary materials (give beanbags).

UDL SUGGESTIONS (continued)

Representation

Means of Representation	Warm-Up	Core Activity 1: Pass the Ball	Core Activity 2: Roll and Catch	Core Activity 3: Throw and Catch	Video 1	Video 2	Cool-Down
Forms of Communication							
Auditory	Glossary of Verbal Prompts						→
Visual	Visual Support Cards						→
Tactile	Give hand-over-hand instruction (hold hands and roll arms).	Give hand-over-hand instruction (hold hands and pass ball overhead).	Give hand-over-hand instruction (sit behind child, hold hands, and roll ball together).	Give hand-over-hand instruction (stand behind child and catch ball together).	Give hand-over-hand instruction as needed.	Give hand-over-hand instruction as needed.	Give hand-over-hand instruction (hold hands and stretch arms).
Multiple Levels of Complexity							
Key vocabulary: define/model	jog jumping jacks roll arms walk (backward)	catch ball pass ball (overhead, between legs)	catch ball kneel roll ball sit	catch ball stand throw ball	Instruct as needed.	Instruct as needed.	bend and stretch play drums roll arms stretch arms wave goodbye

Action & Expression

Means of Expression	Warm-Up	Core Activity 1: Pass the Ball	Core Activity 2: Roll and Catch	Core Activity 3: Throw and Catch	Video 1	Video 2	Cool-Down
Variety of responses	Sing, clap, or hum song. Move in place.	Sing, clap, or hum song. Teacher provides hand-over-hand assistance with passing	Child taps ball instead of catching. Assigned roles vary (ball roller or catcher). Children use wall instead of partner.	Child taps ball instead of catching. Assigned roles vary (ball thrower or catcher). Children use wall instead of partner.	Choose only one to two movements to repeat.	Choose only one to two movements to repeat.	Sit with ball. Sing, clap, or hum song. Only do movements, no singing.

Means of Expression	Warm-Up	Core Activity 1: Pass the Ball	Core Activity 2: Roll and Catch	Core Activity 3: Throw and Catch	Video 1	Video 2	Cool-Down
Complexity of responses	Accept partial movement (airplane arms instead of rolling arms, walking forward instead of backward).	Accept partial movement (children hold ball in front of body instead of overhead). Children pass ball to left or right.	Accept partial movement (children remain seated). Children sit closer or further apart. Children count rolls in another language. Children click tongue after each roll rather than count.	Accept partial movement (children pass ball instead of throwing). Children sit closer or further apart. Children count throws in another language. Children click tongue after each throw rather than count.	Accept partial movement as needed.	Accept partial movement as needed.	Accept partial movement.

SUPPORT SCHOOL READINESS SKILLS

LANGUAGE AND LITERACY	Warm-Up	Core Activity 1: Pass the Ball	Core Activity 2: Roll and Catch	Core Activity 3: Throw and Catch	Cool-Down
Expresses feelings and preferences (hot, thirsty, tired, hungry, sleepy, sweaty)	Ask: *How do you feel after warm-up? Tired? Excited?*	Ask: *Do you like to pass fast or slow?*	Ask: *Do you like to roll fast or slow?*	Ask: *Do you like to throw high or low?*	Ask: *How do you feel when CHAMPPS is over? Tired? Hot? Sweaty?*
Engages in active discussion (shares ideas, asks and answers questions)	Ask children for new movement ideas.	Ask: *How else could you pass the ball? To the side? With your eyes closed?*	Ask: *Who can roll/ catch with one hand?*	Ask: *Who can throw/catch with two hands? With one hand?*	Ask children for cool-down ideas.
Communicates personal experiences and interests	Ask: *What's your favorite warm-up move?*	Ask: *Which do you like better, the overhead pass or between-legs pass?*	Ask: *Do you play any sports? Do you use a ball?*	Ask: *Do you play catch at home? Who do you play with?*	Ask: *Which activity was your favorite today? Which was your least favorite?*
Listens to/uses formal and informal language (listens to/sings songs, uses different voices)	Children listen and sing along.	Children listen and sing along.	Children say their friend's name ("_____, are you ready?").	Children say, "Throw gently, please! I'm over here!"	Children listen and sing along.
Recognizes shapes (circle, square, triangle, rectangle)	Children stand in circle, square, triangle, or rectangle. Make floor markers out of paper in various shapes.	Children stand in circle, square, triangle, or rectangle as they pass the ball.	Children discuss which shapes they see.	Children discuss which shapes they see.	Children sit in circle, square, triangle, or rectangle.
Recognizes letters	Label floor markers with letters. Ask: *Which letter are you standing on?*	Label bean bags or balls with letters. Have children say letters for each as they pass ball/ bean bag.	Say letters of the alphabet with each roll/catch.	Say letters of the alphabet with each throw/catch.	

MATHEMATICS	Warm-Up	Core Activity 1: Pass the Ball	Core Activity 2: Roll and Catch	Core Activity 3: Throw and Catch	Cool-Down
Number recognition (count, one–one correspondence)	Children count steps and arm rolls.	Children count passes.	Children count as they roll/catch.	Children count as they throw/catch.	Children count heartbeats.
Positional words (*above, side to side*)	Forward, backward	Instead of singing, children say positional words (*over, under, between*) when passing the ball. Children create patterns (over, under, over) when passing ball.	Forward, in front of	Forward, in front of	Side to side, left to right

MATHEMATICS	Warm-Up	Core Activity 1: Pass the Ball	Core Activity 2: Roll and Catch	Core Activity 3: Throw and Catch	Cool-Down
Ordinal language (*first, second,* etc.)	Use ordinal words for order of moves (first, jog; second, roll arms, etc.).	Ask: *Who is first in line? Last in line? Middle of the line?*	Use ordinal words for order of positions (first, sit; second, kneel; third, stand, etc.).	Use ordinal words for order of positions (first, sit; second, kneel; third, stand, etc.).	Use ordinal words to describe order of moves.
Categorizing and sorting objects	Say: *Before we start, let's find with our eyes and point to objects of different shapes that are around us* (e.g., circles, rectangles, squares; blue, red, orange things; soft/ hard things; tall, short things).	Provide assortment of objects that can be passed (e.g., beanbag, small football, small soccer ball, scarf). Ask: *Which objects roll/bounce? Let's pass them first. Which objects are made of fabric? Let's pass them.*	Partner children who are both wearing red, both wearing sneakers, etc.	Sort balls by size/color when putting away.	Children sit with other children who are wearing the same color.
Patterns (recognize, describe, reproduce)	Create a movement pattern (e.g., do two jumping jacks, then jog around).	Children line up alternating boy-girl.	Point out A-B pattern rolling back and forth.	Point out A-B pattern throwing back and forth.	Create a movement pattern.

SCIENCE	Warm-Up	Core Activity 1: Pass the Ball	Core Activity 2: Roll and Catch	Core Activity 3: Throw and Catch	Cool-Down
Ask/answer questions together (*Who? What? Where? How?*).	Ask: *Why do we warm-up? What happens to our hearts during CHAMPPS?*	Ask: *How do we push a ball? Show me!*	Ask: *How far will the ball go if you roll it hard? Softly?*	Ask: *How far will the ball go if you throw it hard? Softly?* Ask: *Who is your partner? Where do we stand?*	Ask: *Why do we cool-down?*
Make predictions together (*What if?*).	Ask: *What if we move faster?* Children jog, then pause and feel heartbeat.	Ask: *If we move faster, will it be easier or harder to catch the ball?*	Ask: *If we roll the ball too hard, what happens?*	Ask: *If we throw the ball too hard, what happens?* Children stand closer to partner. Ask: *Is this easy or hard?* Have them stand farther apart and ask the same question.	Ask: *What happens if we do not cool-down?*
Understand weather/seasons, calendar/days of the week.	Ask: *Do we jog in the summer? Fall? Winter? What sports do we play in the winter? Summer?*	Say: *Let's say the days of the week with each pass!*	Ask: *What happens when we roll a snowball? It gets bigger!* Children say days of week, months of year as they roll/catch.	Ask: *What happens when we throw a snowball?* Children say days of week, months of year as they throw/catch.	Ask: *How does your body feel when you come inside after running around outside in the heat/snow? What could you do to cool-down?*

SUPPORT SCHOOL READINESS SKILLS *(continued)*

SCIENCE	Warm-Up	Core Activity 1: Pass the Ball	Core Activity 2: Roll and Catch	Core Activity 3: Throw and Catch	Cool-Down
Discuss characteristics of living things (*humans, animals, plants*).	Say: *Let's talk about animal moves! Birds fly, horses gallop, frogs leap, bunnies jump.* Imitate movements.	Pass various objects—pine cones, leaves, apples, lemons, beanbags, etc. Discuss living and nonliving objects.		Ask: *Do any animals throw things? (Monkeys throw coconuts, squirrels throw nuts.)*	Discuss taking deep breaths, feeling tired, and needing to rest.
Use sensory vocabulary	Ask: *How does it feel to jog on grass—soft? On concrete—hard?*	Ask: *How does the ball feel? Heavy, light, rubbery, squishy?*	Ask: *How does the ball feel? Heavy, light, rubbery, squishy?*	Ask: *How does the ball feel? Heavy, light, rubbery, squishy?*	Say: *Close your eyes. What do you hear? Smell? Feel?*

MOTOR	Warm-Up	Core Activity 1: Pass the Ball	Core Activity 2: Roll and Catch	Core Activity 3: Throw and Catch	Cool-Down
Balance	Children walk (backward) and do jumping jacks.	Children pass ball overhead and between legs.	Children maintain balance while throwing and catching from kneeling position.	Children maintain balance while throwing and catching from standing position.	Children maintain balance while bending and stretching from seated position.
Visual tracking	Children hold scarves and roll their arms.	Children pass and catch ball.	Children roll and catch ball.	Children throw and catch ball.	Say: *Follow the ball with your eyes as we do our cool-down stretches.*
Motor imitation	Children imitate leader/peers.				⟶
Body awareness	Children identify which body parts are needed for the movement.				⟶
Body movement (stationary)	Children roll their arms and do jumping jacks.	Children stand, bend, pass, catch.	Children sit, kneel, stand, pass, roll, catch.	Children stand, pass, throw, bounce, catch.	Children stretch, roll arms, wave.
Strength/speed/duration	Children sustain movement through the song.	Children engage in continuous passing and catching.	Children roll the ball hard or softly.	Children throw the ball hard or softly.	Children slow down movement to cool-down.
Coordination (eye/hand; eye/foot)	Children roll their arms while walking and do jumping jacks.	Children coordinate during passing and catching,	Children coordinate during rolling and catching.	Children coordinate during throwing and catching.	Children hold ball while moving.
Locomotion	Children jog, walk.	Children walk in place while playing pass the ball.	Children retrieve overthrown balls.	Children retrieve overthrown balls.	

MOTOR	Warm-Up	Core Activity 1: Pass the Ball	Core Activity 2: Roll and Catch	Core Activity 3: Throw and Catch	Cool-Down
Directionality (forward, backward, sidesteps)	Children switch direction (*forward, backward*).	Children pass ball forward and backward while standing side by side.	Children roll ball forward or backward.	Children throw ball forward or backward.	Children move side to side.
Personal space	Children use own floor marker.	———————————————————————————————→			
Cross midline reach	Children hug body before and after warm-up and use each hand to pat opposite shoulder.	Children stand in circle and pass balls to the person on their left, then to the person on their right.			Children pat own shoulders to congratulate themselves, using each hand to pat opposite shoulder.
Grasp and release	When children roll their arms, have them open and close hands while making sound effects.	Children catch and pass/release ball.	———————————————————————————————→		
Motor regulation (go slow, go fast, stop)	Children move slowly or quickly.	Children sing/pass ball slower or faster.	Children keep one ball between each pair (few overthrown balls).	Children keep one ball between each pair (few overthrown balls).	Children slow down movement to cool-down.
Music and dance	Children sing.	Children sing.			Children sing.

SOCIAL-EMOTIONAL	Warm-Up	Core Activity 1: Pass the Ball	Core Activity 2: Roll and Catch	Core Activity 3: Throw and Catch	Cool-Down
Recognizes, describes, and regulates emotions	Ask: *How's everyone feeling today for CHAMPPS? Excited?* Discuss various emotion words.	Ask: *How do you feel when you catch the ball?* Discuss emotion words: *happy, ecstatic, excited, lucky, proud.*	Ask: *How do you feel when you miss the ball?* Discuss words: *sad, frustrated, mad, unhappy.*	Ask: *How do you feel now that CHAMPPS is over?*	Ask: *How do you feel when you catch the ball?* Discuss words: *happy, ecstatic, excited, lucky, proud.*
Solves/prevents problems	Establish a rule not to pass friends when moving in circle.	Call out names while passing the ball.	Review passing to partner and not over rolling balls.	Review passing to partner and not overthrowing balls.	Children stay on own floor marker.
Learns independence/self-help	Children go to vacant floor marker without support (e.g., walking child to vacant floor marker, verbal prompt).	Children line up without support (e.g., walking child to line, placing child behind someone already in line, verbal prompt).	Children retrieve balls that are not caught. Children gather their own balls.	Children retrieve overthrown balls. Children gather their own balls.	Children gather and put away their own balls.
Takes turns/waits turn	Children move with classmates and not speed ahead.	Children watch and wait to retrieve the ball.	Children watch and wait to retrieve the ball.	Children watch and wait to retrieve the ball.	Children take turns/wait for turn.

SUPPORT SCHOOL READINESS SKILLS *(continued)*

SOCIAL-EMOTIONAL	Warm-Up	Core Activity 1: Pass the Ball	Core Activity 2: Roll and Catch	Core Activity 3: Throw and Catch	Cool-Down
Helps/supports peers	Have partners help one another through transitions (holding hands).	Children call out peers' names.	Children call out peers' name. Help peer retrieve ball.	Children call out peers' names. Help peer retrieve overthrown ball.	Children hold hands, walking a peer to the floor markers.
Plays cooperatively	Children respectfully pass peers without bumping into them or apologize when bumping into peer.	Children work together to move balls down the line.	Children roll and catch the ball with partner.	Children throw and catch the ball with partner.	
Shares materials		Children share ball with peers.	Children share ball with peers.	Children share ball with peers.	
Socializes with peers	Add CHAMPPS greeting to children's warm-up.	Tell children: *Let's say our friends' names!* Children work together with peers.	Tell children: *Let's say our friends' names!* Children work together with peers.	Tell children: *Let's say our friends' names!* Children work together with peers.	Children wave at peers and say goodbye.

APPROACHES TO LEARNING	Warm-Up	Core Activity 1: Pass the Ball	Core Activity 2: Roll and Catch	Core Activity 3: Throw and Catch	Cool-Down
Transitions into/out of activities	Children return to floor marker at end of song.	Children line up showing respect for peers (e.g., without pushing).	Children transition to working with partner in kneeling position with ease.	Children transition to standing position with ease.	Children move with group to circle.
Listens to/follows directions	Children listen and imitate movement.			→	
Demonstrates focused attention	Children listen for next movement.	Children watch peer retrieve ball.	Children watch peer retrieve ball.	Children watch peer retrieve ball.	Children listen for next movement.
Demonstrates sustained attention	Children sustain movement until end of song.	Children listen for directions (over or under/between).	Children stay with partner.	Children stay with partner.	Children stay on floor marker.
Demonstrates active engagement in small/large group/with partner	Children stay engaged in whole group.	Children take/give ball to peer.	Children stay engaged while rolling ball with partner.	Children stay engaged while throwing ball with partner.	Children sing while doing cool-down movements.
Demonstrates active engagement in independent task	Children sing while completing warm-up movements.	Encourage children to find line on floor and line up independently. Children check their spacing by placing hands on shoulder of person in front of them.	Children retrieve ball and return to partner independently.	Children retrieve ball and return to partner independently.	Children get ball and go to floor marker independently.

Lesson Variations

■ WARM-UP VARIATION

Music/Rhythm/Dance

Variation 1: Music Warm-Up

Structure	Materials	Instructions
Whole group	• Floor markers • Projector with Internet access	1. Before warm-up, select YouTube videos with music at different tempos. For example, choose three familiar songs, one at a slow pace, one medium, and one fast. (See the video selection criteria on Page 269.) 2. Children stand on their floor markers in warm-up circle. 3. Children do the warm-up motor movements at the different paces.

■ CORE ACTIVITY 1: **Pass the Ball** VARIATIONS

Music/Rhythm/Dance

Variation 1: Pass the Instrument

Structure	Materials	Instructions
Whole group	Variety of musical instruments	Children pass musical instruments that will make a noise when passed.

Variation 2: Pass and Freeze

Structure	Materials	Instructions
Whole group	• Floor markers • Balls • Projector with Internet access	1. Before the activity, select a YouTube video of the "freeze dance" or "dance freeze" song. (See the video selection criteria on Page 269.) 2. Children gather in a circle, seated or standing. 3. Have them pass the ball as you play the video with the song. Tell children that when the song says "Freeze!" they must stop passing the ball. The goal of the game is to avoid ending up with the ball when this happens.

■ CORE ACTIVITY 2: **Roll and Catch** VARIATIONS

Music/Rhythm/Dance

Variation 1: Rhythm Roll and Catch

Structure	Materials	Instructions
Whole group	• Floor markers • Balls • Projector with Internet access	1. Before the activity, select several YouTube videos with children's music at different tempos. (See the video selection criteria on Page 269.) 2. Children roll the ball to the beat (fast/slow tempo) of the music.

Arts and Crafts

Variation 2: Roll and Catch Art

Structure	Materials	Instructions
Whole group	• Paper • Markers, crayons, colored pencils, or paints	Children decorate paper balls or decorate a piece of paper before wadding it up to throw and catch. Note: Painted paper needs to dry before rolling into balls.

■ CORE ACTIVITY 3: **Throw and Catch** VARIATIONS

Music/Rhythm/Dance

Variation 1: Motor Moves

Structure	Materials	Instructions
Whole group	Balls	1. Children practice jumping jacks, squats, or turning around in place. 2. Challenge children to try to do a new movement (jumping jack, turn around, or squat) after they throw the ball up in the air, in time to catch it again. 3. Challenge each child to increase the number of times they can do the new movement between throws/catches. 4. Ask the children to come up with different moves besides squats, turns, and jumping jacks.

Home Activities Record

Child: _____   Teacher: _____

Unit: _____   Week: _____

Please return by: _____

Thank you for playing with me! Please tell my teachers if we did CHAMPPS activities this week at home. Write a check (√) if we practiced CHAMPPS at home this week. You can also write comments to tell my teachers how I did when we practiced at CHAMPPS at home! Please give this form to my teacher each week.

Check (√) if you did CHAMPPS practice.	Parent/Child Comments

CHAMPPS: CHildren in Action Motor Program for PreschoolerS by Paddy C. Favazza and Michaelene M. Ostrosky with Melissa Stalega, Hsiu-Wen Yang, Katherine Aronson-Ensign, Martin Block, W. Catherine Cheung, and Yusuf Akemoglu. Copyright © 2023 by Paul H. Brookes Publishing Co., Inc. All rights reserved.

Home Activities Record

CHAMPPS

Child: _____   Teacher: _____

Unit: _____   Week: _____

Please return by: _____

Thank you for playing with me! Please tell my teachers if we did CHAMPPS activities this week at home. Write a check (√) if we practiced CHAMPPS at home this week. You can also write comments to tell my teachers how I did when we practiced CHAMPPS at home! Please give this form to my teacher each week.

Check (√) if you did CHAMPPS practice.	Parent/Child Comments

CHAMPPS: CHildren in Action Motor Program for PreschoolerS by Paddy C. Favazza and Michaelene M. Ostrosky with Melissa Stalega, Hsiu-Wen Yang, Katherine Aronson-Ensign, Martin Block, W. Catherine Cheung, and Yusuf Akemoglu. Copyright © 2023 by Paul H. Brookes Publishing Co., Inc. All rights reserved.

CHAMPPS Home Activities

Hi, Family and Friends!

We are beginning Unit 4 of CHAMPPS at school! I am learning all about how to pass and catch a ball in different ways. Now I want to play CHAMPPS with you! It only takes 10–20 minutes. Thank you for playing with me!

Love, Your Little CHAMP

■ ACTIVITY 1: **Warm-Up**

Materials None
Directions Move and sing with me.

CHAMPPS Warm-Up Song

(Tune: "The Ants Go Marching")

The CHAMPPS go jogging one by one
Hurrah, hurrah!
The CHAMPPS go jogging one by one
Hurrah, hurrah!
The CHAMPPS go jogging one by one
This is the way we have some fun
And we all go jogging on, and on, and on!

Repeat with: roll arms and
do jumping jacks.

■ ACTIVITY 2: **Pass the Ball**

Materials Ball (ball of yarn or rolled-up sock)
Directions

1. Stand in front of me so I'm looking at the back of your head.
2. Sing "Pass the Ball."
3. Pass the ball overhead. Hold the ball over/behind your head and I will take it from you.
4. Pass the ball under your legs. Hold the ball and pass it through your legs. I will take it from you.

Pass the Ball

(Tune: "Frère Jacques/Are You Sleeping?")

Pass the ball, pass the ball
Overhead, overhead
Kee-eep on passing! Kee-eep on passing!
'Til the end! 'Til the end!

Repeat with: between your legs.

■ ACTIVITY 3: **Cool-Down**

Materials None
Directions Stretch and sing with me.

CHAMPPS Cool-Down Song

(Tune: "Here We Go 'Round the Mulberry Bush")

This is the way we stretch our arms
Stretch our arms, stretch our arms
This is the way we stretch our arms
At the end of CHAMPPS

Repeat with: roll our arms, bend and stretch, wave goodbye.

stretch arms

roll arms

bend and stretch

wave goodbye

Read and move together!

Look for this book at your local library: *My Hands* by Aliki.

Dance to this YouTube video: _____

Thank you for playing with me!

CHAMPPS Home Activities

Hi, Family and Friends!

I am still doing CHAMPPS Unit 4 at school! I am learning about how to play catch by rolling the ball. Now I want to play CHAMPPS with you! It only takes 10–20 minutes. Thank you for playing with me!

Love, Your Little CHAMP

■ ACTIVITY 1: **Warm-Up**

Materials None
Directions Move and sing with me.

CHAMPPS Warm-Up Song

(Tune: "The Ants Go Marching")

The CHAMPPS go jogging one by one
Hurrah, hurrah!
The CHAMPPS go jogging one by one
Hurrah, hurrah!
The CHAMPPS go jogging one by one
This is the way we have some fun
And we all go jogging on, and on, and on!

Repeat with: roll arms and
do jumping jacks.

■ ACTIVITY 2: **Roll and Catch**

Materials
Floor marker: A placemat, towel, or sheet of paper
Ball (ball of yarn, rolled-up sock, newspaper rolled into a ball)

Directions

1. Sit on floor marker in front of me.
2. Roll the ball to me on the floor.
3. I catch the ball and roll it back to you. We keep rolling and catching.
4. Next time, we both kneel and then roll and catch.

■ ACTIVITY 3: **Cool-Down**

Materials None
Directions Stretch and sing with me.

CHAMPPS Cool-Down Song

(Tune: "Here We Go 'Round the Mulberry Bush")

This is the way we stretch our arms
Stretch our arms, stretch our arms
This is the way we stretch our arms
At the end of CHAMPPS

Repeat with: roll our arms, bend and stretch, wave goodbye.

stretch arms

roll arms

bend and stretch

wave goodbye

Read and move together!
Look for this book at your local library: *Here Are My Hands* by Bill Martin, Jr., and John Archambault.

Dance to this YouTube video: _____

Thank you for playing with me!

CHAMPPS Home Activities

Hi, Family and Friends!
I am finishing up Unit 4 of CHAMPPS at school! We are learning how to throw and catch a ball! Now I want to play CHAMPPS with you! It only takes 10–20 minutes. Thank you for playing with me!
Love, Your Little CHAMP

■ ACTIVITY 1: **Warm-Up**

Materials None
Directions Move and sing with me.

CHAMPPS Warm-Up Song

(Tune: "The Ants Go Marching")

The CHAMPPS go jogging one by one
Hurrah, hurrah!
The CHAMPPS go jogging one by one
Hurrah, hurrah!
The CHAMPPS go jogging one by one
This is the way we have some fun
And we all go jogging on, and on, and on!

Repeat with: roll arms and
do jumping jacks.

■ ACTIVITY 2: **Throw and Catch**

Materials
Floor marker: A placemat, towel, or sheet of paper on nonskid surface
Ball (ball of yarn, rolled up sock, newspaper rolled up in ball)

Directions

1. Stand or kneel on floor marker in front of me.
2. Drop the ball into my hands.
3. I catch the ball and throw it back to you. Do this three to five times.
4. Then stand or kneel farther away and throw the ball to me.

■ ACTIVITY 3: **Cool-Down**

Materials None
Directions Stretch and sing with me.

CHAMPPS Cool-Down Song

(Tune: "Here We Go 'Round the Mulberry Bush")

This is the way we stretch our arms
Stretch our arms, stretch our arms
This is the way we stretch our arms
At the end of CHAMPPS

Repeat with: roll our arms, bend and stretch, wave goodbye.

| stretch arms | roll arms | bend and stretch | wave goodbye |

Read and move together!
Look for this book at your local library: *Clap Your Hands* by Lorinda Bryan Cauley.

Dance to this YouTube video: _____

Thank you for playing with me!

CHAMPPS: CHildren in Action Motor Program for PreschoolerS by Paddy C. Favazza and Michaelene M. Ostrosky with Melissa Stalega, Hsiu-Wen Yang, Katherine Aronson-Ensign, Martin Block, W. Catherine Cheung, and Yusuf Akemoglu. Copyright © 2023 by Paul H. Brookes Publishing Co., Inc. All rights reserved.

Get Moving: CHAMPPS Motor Skills Units

Throwing

Unit Objectives

1. **Motor Movement.** Focus on throwing objects overhead and overhand. Reinforce previously learned skills such as jogging, jumping, galloping, and catching.

2. **Visual Tracking.** Watch and follow the ball (scarf, balloon) with your eyes.

3. **Grasp and Release.** Hold the ball (balloon, scarf) and let it go. Pass/Roll/Throw ball.

4. **Hand-Eye Coordination.** Watch ball. Eyes guide hands to throw and catch the ball.

5. **Cooperative Play.** Focus on sharing and taking turns with friends, complimenting friends (e.g., good catch, good roll, good throw).

6. **Force.** Throw ball hard (strong force) or soft (light force) to reach target.

7. **Sustained Physical Activity.** Engage in continuous movement during music video.

Key Vocabulary

Body Parts	**arms, elbows, eyes, feet, fingers, hands, knees**
Motor Movement	**catch, hold, jumping jacks, roll arms, swim, throw, watch**
Concepts	**aim, between, fast, hard, overhand, slow, soft, together, underhand**
Pre-academic	Instruments: **drums, piano**
	Weather: **snow, winter**
	Sports: **baseball, bowling**
	Other: **animals, colors, letters, numbers**
Social-Emotional	**friend, partner, team**

UNIT LESSON

Time	Activity	Focus			
3–5 min	WARM-UP	Gathering	Increase Heart Rate		Warm-Up Muscles
5 min	CORE 1: **Snowballs in the Air**	Motor Movement	Hand-Eye Coordination	Visual Tracking	Force
5 min	CORE 2*: **Snowman Throw**				
5 min	CORE 3*: **Bottle Bowling**				
2–4 min	PHYSICAL ACTIVITY: Music Video (Lessons 3–6 only)	Motor Imitation & Sustained Physical Activity			
3 min	COOL-DOWN	Gathering	Decrease Heart Rate		Cool-Down Muscles

* Core 2 and Core 3 occur simultaneously with the class divided into two small groups. After both small groups complete one activity, children remain with their group and the small groups switch locations/activities.

PREPARATION AND MATERIALS

Activity	Materials (class of 15 children with 2 adults)
WARM-UP COOL-DOWN Whole Group	Numbered floor markers (1 per person)
CORE 1 **Snowballs in the Air** Whole Group	Numbered floor markers (same ones used in Warm-Up) Buckets/baskets (at least 4) Beanbags (17, enough for 15 children and 2 adults to have 1 each)
CORE 2* **Snowman Throw** Independent practice	Snowman posters (8, enough for half of children) See Setup notes for making snowman posters. Beanbags (24, enough for 8 children to have 3 each) Small buckets (8, one for each station) Stars of various colors (8)
CORE 3 **Bottle Bowling** Independent practice	Water bottles (24, enough for 8 children to have 3 each) Balls of various sizes (8) Stars of various colors (8)
Visual Support Cards	
Used for these movements: stand, stand in circle, sit, roll arms, jumping jacks, pick up ball, retrieve ball, grasp, put in/take out, roll ball, throw, stretch arms, twist, airplane arms, bend and stretch, wave hand.	
Visit the Brookes Download Hub to download and print the Visual Support Cards for Unit 5.	

* Because Core 2 and Core 3 activities occur simultaneously, use the Planning Notes form to preassign children to Small Group 1 or Small Group 2. Once all children complete one of the two core activities, they switch to the other activity. For smooth transitions to the next activity, you might keep small groups relatively stable once they are set, unless a teacher determines that a child needs to be placed in a different group due to specific support or behavioral needs. During Snowman Throw and Bottle Bowling, teachers circulate around the room to model, support, and encourage children.

SETUP

Warm-Up and Cool-Down

Place floor markers in a circle or square in the middle of the room. (Setup should be similar to Figure U4.1 in Unit 4.)

Snowballs in the Air

Place four buckets in the middle of the warm-up area. Fill each bucket with four to five beanbags, enough for each child and adult to have one beanbag. See Figure U5.1.

Snowman Throw

1. Draw a large snowman on eight posters. (See Figure U5.2.) Attach Velcro on the snowman buttons, and then use Velcro to attach school readiness symbol or photo (animal, letter, color, number) to the snowman buttons. The symbols are used to give children a "target." The symbol or photo can be changed, depending on your focus.

2. Attach posters to the wall to create eight snowman stations (enough for half of the children in your class to use at one time). Each snowman station should have one star (indicating where the child stands), one snowman poster, one bucket, and at least three beanbags. Initially, the star is placed close (3–4 feet) in front of the snowman, with beanbags in a bucket next to the star. The bucket is also used to gather thrown beanbags. The star is moved further back as the child gains success with overhand throwing for accuracy and distance.

Bottle Bowling

1. Fill 24 water bottles with water. Note that full water bottles are heavier and harder to knock over. To encourage interest, children can make water bottles in an art or science lesson using food coloring and/or small sensory objects (glitter, pebbles, gemstones). Velcro symbols (animals, colors, letters, numbers) can be attached to the bottle to address school readiness skills.

2. Set up enough stations for half of the children in your class to use them at one time. Each station should have three bottles, one star (indicating where to stand), and one ball. Initially, the star is placed close (3–4 feet) in front of the bottles, with the ball next to the star. The star is moved further back as the child gains success with bowling for accuracy and distance. See Figure U5.3.

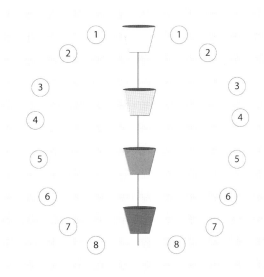

Figure U5.1. Classroom setup for Snowballs in the Air.

Figure U5.2. Classroom setup for Snowman Throw.

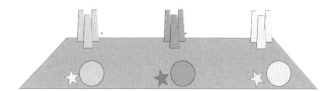

Figure U5.3. Classroom setup for Bottle Bowling.

Featured Interactive Movement Books

- *Clap Hands,* written and illustrated by Helen Oxenbury. Little Simon, 1999.
- *Pete the Cat: The Wheels on the Bus,* written and illustrated by James Dean. Harper Festival, 2015.
- *Hand, Hand, Fingers, Thumb,* written by Al Perkins and illustrated by Eric Gurney. Random House Books for Young Readers, 1998. (Original work published 1969.)

Video Content

For this unit, you will need to select one or two music videos, each approximately 2 minutes long. Given the focus of this unit on throwing, try and find videos that encourage children to use their arms by having them imitate movements such as waving arms; walking; swimming motions such as backstroke, dog paddle, breaststroke, snorkeling, and diving; and twisting as if drying off with towel. Note, you can select a longer (4-minute) music video and use 2 minutes for Lesson 3, 3 minutes for Lesson 4, and the entire 4 minutes for Lessons 5 and 6.

See the recommended list of video sources on Page 265 and the criteria for video selection on Page 270.

BEFORE YOU START

1. Read through the unit. In particular, read through all of the lesson activities. Visualize the space where you will have CHAMPPS and how you will implement each activity with the children with whom you work.
2. Identify the school readiness skills you will focus on in each lesson activity; school readiness skills should correspond to your core curriculum.
3. Identify universal design for learning (UDL) strategies and adaptations to use for particular activities and/or to support individual children. For example, download the visual supports for use with the lesson prior to starting.
4. Review the lesson variations to determine which you will complete, if needed.
5. Plan ahead for how you will shorten the lesson, if needed (see below).
6. Complete the Planning Notes.

If you need to shorten the lesson:
Depending on the needs of the children you teach, you may choose to shorten the lesson on the first day or first two days of Unit 5 to allow children to get used to the CHAMPPS routine. For example, you could do the Warm-Up with the song, one or two core activities, and the Cool-Down with the song. Then, on the third day, you could add the remaining activities.

UNIT 5 PLANNING NOTES

Motor movements to focus on:
Vocabulary to focus on:
Children who will be positioned near an adult for additional support and attention:
Children who will help with setup:
Children who will help with cleanup:
Children in Small Group 1:
Children in Small Group 2:
Partner pairs (if using activity variation):

■ WARM-UP

Structure: Whole group

Get ready! Focus on:
- Gathering
- Increasing heart rate
- Warming up muscles

Total time: 3-5 minutes

Key Vocabulary
- arms, elbows, feet, knees
- jumping jacks, roll arms, swim

1. MOVE: Motor Movements

Children start on their floor marker, warming up their bodies while singing the "CHAMPPS Warm-Up Song" with each movement you model. Verbal prompts are provided below, if needed.

- Children **jog** in a circle. Say: *We are going to jog. A jog is a **slow run. Swing your arms** forward and back and **run slowly.***

- Children **swim** in a circle. Say: *Walk in a circle. One arm forward, one arm back. **Swing your arms** like you are swimming in the water.*

- Children **roll arms** in a circle. Say: *Walk in a circle. Keep arms out straight like **airplane arms.** Roll arms in big (or small) circles forward (or backward).*

- Children do **jumping jacks** on their floor markers. Say: *Time for jumping jacks! Let's **star jump!** Arms up and apart, feet wide. We look like a star! Clap hands together above our head. We look like a tree! **Apart!** We're a star! **Together!** We're a tree! Again! **Apart!** Star! **Together!** Tree! Let's keep going faster. **Apart! Together!** Star! Tree!*

2. ADAPT: UDL Strategies

Adapt the activity to meet the needs of the children with whom you work. See the suggestions in the following table; for additional ways to adapt, use the UDL Suggestions for Unit 5.

Engagement	Representation	Action & Expression
Give children choices. Ask children to choose the next warm-up movement(s).	• Use verbal prompts to encourage movement. See the Glossary of Verbal Prompts. • Use visual supports. See Visual Support Cards for stand, stand in circle, sit, roll arms, and jumping jacks.	Encourage children to sing along. Give children the option to hum or clap to the melody/rhythm.

3. SUPPORT: School Readiness

Choose one to three school readiness skills to focus on. See the suggestions in the following table; for additional ways to support school readiness, turn to Page 165.

Language	Mathematics	Approaches to Learning
• Encourage children to sing along. • Say: *Show me your favorite warm-up movement!* • Say: *Let's review body parts! Where are your knees? Shoulders? Elbows?*	• Say: *Show me fast/slow jogging, swimming arms, and arm rolls.* • Say: *Let's do a pattern with our movements. Two jumping jacks, one arm roll, two jumping jacks, one arm roll.*	• Remind children to return to their floor marker between movements. • Encourage children to listen to directions and imitate movements. • Encourage and compliment children for whole-group engagement.

4. LESSON VARIATIONS

If the children you work with learn these activities quickly and need no further practice, or if you want to vary activities for review days, see Lesson Variations on Page 171.

■ CORE ACTIVITY 1: **Snowballs in the Air**

Structure: Whole group

Total time: 3–5 minutes

Focus on these objectives:
- Underhand throw
- Overhand throw
- Visual tracking
- Force

Key Vocabulary:
- **eyes, fingers, hands**
- **catch, hold, throw, watch**
- **aim, overhand, underhand**
- **snow, winter**

1. MOVE: Motor Movements

- Children remain in warm-up area.
- Demonstrate tossing beanbag to self. **Hold** beanbag with two **hands,** toss the beanbag into the air at **eye** level, **watch,** and **catch** with two **hands.** Children will **toss** beanbag to self and **catch** while singing "Snowballs in the Air." At the end of the song, they all throw their beanbags in the buckets using **underhand throw** and **overhand throw** (see below). Then they will retrieve a beanbag from the bucket using different movements (see below) and return to their floor marker.
- Demonstrate an **underhand throw** by tossing a beanbag into the bucket while standing on your floor marker. Then children will use an **underhand throw** to toss the beanbag into one of the buckets. Say: *Now we're going to throw underhand!*
  - *When I say **ready**, swing your arm back!*
  - *When I say **set**, step forward with one foot!*
  - *When I say **throw**, throw the beanbag! **Ready, set, throw!***
- Demonstrate an **overhand throw** and then let children practice while you and they say, "Ready, set, throw!" Say: *Now we are going to practice throwing overhand!*
  - *Hold the beanbag in your throwing hand.*
  - *Lift your arm, bringing the beanbag back to touch your ear.*
  - *Step forward with one foot.*
  - *Move your arm forward, throwing the beanbag into the bucket.*
  - *You can say it yourself: **Ready, set, throw!***
- Choose a movement (e.g., jog, jump, gallop). Demonstrate using the movement to go to the bucket, retrieve the beanbag, and go back to the floor marker. Children practice by moving (jogging, jumping, galloping) to the bucket, retrieving one beanbag, and moving (jogging, jumping, galloping) back to the floor marker.
- Repeat the song "Snowballs in the Air" as children toss the beanbags to themselves and catch them. At the end of the song, tell the children which throw to use to toss the beanbag into the bucket: overhand or underhand. Repeat by alternating between **underhand throw** and **overhand throw** for 3–5 minutes.

2. ADAPT: UDL Strategies

Adapt the activity to meet the needs of the children with whom you work. See the suggestions in the following table; for additional ways to adapt, use the UDL Suggestions for Unit 5.

Engagement	Representation	Action & Expression
Increase challenge by asking children to throw the beanbag into a bucket of a certain color.	• Model the movement(s) for children and then have them imitate the movement(s). • Use verbal prompts for each movement. See the Glossary of Verbal Prompts. • Use visual supports. See Visual Support Cards for stand, stand in circle, grasp, put in/take out, catch, and throw.	Provide hand-over-hand support to assist in **throw** and **catch.**

3. SUPPORT: School Readiness

Choose one to three school readiness skills to focus on. See the suggestions in the following table; for additional ways to support school readiness, turn to Page 165.

Language	Mathematics	Social	Approaches to Learning
• Encourage children to sing along. • Ask: *What are things we can do in the snow?* • Ask: *What shape is the beanbag? Let's trace the shape of the beanbag.*	• Emphasize positional words (*up, down, high, low*). • Ask: *What else can we make with snow?*	• Ask: *Who likes to throw snowballs in the air?* • Encourage children to gather and put away their own beanbag.	• Encourage children to return to floor marker after retrieving their beanbag. • Encourage children to listen for the next movement.

4. LESSON VARIATIONS

If the children you work with learn these activities quickly and need no further practice, or if you want to vary activities for review days, see Lesson Variations on Page 171.

■ CORE ACTIVITY 2: **Snowman Throw**

Structure: Independent practice

Focus on these objectives:
- Overhand throw
- Hand-eye coordination
- Cooperative play
- Force

Total time: 3-5 minutes

Key Vocabulary:
- **eyes, fingers, hands**
- **throw**
- **aim, hard, overhand, soft**
- **letters, numbers**

1. MOVE: Motor Movements

- Children form two small groups. Half the class goes to the snowman station, and half the class goes to the bowling station.
- At the snowman station, each child has one star and one bucket with three beanbags placed 3-4 feet away from one snowman poster.
- Children start off standing on the star. Tell children to pick up one beanbag with their throwing **hand** and look at the snowman poster at their station.
- Tell children to **throw** the beanbag **overhand, aiming** at each of the snowman circles. Children continue **throwing** until all three beanbags are thrown.
- Children retrieve their beanbags using their bucket and return to their star.
- Repeat, asking children to **aim** for the symbols or photo on the snowman (color, animal, **letter,** or **number**).

2. ADAPT: UDL Strategies

Adapt the activity to meet the needs of the children with whom you work. See the suggestions in the following table; for additional ways to adapt, use the UDL Suggestions for Unit 5.

Engagement	Representation	Action & Expression
Vary children's distance from the snowman target depending on the needs of each child.	• Use verbal prompts to describe **overhand throw** and model the throw for children. See the Glossary of Verbal Prompts. • Use visual supports. See Visual Support Cards for stand, retrieve ball, grasp, and throw.	Vary complexity of response by allowing child to walk, touch beanbag to target, and then drop beanbag to floor instead of **throwing** from a distance.

3. SUPPORT: School Readiness

Choose one to three school readiness skills to focus on. See the suggestions in the following table; for additional ways to support school readiness, turn to Page 165.

Mathematics	Science	Approaches to Learning
• Encourage shape recognition and letter recognition. • Ask: *What do you want to use on your snowman: animals, letters, colors, or numbers?*	• Discuss force (throw **hard** versus **soft**). • Ask: *What do you wear in winter? Do animals wear coats? Where do animals live in winter?* • Ask: *How do you make a snowman?*	• Encourage children to follow directions. • Encourage children to remain at their snowman station. • Praise children for picking up their beanbags and repeating the Snowman Throw activity.

4. LESSON VARIATIONS

If the children you work with learn these activities quickly and need no further practice, or if you want to vary activities for review days, see Lesson Variations on Page 171.

■ CORE ACTIVITY 3: **Bottle Bowling**

Structure: Independent practice

Total time: 3–5 minutes

Focus on these objectives:
- Underhand throw/roll
- Hand-eye coordination
- Cooperative play
- Force

Key Vocabulary:
- eyes, fingers, hands
- hold, throw
- aim, hard, soft, underhand
- bowling

1. MOVE: Motor Movements

- Children form two small groups. Half the class goes to the snowman station, and half the class goes to the bowling station. For bowling, each child has their own bowling station.
- Children start by standing on a star. Tell children to **hold** their ball in their throwing hand and look at the bottles at their station.
- Tell children to **roll** the ball using the steps for an **underhand throw, aiming** at the bottles. Children should try to knock down all three bottles at the same time.
- Demonstrate an underhand roll by rolling a ball toward the water bottles while standing on a floor marker. Then have children use an **underhand throw** to roll the ball into the water bottles. Say: *Now we're going to roll the ball using an underhand throw!*
  - *When I say **ready**, swing your arm back!*
  - *When I say **set**, step forward with one foot!*
  - *When I say **roll**, roll the ball into the bottles! **Ready, set, roll!***
- Children continue **rolling the ball** until all bottles are knocked down.
- Show children how to reset bottles, retrieve ball, and return to star.

2. ADAPT: UDL Strategies

Adapt the activity to meet the needs of the children with whom you work. See the suggestions in the following table; for additional ways to adapt, use the UDL Suggestions for Unit 5.

Engagement	Representation	Action & Expression
Increase or decrease water levels in each bottle to add challenge or simplify the activity for each child.	• Use verbal prompts to describe **underhand roll** and model the movement for children. See the Glossary of Verbal Prompts. • Use visual supports. See Visual Support Cards for stand, pick up ball, retrieve ball, and throw.	Vary complexity of response by allowing children to sit and roll ball instead of standing and **rolling** it to water bottles.

3. SUPPORT: School Readiness

Choose one to three school readiness skills to focus on. See the suggestions in the following table; for additional ways to support school readiness, turn to Page 165.

Mathematics	Science	Approaches to Learning
• Say: *Count the bottles remaining to be knocked over.* • Say: *Count the number of times it takes you to knock down three bottles.*	Ask: *Which is harder to knock over: a bottle full of water or a half-empty bottle?*	• Encourage children to remain at their bowling station. • Compliment children for remaining focused. • Compliment children for resetting their bottles independently.

4. LESSON VARIATIONS

If the children you work with learn these activities quickly and need no further practice, or if you want to vary activities for review days, see Lesson Variations on Page 171.

◼ PHYSICAL ACTIVITY: **Music Video**

Structure: Whole group   **Total time:** 2-4 minutes
Focus on this objective:
Sustained physical activity

1. MOVE: Motor Movements

Children stand on their floor marker. Spread out for enough space for floor movement. Say: ***Arms out.*** *Make wide,* ***airplane arms. Make sure you are not touching a friend.***

Children move to the music video you selected.

Lesson	Video	Total Time
3	Video 1: arm movements such as waving arms; swimming motions such as backstroke, dog paddle, and breaststroke	2 minutes
4	Video 2: same as above	3 minutes
5	Videos 1 and/or 2	4 minutes
6		

2. ADAPT: UDL Strategies

Adapt the activity to meet the needs of the children with whom you work. See the suggestions in the following table; for additional ways to adapt, use the UDL Suggestions for Unit 5.

Engagement	Representation	Action & Expression
Provide specific praise and encouragement (e.g., *I love your dance moves!* Or *Excellent job, keep moving!*)	• Use verbal prompts to describe movement. See the Glossary of Verbal Prompts. • Use visual supports. See Visual Support Cards for stand, stand in circle, sit, and airplane arms.	Stand in close proximity to children and model modified movements (e.g., bend knees instead of sitting).

3. SUPPORT: School Readiness

During the music video, the primary goal is to have all children maintain sustained/increased physical activity levels. To achieve this goal, teachers can provide models/prompts for motor imitation (imitate actions/songs from video, maintain personal space) and approaches to learning (active engagement, following instructions from video).

4. LESSON VARIATIONS

If the children you work with learn these activities quickly and need no further practice, or if you want to vary activities for review days, see Lesson Variations on Page 171.

■ COOL-DOWN

Structure: Whole group

Wrap up: Focus on
- Gathering
- Decreasing heart rate
- Cooling down muscles

Total time: 3-5 minutes

Key Vocabulary:
- arms, fingers, knees
- hold, roll arms
- between, together
- hard, soft
- drums, piano

1. MOVE: Motor Movements

Children sit on their floor marker and cool-down their bodies with the movements listed below. Once you have modeled each movement, sing the "CHAMPPS Cool-Down Song" while doing the movements (see "CHAMPPS Cool-Down Song," Page 159).

- Stretch **arms.** Say: *Hold ball with one hand.* **Make an X.** *Bend your arm. Touch ball to shoulder.*
- **Roll arms.** Say: *Sit with a straight back. Hold ball with two hands.* **Arms out straight. Roll your arms** *and* **make a circle.**
- Play **piano/drums.** Say: **Bend your knees. Squeeze ball** *between your knees.* **Let's play the piano** *[or drums].* (*Note:* This activity should be done seated on the floor.)
- Wave goodbye. Say: *Look at your friends. Hold out your hand and* **wave** *goodbye.*

Optional: End with yoga.

- Cow Pose. (See Figure U5.4.) Say: *Start in a kneeling position. Plant your hands on the floor. Pretend you are a table. Look toward the ceiling.*
- Cat Pose. (See Figure U5.5.) Say: *From Cow Pose, look down at your knees, rounding your back toward the ceiling. Pretend you are a cat stretching your back.*

Figure U5.4. Cow Pose.

Figure U5.5. Cat Pose.

2. ADAPT: UDL Strategies

Adapt the activity to meet the needs of the children with whom you work. See the suggestions in the following table; for additional ways to adapt, use the UDL Suggestions for Unit 5.

Engagement	Representation	Action & Expression
Vary volume of voice and pace of instructions to match the cool-down movement and pace of movement.	• Use verbal prompts to describe movement. See the Glossary of Verbal Prompts. • Use visual supports. See Visual Support Cards for sit, roll arms, stretch arms, bend and stretch, and wave hand.	Begin with simple movements and no singing.

3. SUPPORT: School Readiness

Choose one to three school readiness skills to focus on. See the suggestions in the following table; for additional ways to support school readiness, turn to Page 165.

Language	Mathematics	Approaches to Learning
• Encourage sing-along. • Ask: *How do you feel when CHAMPPS is over?* • Ask: *Which activity was your favorite today?*	• Ask: *What movement will we do first, second, and third?* • Say: *As we slowly curve our back into the Cat Pose, let's count.*	• Compliment children who transition smoothly to next movements. • Say: *Let's see who can put away the balls and line up to go back to class.*

4. LESSON VARIATIONS

If the children you work with learn these activities quickly and need no further practice, or if you want to vary activities for review days, see Lesson Variations on Page 171.

1	**Warm-Up**	
	Gathering, increase heart rate, warm-up muscles	
	MATERIALS	• Numbered floor markers (1 per person)
	ACTIVITIES	Sing "CHAMPPS Warm-Up Song." Children jog, swim, roll arms, and do jumping jacks.

2	**Core Activity 1: Snowballs in the Air**	
	Physical movement, hand–eye coordination, visual tracking	
	MATERIALS	• Numbered floor markers • 4–5 buckets containing at least 16–20 beanbags total
	ACTIVITIES	First: Sing "Snowballs in the Air." Children jog, jump, and/or gallop to bucket, pick up beanbag, and return to floor marker. Then: Children throw beanbag into bucket underhand. Next: Repeat with overhand throw.

3	**Core Activity 2: Snowman Throw**	
	Physical movement, hand–eye coordination, grasp and release, cooperative play, force	
	MATERIALS	• Numbered floor markers • 1 snowman target per child • 1 bucket of beanbags per child
	ACTIVITIES	First: Children throw beanbags overhand at snowman target. Then: Children retrieve beanbags and repeat.

4	**Core Activity 3: Bottle Bowling**	
	Physical movement, hand–eye coordination, grasp and release, cooperative play, force	
	MATERIALS	• 1 floor marker per child • Balls of various sizes (1 per child) • 3 water bottles per child
	ACTIVITIES	First: Children throw ball underhand at water bottles. Then: Children reset water bottles, retrieve ball, and repeat.

5	**Physical Activity: Music Video**		
	Sustained physical activity		
	MATERIALS	Video, video player, wall or screen for viewing	
	Lesson 3 Video 1 (2 minutes)	**Lesson 4** Video 2 (3 minutes)	**Lessons 5 and 6** Videos 1 and/or 2 (4 minutes)

6	**Cool-Down**	
	Gathering, lower heart rate, cool-down muscles	
	MATERIALS	Numbered floor markers
	ACTIVITIES	First: Sing "CHAMPPS Cool-Down Song." Stretch arms, roll arms, play piano/drums, and wave goodbye. Then: Do yoga poses: Cow Pose and Cat Pose.

Walk-Around Card

CHAMPPS Warm-Up Song

(Sung to the tune of "The Ants Go Marching")

The CHAMPPS go **jogging** one by one
Hurrah! Hurrah!
The CHAMPPS go **jogging** one by one
Hurrah! Hurrah!
The CHAMPPS go **jogging** one by one
This is the way we have some fun
And we all go **jogging** on, and on, and on, and on

(Repeat with **swimming** and **roll arms**)

Snowballs in the Air

(Sung to the tune of "The Farmer in the Dell")

Snowballs in the air
Snowballs in the air
Heigh-ho, the snowballs go
Snowballs in the air

CHAMPPS Cool-Down Song

(Sung to the tune of "Here We Go 'Round the Mulberry Bush")

This is the way we **roll our arms**
Roll our arms, **roll our arms**
This is the way we **roll our arms**
At the end of CHAMPPS

(Repeat with **stretch our arms, play piano/drums,** and **wave goodbye**)

GLOSSARY OF VERBAL PROMPTS

Do (Movement)	Say (Verbal Prompt)	Use
Bend and stretch	Reach, side, hold	Sit crisscross and **reach** above your head! Now lean to the **side** and **hold** it there! Feel the stretch!
Catch the ball	Hands ready	You need to catch the beanbag! Have your **hands ready** with palms up and fingers spread apart!
	Eyes ready	Have your **eyes ready** by watching the beanbag! Don't look away!
Gallop	Lean back, hop forward	Now let's gallop like horses! **Lean back** and **hop forward!** Keep one foot in front! Neigh!
Jog	Slow run	We are going to jog. A jog is a **slow run.**
	Swing arms	*Swing your arms* and *run slowly.*
Jump	Bend knees, push up	Let's jump! **Bend your knees** down low, and then **push up!** Great jumping!
Jumping jacks	Star jump	Time for jumping jacks! Let's **star jump!** Arms up. Feet wide. We look like a star!
	Apart, together	Now feet together. Hands together. We look like a tree! **Apart!** We're a star! **Together!** We're a tree! Again! **Apart!** Star! **Together!** Tree! Let's keep going faster. **Apart! Together!** Star! Tree!
Overhand throw	Touch your ear	Put the bean bag in your hand and **touch it to your ear** for an overhand **throw**! Move your hand in a forward motion and release.
	Swing forward, throw	
Roll arms	Airplane arms	Now let's roll those arms! First, **make airplane arms**, stretched out wide!
	Circles	Make little **circles** with your arms. Feel the stretch!
Stretch arms	Make an X	Arms out straight. **Make an X.**
	Kiss your shoulder	Take your ball and touch your opposite shoulder (**kiss your shoulder**). *kiss sound* Repeat with the other arm!
Swim	Reach, pull	Let's go swimming! **Reach** out with one hand, then **pull** it back to you! Now other hand! **Reach, pull!**
Touch toes	Reach forward, hold	Sit with your legs straight! Now **reach forward** to touch your toes! **Hold** that pose!
Underhand roll	Ready, set, roll	Now we're going to underhand roll! When I say **ready**, swing your arm back! When I **say** set, step forward! And then **roll! Ready, set, roll!**
Underhand throw	Ready, set, throw	Now we're going to underhand throw! When I say **ready**, swing your arm back! When I say set, step forward! And then **throw! Ready, set, throw!**

UDL SUGGESTIONS

Engagement							
Means of Engagement	**Warm-Up**	**Core Activity 1: Snowballs in the Air**	**Core Activity 2: Snowman Throw**	**Core Activity 3: Bottle Bowling**	**Video 1**	**Video 2**	**Cool-Down**
Recruit Interest							
Child choice	Warm-up moves	Motor movement	Target	Distance from the bottles	Which video to play	Which video to play	Cool-down movements
Novel/familiar	Familiar moves (jog, roll arms) Consistent structure (whole group)	Familiar moves (throw, catch) New tune ("Farmer in the Dell")	Familiar materials (beanbags) New structure (independent)	Familiar materials (beanbags) New structure (independent)	New video Optional: Repeat video	New video Optional: Repeat video	Familiar moves (roll arms, touch toes, bend and stretch, wave goodbye)
Sustain Effort and Persistence							
Praise/ encourage	Say: *Great! Keep moving to warm-up our bodies and get ready for CHAMPPS!*	Say: *I like how you stayed on your own spot and caught your snowballs!* Say: *I love hearing you sing!*	Say: *Super throw! Wow! You hit the target!*	Say: *You got a strike!* Say: *Wow— strong throw! You knocked over all the bottles!*	Say: *Beautiful dancing! I can tell you're happy!* Say: *Nice job going "up" and "down"!*	Say: *Excellent swimming; it's like we're in a pool!* Say: *I love how you're looking and copying the video!*	Say: *I love seeing your faces when you look at all your friends to say goodbye.*
Vary complexity	Increase/ decrease number of moves.	Increase/ decrease number of beanbags.	Vary distance from target (close/far).	Vary distance from target (close/far). Vary ball size/weight.	Increase/ decrease length of video.	Increase/ decrease length of video.	Increase/ decrease number of moves.
Vary setup, directions	Sing softly/ loudly. Move slowly/ fast.	Sing softly/ loudly. Move slowly/ fast.	Have partners do activity. Change targets (animal stickers, numbers).	Have partners do activity. Change targets (cones).	Vary materials (give instruments, scarves).	Vary materials (give instruments, scarves).	Vary materials (balls, beanbags, scarves).

UDL SUGGESTIONS *(continued)*

Representation

Means of Representation	Warm-Up	Core Activity 1: Snowballs in the Air	Core Activity 2: Snowman Throw	Core Activity 3: Bottle Bowling	Video 1	Video 2	Cool-Down
Forms of Communication							
Auditory	Glossary of Verbal Prompts						→
Visual	Visual Support Cards						→
Tactile	Give hand-over-hand instruction (hold child's hands and roll arms).	(hold child's hands and throw) Present materials when explaining activity (beanbags).	(hold child's hands and throw) (beanbags)	(hold child's hands and roll) (water bottles, balls)	(as needed)	(as needed)	(hold child's hands and stretch arms)
Multiple Levels of Complexity							
Key vocabulary: define/model	jog jumping jacks roll arms swim	catch gallop jog jump throw (underhand)	retrieve beanbags throw (overhand)	retrieve ball roll underhand	Instruct as needed.	Instruct as needed.	bend and stretch roll arms stretch arms touch toes wave goodbye

Action & Expression

Means of Representation	Warm-Up	Core Activity 1: Snowballs in the Air	Core Activity 2: Snowman Throw	Core Activity 3: Bottle Bowling	Video 1	Video 2	Cool-Down
Variety of responses	Sing, clap, or hum song. Move in place.	Sing, clap, or hum song. Throw and watch beanbag fall (no catch), and/or use scarf instead of beanbag.	Children throw underhand or overhand. Children touch beanbag to target.	Children sit and roll ball to bottles.	Vary as needed	Vary as needed	Sing, clap, or hum song.
Complexity of responses	Accept partial movement (airplane arms instead of rolling arms).	Accept partial movement (children lift and lower beanbags instead of throwing).	Accept partial movement (children throw beanbag; a partner or leader retrieves it).	Accept partial movement (initially, children roll ball; when they gain more control of ball, have them try a soft underhand throw).	Accept partial movement as needed.	Accept partial movement as needed.	Accept partial movement (touch knees rather than toes).

SUPPORT SCHOOL READINESS SKILLS

LANGUAGE AND LITERACY	Warm-Up	Core Activity 1: Snowballs in the Air	Core Activity 2: Snowman Throw	Core Activity 3: Bottle Bowling	Cool-Down
Expresses feelings and preferences (hot, thirsty, tired, hungry, sleepy, sweaty)	Ask: *How do you feel now?* (hot, thirsty, tired, hungry, sweaty)	Ask: *Is snow cold or hot? Is it cold or hot in the winter?*	Ask: *Who likes snow? What do you like about snow?*	Ask: *How do you feel when you knock the bottles over?* (happy, proud, excited)	Ask: *How do you feel when CHAMPPS is over? Tired? Hot? Sweaty?*
Engages in active discussion (shares ideas, asks and answers questions)	Ask: *Do you have any new ideas for warm-up movements?*	Ask: *What else could we do in the snow?*	Ask: *What are things you can do in winter?* (ski, skate, play in snow)	Ask: *Who has been bowling? What do you do when you go bowling?* (get shoes, select ball, keep score)	Ask: *How do you cool off when you get hot or sweaty?*
Communicates personal experiences and interests	Ask: *What's your favorite warm-up move?*	Ask: *Who has thrown a snowball before?*	Ask: *Have you ever made a snowman? What do you like to do in the snow?*	Ask: *What do you like about bowling?*	Ask: *Which activity was your favorite today? Which was your least favorite?*
Listens to/uses formal and informal language (listens to/sings songs, uses different voices)	Children listen and sing along.	Children listen and sing along.	Ask: *How do you make a snowman?*	Ask: *What is a strike in bowling?* Say: *Yippee! Strike!*	Ask: *Let's make cow and cat sounds as we do our Cat and Cow yoga poses.*
Recognizes shapes (circle, square, triangle, rectangle)	Children stand in circle.	Children stand in circle. Ask: *What shape is your beanbag?* (Square!) Say: *Let's trace the shape with your pointer finger!*	Use circle targets. Ask: *What shapes do you see on the snowman target?*	Ask: *What shape is your floor marker?* (Star!)	Children sit in circle, square, triangle, or rectangle. Ask: *How many sides does a square, triangle, or circle have?*
Recognizes letters	Pass out letter cards for children to hold during warm-up. Ask: *What letter are you holding? What letter is _____ (a peer) holding?*	Children sing their ABCs while throwing.	Use letter targets (A, B, C, etc.). Ask: *What letters are on the snowman? On your beanbags?*	Use letter targets (A, B, C, etc.). Ask: *What letters are on the bottles?*	Pass out letter cards for children to hold during stretches. Ask: *What letter are you holding? What letter is _____ (a peer) holding?*

MATHEMATICS	Warm-Up	Core Activity 1: Snowballs in the Air	Core Activity 2: Snowman Throw	Core Activity 3: Bottle Bowling	Cool-Down
Number recognition (count, one–one correspondence)	Children count moves.	Children count throws.	Children count targets hit.	Children count bottles knocked down.	Say: *Let's count how many times we touch our toes!*
Positional words (*above, side to side*)	Forward/backward Up/down	High/low Up/down	Forward/backward Up/down	Forward/backward Up/down	Left/right Side to side

SUPPORT SCHOOL READINESS SKILLS (continued)

MATHEMATICS	Warm-Up	Core Activity 1: Snowballs in the Air	Core Activity 2: Snowman Throw	Core Activity 3: Bottle Bowling	Cool-Down
Ordinal language (*first, second,* etc.)	Use ordinal words for order of moves (first, jog; second, swim, etc.).	Use ordinal words for movements (first, get the beanbag; second, toss the ball in air; third, throw ball into bucket).	Use ordinal words for movements (first, get the beanbag; second, throw a beanbag with an overhand throw aiming for the snowman; third, pick up beanbags and place in bucket).	Use ordinal words for movements (first, get ball; second, throw ball with underhand throw aiming for bottles until all bottles are down; third, retrieve ball and reset bottles).	Use ordinal words to discuss order of moves. Ask: *What will we do first? Second? Third?*
Categorizing and sorting objects	Say: *Show me fast moves!* (jog, swim quickly) *Slow moves!* (jog, swim slowly)	Ask: *What else can we make out of snow? Snowmen? Igloos?*	Say: *Let's throw the blue beanbags first; then we'll throw the red ones!*	Color the water in the bottles. Say: Let's knock over the red/blue bottle first!	Children sit with other children who are wearing the same color.
Patterns (recognize, describe, reproduce)	Create a movement pattern (e.g., do two jumping jacks, then roll arms once; repeat).		Say: *Let's make a pattern. Throw three times close to snowman, three times farther away from snowman, and three times close to snowman.*	Color the water in the bottles. Say: *Let's make a pattern while bowling! Knock over the red bottle first, then the blue one, then the red bottle.*	Create a movement pattern, alternating stretches.

SCIENCE	Warm-Up	Core Activity 1: Snowballs in the Air	Core Activity 2: Snowman Throw	Core Activity 3: Bottle Bowling	Cool-Down
Ask/answer questions together (*Who? What? Where? How?*).	Ask: *Why do we warm-up? What are other activities you should warm-up before?*	Ask: *What happens when snow gets warm? When water gets cold?*	Ask: *How do you make a snowman? What makes a snowman melt?*	Ask: *If the bottles were heavier, would they be easier or harder to knock down?*	Ask: *Why do we cool-down?*
Make predictions together (*What if?*).	Ask: *What if we move faster? Slower?*	Ask: *What if you got hit with a snowball? Would it hurt?*	Ask: *What happens if we throw the beanbag harder? Gentler?*	Ask: *What happens if we throw the ball harder? Gentler?*	Ask: *What happens to our heart rate if we do not cool-down? What happens to our heart rate when we cool-down?*
Understand weather/seasons, calendar/days of the week.	Ask: *Do we jog in the summer? Fall? Winter?*	Ask: *During which months do we get snow?*	Ask: *What months are winter months? What holidays do you celebrate during winter?*	Ask: *What happens to the water in the bottles if we keep the bottles of water in the sun? In the snow?*	Say: *Let's do a slow swim to stretch out arms.* Ask: *In which season do we swim outdoors?*

SCIENCE	Warm-Up	Core Activity 1: Snowballs in the Air	Core Activity 2: Snowman Throw	Core Activity 3: Bottle Bowling	Cool-Down
Discuss characteristics of living things (*humans, animals, plants*).	Ask: *What animals like to run? Walk? Jump?*	Ask: *What happens to plants in the winter? Trees?*	Ask: *What animals do you see in the wintertime?*	Ask: *Do any animals knock stuff down? How? (My cat knocks things over with her paws.)*	Discuss how all living things need air. Ask: *What do we (humans) do to get air?* Practice taking slow deep breaths.
Use sensory vocabulary.	Ask: *How does it feel to jog on sand—soft? On the floor—hard?*	Ask: *How does snow feel? Cold? Wet?*	Ask: *How does snow feel? Cold? Wet?*	Ask: *What does it sound like when the bowling pins are knocked over?*	Say: *Close your eyes.* Ask: *What do you hear? Smell? Feel?*

MOTOR	Warm-Up	Core Activity 1: Snowballs in the Air	Core Activity 2: Snowman Throw	Core Activity 3: Bottle Bowling	Cool-Down
Balance	Children do jumping jacks and roll their arms.	Children take a stance while throwing.	Children do overhand throw standing on two feet, standing on one foot.	Children do underhand throw standing on two feet, standing on one foot.	Encourage children to do long, slow bend and stretch to left and right, without losing their balance.
Visual tracking	Children hold scarves or balls and roll their arms.	Children watch the beanbag as they throw/catch it and as they throw it into bucket.	Children watch the beanbag as they throw it at the snowman target.	Children watch the ball as they throw it at bottles.	Children hold ball or visual support cards (animals, numbers, letters, colors). Encourage them to stretch while holding the card and follow the card with their eyes.
Motor imitation	Children imitate leader/peers.	⟶			⟶
Body awareness	Children identify which body parts are needed for each movement.	⟶			⟶
Body movement (stationary)	Children roll their arms and do jumping jacks.	Children throw underhand and catch their own beanbag.	Children throw overhand.	Children throw underhand.	Children roll and stretch arms, bend and stretch, touch toes, wave goodbye.
Strength/speed/duration	Children sustain movement through the song.	Children sustain movement through the song.	Children throw the beanbag hard or softly.	Children throw the ball hard or softly.	Children slow down movement to cool-down.

SUPPORT SCHOOL READINESS SKILLS *(continued)*

MOTOR	Warm-Up	Core Activity 1: Snowballs in the Air	Core Activity 2: Snowman Throw	Core Activity 3: Bottle Bowling	Cool-Down
Coordination (eye/hand; eye/foot)	Children roll their arms while walking and do jumping jacks.	Children coordinate throwing and catching beanbag.	Children throw at a target.	Children throw at a target.	Children hold ball while moving.
Locomotion	Children jog, walk, or use swimming arms.	Children jog, jump, or gallop.	Children retrieve overthrown beanbags/balls.	Children retrieve overthrown balls.	
Directionality (forward, backward, sidesteps)	Children switch direction (forward, backward) for motor movements.	Ask: *In what direction did you step to catch your beanbag (forward, backward, sideways)?*	Say: *Take one giant step forward (toward snowman) before throwing. Take one giant step backward (away from snowman) before throwing.*	Say: *Take one giant step forward (toward bottles) before throwing. Take one giant step backward (away from bottles) before throwing.*	Once seated, ask children to move their body leaning to the right side and then to the left side. When stretching, say: *Bend forward to touch your toes. Bend backward to sit back up.*
Personal space	Children use own floor marker.	Children use own floor marker.	Children stay in their own station.	Children stay in their own station.	Children use own floor marker.
Cross midline reach	Children hug body before and after warm-up.	Children toss beanbag with one hand and catch beanbag with opposite hand.	Children hold beanbag and touch it to opposite shoulders before going to snowman station.	Children hold ball and touch it to opposite shoulders before going to bowling station.	Children pat own shoulders to congratulate themselves, using each hand to pat opposite shoulder.
Grasp and release		Children throw and catch beanbag.	Children throw beanbag.	Children throw ball.	Children hold ball during stretch.
Motor regulation (go slow, go fast, stop)	Children sing and move slowly or quickly.	Children sing and move slowly or quickly.	Children stay at station. Children respond to group directions to throw slowly, throw quickly, and freeze (stop).	Children stay at station. Children respond to group directions to throw slowly, throw quickly, and freeze (stop).	Children slow down movement to cool-down.

SOCIAL-EMOTIONAL	Warm-Up	Core Activity 1: Snowballs in the Air	Core Activity 2: Snowman Throw	Core Activity 3: Bottle Bowling	Cool-Down
Recognizes, describes, and regulates emotions	Ask: *How's everyone feeling? Who is having a good day? Why?*	Ask: *Who likes to throw snowballs in the air?*	Ask: *How do you feel when you hit/miss the target?*	Ask: *How do you feel when you knock all the pins down?*	Ask: *How do you feel now that CHAMPPS is over?*

SOCIAL-EMOTIONAL	Warm-Up	Core Activity 1: Snowballs in the Air	Core Activity 2: Snowman Throw	Core Activity 3: Bottle Bowling	Cool-Down
Solves/prevents problems	Children move in line around circle.	Children each stay on own floor marker.	Say: *Let's throw the beanbag safely! Stay in your personal space!*	Say: *Let's roll the ball safely! Stay in your personal space!*	Say: *Let's move safely! Stay in your personal space!*
Learns independence/self-help	Each child independently finds own floor marker.	Children gather and put away own beanbags.	Children retrieve overthrown beanbags. Children gather their own beanbags.	Children retrieve overthrown balls. Children gather their own balls.	Children gather and put away their own balls.
Takes turns/waits turn	Children move with classmates and do not speed ahead.	Children wait until everyone has a beanbag before they begin throwing.	Children share a station and wait their turn.	Children share a station and wait their turn.	Ask: *Who wants to pick the first movement? Who is next?*
Helps/supports peers	Partners help one another through transitions (holding hands).	Ask: *Who can help pass out beanbags?*	Ask: *What can you say/do when your friend hits/misses the snowman target?*	Ask: *What can you say/do when your friend hits/misses the bottles?*	Ask: *Who can help pass out balls?*
Plays cooperatively	Say: *Let's hold hands and make a big circle!*	Establish a rule that children only throw beanbags at target, not at peers.	Ask: *How should you leave your snowman station for the next person?*	Ask: *How should you leave your bowling station for the next person?* Encourage children to help a friend. Say: *Help your friend retrieve the ball and set up the pins!*	Ask: *What can you say to encourage a friend?*
Shares materials	Ask: *We are using beanbags and balls today. What can you do if someone wants the same ball/beanbag that you want?*	Children share beanbags with peers.	Children take turns using the same snowman station.	Children take turns using the same bowling station.	Children share/trade balls (or visual support cards) with a friend.
Socializes with peers	Ask: *What can we say to our CHAMPPS helpers? Good morning! Good afternoon!*	Say: *Shake hands with a friend near you and wish him/her good luck in throwing and catching.*	Children share a station and cheer on their partner.	Tell children: *Let's say our friends' names!* Children work together with peers.	Say: *We all like to get compliments. Share a compliment that you want to give for a friend.* (Example: Mindy was great at bowling today!) Children wave at peers and say goodbye.

SUPPORT SCHOOL READINESS SKILLS *(continued)*

APPROACHES TO LEARNING	Warm-Up	Core Activity 1: Snowballs in the Air	Core Activity 2: Snowman Throw	Core Activity 3: Bottle Bowling	Cool-Down
Transitions into/out of activities	Children return to floor markers in between movements.	Children get beanbag and return to floor marker.	Children change stations between independent activities.	Children change stations between independent activities.	Children return to floor marker.
Listens to/follows directions	Children complete instructed movement.				→
Demonstrates focused attention	Children listen for next movement.	Children maintain attention and focus on throwing and retrieving beanbag with partner.	Children maintain attention and focus on throwing/retrieving their own beanbag.	Children maintain attention and focus on rolling/retrieving ball and setting up their bowling pins.	Children listen for next movement.
Demonstrates sustained attention	Children sustain movement until end of song.	Children sustain movement until end of song.	Children stay at own station.	Children stay at own station.	Children stay at own floor marker.
Demonstrates active engagement in small/large group	Children stay engaged in whole group.	Children stay engaged in whole group.	Children stay engaged in small-group/independent activity.	Children stay engaged in small-group/independent activity.	Children stay engaged in whole-group activity.
Demonstrates active engagement in independent task	Children imitate movements.	Children throw and retrieve beanbags from bucket independently.	Children engage in independent throwing.	Children engage in independent rolling and ball retrieval.	Children retrieve own balls.

Lesson Variations

■ CORE ACTIVITY 1: **Snowballs in the Air** VARIATIONS

Music/Rhythm/Dance

Variation 1: Rhythm Throw

Structure	Materials	Instructions
Whole group	• Balls of various sizes • Projector with Internet access	1. Before warm-up, select children's song(s) with a strong rhythm from YouTube or another online source. (See the video selection criteria on Page 268.) 2. Children throw balls in the air and catch them to the rhythm of the song (e.g., *1-2-3-throw, 1-2-3-throw*).

Variation 2: Throw and Dance

Structure	Materials	Instructions
Whole group	Balls of various sizes	1. Children throw ball up in the air and then do a dance movement. 2. Children skip or dance around space while throwing the ball in the air.

Sports/Games

Variation 3: Toss and Hit

Structure	Materials	Instructions
Whole group	Balls of various sizes	1. Children toss their ball up in the air and then try to hit it with their hand. Guide them to use an overhand motion similar to a tennis or volleyball serve. 2. Children toss their ball up in the air and then try to catch it, similar to catching a pop fly in baseball.

Variation 4: Partner Toss

Structure	Materials	Instructions
Partners	Balls of various sizes	Children toss their ball up in the air and then have a peer try to catch it.

Arts and Crafts

Variation 5: Rainbow Snowballs

Structure	Materials	Instructions
Whole group	• Recycled paper • Paint or colored duct tape	1. Children make their own snowballs by wadding up recycled paper. 2. Children decorate their snowballs by painting them different colors or covering them with different-colored duct tape. 3. Children use the rainbow snowballs to play snowball games. 4. Send rainbow snowballs home with children to encourage use at home.

Other

Variation 6: Toss and Freeze

Structure	Materials	Instructions
Whole group	Balls of various sizes	Children toss their ball up in the air and then freeze, posing in a position like a statue.

■ CORE ACTIVITY 2: **Snowman Throw** VARIATIONS

Sports/Games

Variation 1: Overhand Statue Throw

Structure	Materials	Instructions
Whole Group	Balls of various sizes	1. Children start standing still in a pose, like a statue. 2. Say "Ready, set, throw!" and children perform the overhand throw.

Arts and Crafts

Variation 2: Snowman Art

Structure	Materials	Instructions
Whole group	• Paper • Crayons, markers, or colored pencils • Laminator • Beanbags	1. Have each child draw a snowman with three circles on poster paper and instruct them to include the following in their snowman drawing: hat, scarf, eyes, nose, mouth, arms, mittens, etc. 2. Laminate the snowman drawings. 3. Place the laminated drawings on the floor. 4. Call out the body parts or items of clothing that children included. 5. Children use an underhand throw to throw a beanbag at each body part or clothing item named.

■ CORE ACTIVITY 3: **Bottle Bowling** VARIATIONS

Music/Rhythm/Dance

Variation 1: Dance and Roll

Structure	Materials	Instructions
Whole group	Balls of various sizes	1. Designate an area for rolling the ball. 2. Children start from across the room. 3. Children dance to the designated area and then stop and roll the ball.

Sports/Games

Variation 2: Leg Roll

Structure	Materials	Instructions
Partners	Balls of various sizes	Children roll the ball between a peer's legs toward the bowling pins.

Variation 3: Host a Bowling League/Club

Structure	Materials	Instructions
Whole group, field trip	Bowling alley	1. Go bowling with children. Invite families. 2. Link to math by learning to keep score.

Art or Science Lesson

Variation 4: Make Your Own Bowling Pins

Structure	Materials	Instructions
Whole group	• Recycled water bottles • Food coloring and water, sand, pebbles, gemstones, or glitter • Velcro • Index cards with symbols (animals, colors, letters, numbers) • Balls of various sizes	1. Have families collect recycled water bottles, enough so children have 6-12 bottles each. 2. Invite parents in to help make pins. 3. Fill bottles with different amounts of colored water or sand, gemstones, glitter, or pebbles. 4. Use Velcro to attach symbols on bottles. 5. Children use underhand roll to bowl with their own set. 6. Send bowling pins home to play at home.

Other

Variation 5: Underhand Roll

Structure	Materials	Instructions
Whole group	Balls of various sizes	1. Children start standing on a floor marker 3-5 feet away from a laundry basket (placed on its side). 2. Say "Ready, set, roll!" and children use the underhand roll to roll balls into the laundry basket.

Home Activities Record

CHAMPPS

Child: _____   Teacher: _____
Unit: _____   Week: _____
Please return by: _____

Thank you for playing with me! Please tell my teachers if we did CHAMPPS activities this week at home. Write a check (✓) if we practiced CHAMPPS at home this week. You can also write comments to tell my teachers how I did when we practiced CHAMPPS at home! Please give this form to my teacher each week.

Check (✓) if you did CHAMPPS practice.	Parent/Child Comments

CHAMPPS: CHildren in Action Motor Program for PreschoolerS by Paddy C. Favazza and Michaelene M. Ostrosky with Melissa Stalega, Hsiu-Wen Yang, Katherine Aronson-Ensign, Martin Block, W. Catherine Cheung, and Yusuf Akemoglu. Copyright © 2023 by Paul H. Brookes Publishing Co., Inc. All rights reserved.

Home Activities Record

CHAMPPS

Child: _____   Teacher: _____
Unit: _____   Week: _____
Please return by: _____

Thank you for playing with me! Please tell my teachers if we did CHAMPPS activities this week at home. Write a check (✓) if we practiced CHAMPPS at home this week. You can also write comments to tell my teachers how I did when we practiced CHAMPPS at home! Please give this form to my teacher each week.

Check (✓) if you did CHAMPPS practice.	Parent/Child Comments

CHAMPPS: CHildren in Action Motor Program for PreschoolerS by Paddy C. Favazza and Michaelene M. Ostrosky with Melissa Stalega, Hsiu-Wen Yang, Katherine Aronson-Ensign, Martin Block, W. Catherine Cheung, and Yusuf Akemoglu. Copyright © 2023 by Paul H. Brookes Publishing Co., Inc. All rights reserved.

CHAMPPS Home Activities

Hi, Family and Friends!
We are beginning Unit 5 of CHAMPPS at school! I am learning how to throw and catch. Now I want to play CHAMPPS with you! It only takes 10–20 minutes. Thank you for playing with me!
Love, Your Little CHAMP

◼ ACTIVITY 1: **Warm-Up**

Materials None
Directions Move and sing with me.
CHAMPPS Warm-Up Song
(Tune: "The Ants Go Marching")

The CHAMPPS go jogging one by one
Hurrah, hurrah!
The CHAMPPS go jogging one by one
Hurrah, hurrah!
The CHAMPPS go jogging one by one
This is the way we have some fun
And we all go jogging on, and on, and on!

Repeat with: swimming and roll arms.

◼ ACTIVITY 2: **Snowballs in the Air**

Materials
- Floor marker (placemat, small towel, sheet of paper)
- Ball (can be ball of yarn, rolled-up sock or newspaper, or beanbag)
- Bucket (laundry basket, cooking pot, empty trash bin)

Directions
1. I stand on my floor marker. Watch as I throw the ball in the air and catch it.
2. Sing "Snowballs in the Air."
3. At the end of the song, I will throw the ball into the bucket.
4. Now you take a turn!

Snowballs in the Air
(Tune: "The Farmer in the Dell")

Snowballs in the air
Snowballs in the air
Heigh-ho, the snowballs go
Snowballs in the air

◼ ACTIVITY 3: **Cool-Down**

Materials None
Directions Stretch and sing with me.
CHAMPPS Cool-Down Song
(Tune: "Here We Go 'Round the Mulberry Bush")

This is the way we roll our arms
Roll our arms, roll our arms
This is the way we roll our arms
At the end of CHAMPPS

Repeat with: stretch our arms, play piano/drums, and wave goodbye.

stretch arms

roll arms

bend and stretch

wave goodbye

Read and move together!
Look for this book at your local library: *Clap Hands* by Helen Oxenbury.
Dance to this YouTube video: _____

Thank you for playing with me!

CHAMPPS Home Activities

Hi, Family and Friends!

I am still doing CHAMPPS Unit 5 at school! I am learning to throw a ball at a target. Now I want to play CHAMPPS with you! It only takes 10–20 minutes. Thank you for playing with me!

Love, Your Little CHAMP

■ ACTIVITY 1: **Warm-Up**

Materials None

Directions Move and sing with me.

CHAMPPS Warm-Up Song

(Tune: "The Ants Go Marching")

The CHAMPPS go jogging one by one
Hurrah, hurrah!
The CHAMPPS go jogging one by one
Hurrah, hurrah!
The CHAMPPS go jogging one by one
This is the way we have some fun
And we all go jogging on, and on, and on!

Repeat with: swimming and roll arms.

■ ACTIVITY 2: **Snowman Throw**

Materials
- Floor marker (placemat, small towel, sheet of paper)
- Ball (can be ball of yarn, rolled-up sock or newspaper, or beanbag)
- Three buckets (laundry basket, cooking pot, empty trash bin)

Directions
1. I stand on my floor marker. Place three buckets at different distances from me, close and far.
2. I throw a ball into the different buckets, close and far.
3. Now you take a turn!

■ ACTIVITY 3: **Cool-Down**

Materials None

Directions Stretch and sing with me.

CHAMPPS Cool-Down Song

(Tune: "Here We Go 'Round the Mulberry Bush")

This is the way we roll our arms
Roll our arms, roll our arms
This is the way we roll our arms
At the end of CHAMPPS

Repeat with: stretch our arms, play piano/drums, and wave goodbye.

stretch arms

roll arms

bend and stretch

wave goodbye

Read and move together!
Look for this book at your local library: *Pete the Cat: The Wheels on the Bus* by James Dean.
Dance to this YouTube video: _____

Thank you for playing with me!

CHAMPPS Home Activities

Hi, Family and Friends!

I am finishing up Unit 5 of CHAMPPS at school! We are learning how to bowl with a ball! Now I want to play CHAMPPS with you! It only takes 10–20 minutes. Thank you for playing with me!

Love, Your Little CHAMP

■ ACTIVITY 1: **Warm-Up**

Materials None
Directions Move and sing with me.

CHAMPPS Warm-Up Song

(Tune: "The Ants Go Marching")

The CHAMPPS go jogging one by one
Hurrah, hurrah!
The CHAMPPS go jogging one by one
Hurrah, hurrah!
The CHAMPPS go jogging one by one
This is the way we have some fun
And we all go jogging on, and on, and on!

Repeat with: swimming and roll arms.

■ ACTIVITY 2: **Bottle Bowling**

Materials
• Floor marker (placemat, small towel, sheet of paper)
• Ball (can be ball of yarn or rolled-up sock or newspaper)
• Three plastic bottles (or use tall blocks or plastic cups)

Directions
1. I stand on my floor marker. Place the three bottles in front of me.
2. I roll the ball to knock down the bottles.
3. Then I run to reset the bottles, get the ball, and go again!
4. You can take a turn too.

■ ACTIVITY 3: **Cool-Down**

Materials None
Directions Stretch and sing with me.

CHAMPPS Cool-Down Song

(Tune: "Here We Go 'Round the Mulberry Bush")

This is the way we roll our arms
Roll our arms, roll our arms
This is the way we roll our arms
At the end of CHAMPPS

Repeat with: stretch our arms, play piano/drums, and wave goodbye.

stretch arms

roll arms

bend and stretch

wave goodbye

Read and move together!
Look for this book at your local library: *Hand, Hand, Fingers, Thumb* by Al Perkins.
Dance to this YouTube video: _____

Thank you for playing with me!

Get Moving: CHAMPPS Motor Skills Units

UNIT 6

Striking

Unit Objectives

1. **Motor Movement.** Focus on striking with two hands. Reinforce previously learned skills such as jogging, lunging, and rolling arms. Introduce twisting and swinging.

2. **Hand-Eye Coordination.** Watch balloon/ball. Eyes guide hands to strike (with hands, bat, or hockey stick).

3. **Visual Tracking.** Watch and strike balloon/ball.

4. **Cooperative Play.** Focus on sharing and taking turns with friends, complimenting friends (e.g., good swing, good hit)

5. **Force.** Strike hard versus soft.

6. **Sustained Physical Activity.** Engage in continuous movement during music video.

Key Vocabulary

Body Parts	arms, eyes, hands, knees, legs, stomach, waist
Motor Movement	lunge, strike, swing, tap, twist
Concepts	aim, around, backward, bat, forward, goal, hard, hockey stick, puck (ball), racquet, side to side, soft
Pre-academic	circle

179

UNIT LESSON

Time	Activity	Focus			
3–5 min	WARM-UP	Gathering	Increase Heart Rate		Warm-Up Muscles
5 min	CORE 1: **Balloons in the Sky**	Motor Movement	Hand-Eye Coordination	Visual Tracking	Force
5 min	CORE 2*: **Tee-Ball**				
5 min	CORE 3*: **Hockey**				
2–4 min	PHYSICAL ACTIVITY: Music Video (Lessons 3-6 only)	Motor Imitation & Sustained Physical Activity			
3 min	COOL-DOWN	Gathering	Decrease Heart Rate		Cool-Down Muscles

*Core 2 and Core 3 occur simultaneously with the class divided into two small groups. After both small groups complete one activity, children remain with their group and the small groups switch locations/activities.

PREPARATION AND MATERIALS

Activity	Materials (class of 15 children with 2 adults)
WARM-UP **COOL-DOWN** Whole group	Numbered floor markers (1 per person)
CORE 1 **Balloons in the Sky** Whole group	Numbered floor markers (1 per person) Baskets/buckets (at least 4) Balloons of assorted colors (1 per person) Bell (1)
CORE 2* **Tee-Ball** Small group/ Independent	Floor markers (1 per person) Cones (enough for half the children in your class) Foam baseballs (enough for half the children in your class) Foam baseball bats** (enough for half the children in your class) Blocks (7–10) Bell (1)
CORE 3* **Hockey** Small group/ Independent	Stars (enough for half the children in your class) Balls (enough for half the children in your class) Laundry baskets (enough for half the children in your class) Striking tools (child-size racquets, hockey sticks, brooms, or foam baseball bats)** (enough for half the children in your class) Assorted balls (7–10) Bell (1) Wrist bells (1 attached to each basket)
Visual Support Cards Used for these movements: stand, stand in circle, sit, roll arms, tap balloon, catch, strike with bat, strike with hockey stick, pick up ball, retrieve ball, grasp, put in/take out, stretch arms, twist, airplane arms, bend and stretch, touch toes, wave hand, play drums. Visit the Brookes Download Hub to download and print the Visual Support Cards for Unit 6.	

*Because Core 2 and Core 3 activities occur simultaneously, use the Planning Notes form to preassign children to Small Group 1 or Small Group 2. Once all children complete one of the two core activities, they switch to the other activity. For smooth transitions to the next activity, teachers might keep small groups relatively stable once they are set, unless a teacher determines that a child needs to be placed in a different group due to specific support or behavioral needs. During Tee-Ball and Hockey, teachers circulate around the room to model, support, and encourage children.

**A variety of striking tools can be used for Tee-Ball or Hockey to match the children's height and ability, including child-size racquets, child-size hockey sticks, or child-size foam bats.

SETUP

Warm-Up, Balloons in the Sky, and Cool-Down

1. Place floor markers in a circle in the middle of the room.

2. Place balloons of assorted colors in a basket (or in baskets) in the middle. See Figure U6.1.

Tee-Ball

1. Set up tee-ball stations at least 5 feet apart. The number of stations should be half the number of children in your classroom (e.g., seven stations for a class size of 14).

2. Each station should have one cone with a foam baseball on top, two floor markers on the floor next to the cone, and one foam baseball bat.

3. Set blocks aside so they are ready for use. Blocks can be placed underneath cones in order to raise the height of the tee-ball as needed, depending on the height of

each child. For ease of ball retrieval, position the child and tee-ball facing a wall for each station. See Figure U6.2.

Hockey

1. Set up hockey stations at least 5 feet apart. The number of stations should be half the number of children in your classroom (e.g., seven stations for a class size of 14).

2. Each station should have one star, one goal (laundry basket on its side) placed 3-4 feet in front of the star, one striking tool (child-size racquet, hockey stick, baseball ball bat, or broom), and one ball. For ease of ball retrieval, children should be positioned so that they face a wall.

3. Set striking tools (assorted sizes of racquets or hockey sticks) and balls (assorted sizes) aside so they are ready for use. Materials can be swapped depending on the needs of each child. See Figure U6.3.

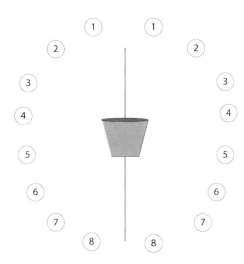

Figure U6.1. Classroom setup for Warm-Up, Balloons in the Sky, and Cool-Down.

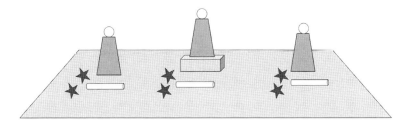

Figure U6.2. Classroom setup for Tee-Ball.

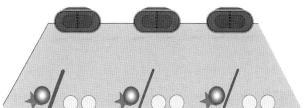

Figure U6.3. Classroom setup for Hockey.

Featured Interactive Movement Books

- *Thump, Thump, Rat-a-Tat-Tat,* written by Gene Baer and illustrated by Lois Ehlert. HarperCollins, 1991.
- *Whoosh Around the Mulberry Bush,* written by Jan Ormerod and illustrated by Lindsey Gardiner. Oxford University Press, 2007.
- *The Animal Boogie,* written and illustrated by Debbie Harter; sing-along CD sung by Fred Penner. Barefoot Books, 2000.

Video Content

For this unit, you will need to select two music videos, each approximately 2-4 minutes long, illustrating side-to-side and up-and-down motions, such as twisting/dancing motions, reaching arms up on each side, jogging or wiggling in place, wiggling fingers, wiggling hips, and moving knees out and in. Note, you can select a longer (4-minute) music video and use 2 minutes for Lesson 3, 3 minutes for Lesson 4, and the entire 4 minutes for Lessons 5 and 6.

See the recommended list of video sources on Page 265 and the criteria for video selection on Page 271.

BEFORE YOU START

1. Read through the unit. In particular, read through all of the lesson activities. Visualize the space where you will have CHAMPPS and how you will implement each activity with the children with whom you work.
2. Identify the school readiness skills you will focus on in each lesson activity; school readiness skills should correspond to your core curriculum.
3. Identify universal design for learning (UDL) strategies and adaptations to use for particular activities and/or to support individual children. For example, download the visual supports for use with the lesson prior to starting.
4. Review the lesson variations to determine which you will complete, if needed.
5. Plan ahead for how you will shorten the lesson, if needed (see below).
6. Complete the Planning Notes.

If you need to shorten the lesson:
Depending on the needs of the children you teach, you may choose to shorten the lesson on the first day or first two days of Unit 6 to allow children to get used to the CHAMPPS routine. For example, you could do the Warm-Up with the song, one or two core activities, and the Cool-Down with the song. Then, on the third day, you could add the third core activity.

UNIT 6 PLANNING NOTES

Motor movements to focus on:
Vocabulary to focus on:
Children who will be positioned near an adult for additional support and attention:
Children who will help with setup:
Children who will help with cleanup:
Children in Small Group 1:
Children in Small Group 2:
Partner pairs (if using activity variation):

■ WARM-UP

Structure: Whole group

Get ready! Focus on:
- Gathering
- Increasing heart rate
- Warming up muscles

Total time: 3-5 minutes

Key Vocabulary:
- **arms, knees, legs, stomach**
- **lunge, twist**
- **around backward, forward, side to side**
- **circle**

1. MOVE: Motor Movements

Children start on their floor marker, warming up their bodies while singing the "CHAMPPS Warm-Up Song" with each movement you model. Verbal prompts are provided below, if needed.

- Children **jog** in a circle. Say: *Remember, a jog is a **slow run**. Jog slowly and **pump your arms!***

- Children **roll arms** in a circle. Say: *Time to roll our arms! Make **airplane arms**. Great job! Now spin them in a **circle**, forward (or backward).*

- Children **twist**. Say: *Stand tall on your circle. Feet together. Let's see your **airplane arms** again, but now turn in a circle side to side. Now your arms are spinning side to side. Make sure you **twist your tummy!***

- Children **lunge**. Say: *Stand tall. **Step** one foot forward. Keep the other foot on your circle. **Bend** your knees and lunge forward. Now let's switch to the other side!*

2. ADAPT: UDL Strategies

Adapt the activity to meet the needs of the children with whom you work. See the suggestions in the following table; for additional ways to adapt, use the UDL Suggestions for Unit 6.

Engagement	Representation	Action & Expression
• Give children choices. Ask children to choose the next warm-up movement(s).	• Use verbal prompts to encourage movement. See the Glossary of Verbal Prompts. • Use visual supports. See Visual Support Cards for stand, stand in circle, sit, roll arms, and twist.	• Encourage children to sing along. Give children the option to hum or clap to the melody/rhythm.

3. SUPPORT: School Readiness

Choose one to three school readiness skills to focus on. See the suggestions in the following table; for additional ways to support school readiness, turn to Page 194.

Language	Mathematics	Approaches to Learning
• Encourage children to sing along. • Children listen for verbal prompts. • Children identify body parts.	Use ordinal language (*first, second, third*) with children.	• Create a smooth transition between movements. • Children follow directions. • Guide children to remain focused and continue moving. • Encourage whole-group engagement.

4. LESSON VARIATIONS

If the children you work with learn these activities quickly and need no further practice, or if you want to vary activities for review days, see Lesson Variations on Page 198.

■ CORE ACTIVITY 1: **Balloons in the Sky**

Structure: Whole group

Total time: 3–5 minutes

Focus on these objectives:
- Striking a moving object
- Visual tracking
- Hand-eye coordination
- Force

Key Vocabulary:
- **eyes, hands**
- **tap**
- **hard, soft**
- **circle**
- **freeze** (stop right where you are and hold object such as balloon or ball)

1. MOVE: Motor Movements

- Children remain in warm-up area, spaced apart so they can tap their balloon without being near peers.
- Each child retrieves one balloon. Children sing "Balloons in the Sky" with each movement.
- Children toss and catch for 1–2 minutes. Children gently toss the balloon in the air, catch it with two **hands,** and repeat.
- Children strike and catch for 1–2 minutes. Children gently toss the balloon in the air. As the balloon begins to fall, children gently **tap** their balloon with their fingers so it goes back up. Children catch the balloon at the end of the song.
- Periodically ring the bell while saying **"Freeze"** to teach children to stop moving and hold their balloon.

2. ADAPT: UDL Strategies

Adapt the activity to meet the needs of the children with whom you work. See the suggestions in the following table; for additional ways to adapt, use the UDL Suggestions for Unit 6.

Engagement	Representation	Action & Expression
Challenge children by starting with strike and catch. Ask children to **tap** the balloon a little **harder** so that the balloon goes higher into the air.	• Model the movement(s) for children and then have them imitate. • Use verbal prompts to describe **tapping** the balloon versus hitting (**soft** versus **hard**). See the Glossary of Verbal Prompts. • Use visual supports. See Visual Support Cards for stand, stand in circle, grasp, put in/take out, tap balloon, and catch.	Vary the complexity of response by asking children to sit on the floor. Place the balloons on the floor in front of the children. The children can **tap** the balloon from **hand** to **hand** and watch it roll **side to side** on the floor.

3. SUPPORT: School Readiness

Choose one to three school readiness skills to focus on. See the suggestions in the following table; for additional ways to support school readiness, turn to Page 194.

Language	Mathematics	Approaches to Learning
• Encourage children to sing along. • Children listen for verbal prompts.	Emphasize positional words (*up, down; high, low*) with children.	• Children follow directions. • Encourage children to stay engaged during the whole-group activity.

4. LESSON VARIATIONS

If the children you work with learn these activities quickly and need no further practice, or if you want to vary activities for review days, see Lesson Variations on Page 198.

◼ CORE ACTIVITY 2: **Tee-Ball**

Structure: Independent practice

Total time: 3-5 minutes

Focus on these objectives:
- Strike a stationary object
- Hand-eye coordination
- Cooperative play
- Force

Key Vocabulary:
- **arms, hands, knees, waist**
- **aim, bat, swing, twist**

1. MOVE: Motor Movements

Children form small groups. Each child should have their own tee-ball station that includes one cone with a foam baseball on top, two floor markers on the floor next to the cone, and one foam baseball bat.

Teacher models: Stand on floor markers with toes pointing at cone. Place ball on cone. Grasp bat with two hands, twist at waist while swinging bat, and hit the ball. Retrieve the ball. Children imitate the teacher's actions:

- Children start off standing with each foot on a floor marker and their toes pointing at the cone.
- Tell children to place two **hands** on the bat and hold the bat behind the ball. Children **twist** at the waist to **swing** and hit the ball.
- Children retrieve their ball, place it back on the cone, and repeat.
- Use bell to signal activity transitions.

2. ADAPT: UDL Strategies

Adapt the activity to meet the needs of the children with whom you work. See the suggestions in the following table; for additional ways to adapt, use the UDL Suggestions for Unit 6.

Engagement	Representation	Action & Expression
Vary the type of bat to suit children's ability/preference. For instance, have younger children use a thicker bat, or let children choose color of bat, foam or plastic bat, etc.	• Use verbal prompts for each part of the **ready, set, swing** sequence as you model for children. See the Glossary of Verbal Prompts. • Use visual supports. See Visual Support Cards for stand, strike with bat, swing, twist, pick up ball, and retrieve ball.	Vary complexity of response by asking children to gently **tap** the ball off the cone rather than completing a full **swing**.

3. SUPPORT: School Readiness

Choose one to three school readiness skills to focus on. See the suggestions in the following table; for additional ways to support school readiness, turn to Page 194.

Mathematics	Science	Approaches to Learning
Emphasize positional words (*high, low*).	Make predictions. Ask: *What happens if we throw the ball harder? Gentler?*	Children work independently and set up their own tee-ball station.

4. LESSON VARIATIONS

If the children you work with learn these activities quickly and need no further practice, or if you want to vary activities for review days, see Lesson Variations on Page 198.

■ CORE ACTIVITY 3: **Hockey**

Structure: Independent practice

Focus on these objectives:
- Strike a stationary object
- Strike a moving object
- Hand-eye coordination
- Cooperative play
- Force

Total time: 3-5 minutes

Key Vocabulary
- **arms, hands, knees**
- **aim, strike, swing, twist**
- **goal, hockey stick, puck (ball), racquet**

1.   MOVE: Motor Movements

Children form small groups. Each child in the group should have their own hockey station that includes one star with one goal (laundry basket with wrist bell attached to each) placed on its side 3-4 feet away, two floor markers on the floor next to the star, a ball, and a racquet or hockey stick.

Teacher models: Stand on floor markers with toes pointing at star. Place ball on star. Grasp the racquet with two hands, and twist at the waist while swinging the racquet, aiming the ball toward the goal. Retrieve the ball. Children repeat actions:

- Children start off standing with each foot on a floor marker, pointing their toes at the star. Place the ball on the star.
- Tell children to place two **hands** on the racquet and hold the racquet behind the ball. Children look at the goal. Children **swing** the racquet to **aim** the ball toward the goal.
- Children retrieve their ball and repeat action.

The bell on each goal serves as a reinforcement; it rings when ball goes in goal or bumps the goal.

- Use another bell to signal activity transitions.

2.   ADAPT: UDL Strategies

Adapt the activity to meet the needs of the children with whom you work. See the suggestions in the following table; for additional ways to adapt, use the UDL Suggestions for Unit 6.

Engagement	Representation	Action & Expression
Challenge children by asking them to **tap** the ball and walk **forward** toward the goal like they are skating down the ice with a hockey puck. This focuses the child's attention on striking a moving object.	• Use verbal prompts for each part of the **ready, set, swing** sequence as you model for children. See the Glossary of Verbal Prompts. • Use visual supports. See Visual Support Cards for stand, strike with hockey stick, twist, pick up ball, and retrieve ball.	Vary complexity of response by asking children to gently **tap** the ball **forward** rather than completing a full **swing**.

3.   SUPPORT: School Readiness

Choose one to three school readiness skills to focus on. See the suggestions in the following table; for additional ways to support school readiness, turn to Page 194.

Language	Social-Emotional	Approaches to Learning
• Children listen for verbal prompts. • Ask: *How do you feel when you miss the ball? When you score a goal?*	• Children retrieve balls for peers. • Children cheer on their peers.	• Children follow directions. • Children work independently and set up their own hockey station.

4.   LESSON VARIATIONS

If the children you work with learn these activities quickly and need no further practice, or if you want to vary activities for review days, see Lesson Variations on Page 198.

■ PHYSICAL ACTIVITY: **Music Video**

Structure: Whole group

Total time: 2-4 minutes

Focus on this objective:
Sustained physical activity

1. MOVE: Motor Movements

Children stand on their floor marker. Spread out for enough space for floor movement. Say: ***Arms out.*** *Make wide,* ***airplane arms.*** *Make sure you are not touching a friend.* Children move to the music video you selected.

Lesson	Video	Total Time
3	Video 1: side-to-side and up-and-down motions	2 minutes
4	Video 2: dancing motions, such as reaching arms up on each side, twisting waist, jogging or wiggling in place, moving forward and backward, wiggling fingers, and moving knees out and in	3 minutes
5	Videos 1 and/or 2	4 minutes
6		

2. ADAPT: UDL Strategies

Adapt the activity to meet the needs of the children with whom you work. See the suggestions in the following table, along with additional ways to adapt using the UDL Suggestions on Page 192.

Engagement	Representation	Action & Expression
Provide specific praise and encouragement (e.g., *I love your dance moves! Or Excellent job, keep moving!*)	• Use verbal prompts to describe movement. See the Glossary of Verbal Prompts. • Use visual supports. See Visual Support Cards for stand, stand in circle, sit, and airplane arms.	Stand in close proximity to children and model modified movements (e.g., bend knees instead of sitting).

3. SUPPORT: School Readiness

During the music video, the primary goal is to have all children maintain sustained/increased physical activity levels. To achieve this goal, teachers can provide models/prompts for motor imitation (imitate actions/songs from video, maintain personal space) and approaches to learning (active engagement, following instructions from video).

4. LESSON VARIATIONS

If the children you work with learn these activities quickly and need no further practice, or if you want to vary activities for review days, see Lesson Variations on Page 198.

■ COOL-DOWN

Structure: Whole group

Total time: 3-5 minutes

Wrap up: Focus on
• Gathering
• Decreasing heart rate
• Cooling down muscles

Key Vocabulary:
• **arms, knees, legs**
• **around, backward, forward, side to side**
• **hard, soft**
• **circle**

1. MOVE: Motor Movements

- Children sit on their floor marker and cool-down their bodies with the movements listed below. Once you have modeled each movement, sing the "CHAMPPS Cool-Down Song" while doing the movements (see "CHAMPPS Cool-Down Song," Page 190).
  - Stretch **arms.** Say: *Hold ball with one hand.* **Make an X.** *Bend your arm. Touch ball to shoulder.*
  - **Roll arms.** Say: *Sit with a straight back. Hold ball with two hands.* **Arms out straight. Roll your arms** *and* **make a circle.**
  - Touch toes. Say: *Sit with your legs out straight! Now* **reach forward** *to touch your toes!* **Hold** *that pose!*
  - Play piano/drums. Say: *Bend your knees. Squeeze the ball between your knees. Let's play the piano (tapping fingers on ball) or drums (tapping hands on ball).*
  - Wave goodbye. Say: *Look at your friends. Hold out your hand and wave goodbye.*
- End with yoga poses: Star Pose and Fold Pose.
  - Star Pose. (See Figure U6.4.) Say: *Spread your feet out wide. Reach your arms up and out wide.* **Make an X.** *Roll out your wrists and shake your hips side to side.*
  - Fold Pose. (See Figure U6.5.) Say: *Stay in Star Pose. Now reach your* **hands to the floor.** *Let's stay here for 10 seconds.*

Figure U6.4.   Star Pose.   **Figure U6.5.**   Fold Pose.

2. ADAPT: UDL Strategies

Adapt the activity to meet the needs of the children with whom you work. See the suggestions in the following table; for additional ways to adapt, use the UDL Suggestions for Unit 6.

Engagement	Representation	Action & Expression
Vary volume of voice to match the pace of movement.	• Use verbal prompts to describe movement. See the Glossary of Verbal Prompts. • Use visual supports. See Visual Support Cards for sit, roll arms, stretch arms, bend and stretch, wave hand, and play drums.	Begin with simple movements and no singing.

3. SUPPORT: School Readiness

Choose one to three school readiness skills to focus on. See the suggestions in the following table; for additional ways to support school readiness, turn to Page 194.

Language	Mathematics	Approaches to Learning
• Encourage sing-along. • Children listen for verbal prompts. • Children identify body parts.	• Use ordinal language (*first, second, third*). • Patterns: Create a movement pattern (e.g., reach up, then touch toes; repeat).	• Create a smooth transition between movements. • Children follow directions. • Children remain focused and keep moving.

4. LESSON VARIATIONS

If the children you work with learn these activities quickly and need no further practice, or if you want to vary activities for review days, see Lesson Variations on Page 198.

Walk-Around Card

CHAMPPS

1	**Warm-Up**	
	Gathering, increase heart rate, warm-up muscles	
	MATERIALS	• Numbered floor markers (1 per person)
	ACTIVITIES	Sing "CHAMPPS Warm-up Song." Children twist, jog, lunge, and roll arms.
2	**Core Activity 1: Balloons in the Sky**	
	Physical movement, hand-eye coordination, visual tracking	
	MATERIALS	• Numbered floor markers (1 per person) • 1–2 baskets containing balloons in assorted colors (1 per person) • 1 bell (for teacher)
	ACTIVITIES	First: Sing "Balloons in the Sky." Next: Children toss and catch balloon and/or strike and catch it. Then: Say *Freeze* and ring bell for children to stop tossing balloons
3	**Core Activity 2: Tee-Ball**	
	Physical movement, hand-eye coordination, visual tracking, force	
	MATERIALS	Set up half as many tee-ball stations as there are children in your class. Each has: • 2 floor markers • 1 foam baseball bat • 1 cone • 1 bell (for teacher) • 1 foam baseball
	ACTIVITIES	First: Children strike the ball with their bat. Next: Children retrieve ball and repeat. Then: Ring bell to signal transition to next activity
4	**Core Activity 3: Hockey**	
	Physical movement, hand-eye coordination, visual tracking, force	
	MATERIALS	Set up half as many hockey stations as there are children in your class. Each station has: • 2 floor markers • 1 child-size hockey stick (stick, racquet, bat, or broom) • 1 star • 1 goal with wrist bells attached • 1 ball • 1 bell (for teacher)
	ACTIVITIES	First: Children strike the ball with their hockey stick, aiming for goal. Bells on goal ring if ball goes in goal or bumps the goal. Next: Children retrieve the ball and repeat actions. Then: Ring bell to signal transition
5	**Physical Activity: Music Video**	
	Sustained physical activity	
	MATERIALS	Video, video player, wall or screen for viewing

Lesson 3 Video 1 (2 minutes)	**Lesson 4** Video 2 (3 minutes)	**Lessons 5 and 6** Videos 1 and/or 2 (4 minutes)

6	**Cool-Down**	
	Gathering, lower heart rate, cool-down muscles	
	MATERIALS	• Numbered floor markers (1 per person)
	ACTIVITIES	First: Sing "CHAMPPS Cool-Down Song." Roll arms, stretch arms, touch toes, play piano/drums, and wave goodbye. Then: Do yoga poses: Star Pose and Fold Pose.

Walk-Around Card

CHAMPPS Warm-Up Song

(Sung to the tune of "The Ants Go Marching")

The CHAMPPS go **twisting** one by one
Hurrah! Hurrah!
The CHAMPPS go **twisting** one by one
Hurrah! Hurrah!
The CHAMPPS go **twisting** one by one
This is the way we have some fun
And we all go **twisting** on, and on, and on

(Repeat with **jogging, lunging,** and **rolling arms**)

Balloons in the Sky

(Sung to the tune of "The Farmer in the Dell")

Balloons in the sky
Balloons in the sky
Heigh-ho, the balloons go
Balloons in the sky

CHAMPPS Cool-Down Song

(Sung to the tune of "Here We Go 'Round the Mulberry Bush")

This is the way we **roll our arms**
Roll our arms, roll our arms
This is the way we **roll our arms**
At the end of CHAMPPS

(Repeat with **stretch our arms, play piano/drums, touch our toes,** and **wave goodbye**)

GLOSSARY OF VERBAL PROMPTS

Do (Movement)	Say (Verbal Prompt)	Use
Bend and stretch	Reach, side, hold	Sit crisscross and **reach** above your head! Now lean to the **side** and **hold** it there! Feel the stretch!
Jog	Slow run	We are going to jog. A jog is a **slow run.**
	Swing arms	**Swing your arms** and **run slowly.**
Roll arms	Airplane arms	Time to roll our arms! Make **airplane arms.** Great job! Now spin them in a *circle!*
	Circle	
Stretch arms	Make an X	This is how we stretch our arms. **Make an X** with your arms in front of your body.
	Kiss your shoulder	Then **kiss your shoulder** with one hand!
Strike moving object	Toss balloon	First **toss the balloon,** and make sure you **watch the balloon!**
	Watch balloon	
	Tap	Now, **tap** it with your fingers/hand!
	Catch	Great job. Time to **catch** the balloon!
Strike stationary object	Eyes on the ball	First, keep your **eyes on the ball!** Make sure you're looking at it!
	Ready, set, swing	Model the ready-set-swing sequence. Say: **Ready** . . . (stand on floor marker facing tee) **Set** . . . (bend knees, hold racquet or bat behind the ball) **Swing!** (twist at waist to swing and hit ball)
	Follow the ball	Follow through with your swing! **Follow the ball** with your bat!
Touch toes	Reach forward, hold	Sit with your legs straight! Now **reach forward** to touch your toes! **Hold** that pose!
Twist	Airplane arms	Let's see your **airplane arms** again, but now turn in a circle side to side.
	Twist tummy	Now your arms are spinning side to side. Make sure you **twist your tummy!**

UDL SUGGESTIONS

Engagement							
Means of Engagement	**Warm-Up**	**Core Activity 1: Balloons in the Sky**	**Core Activity 2: Tee-Ball**	**Core Activity 3: Hockey**	**Video 1**	**Video 2**	**Cool-Down**
Recruit Interest							
Child choice	Warm-up moves	Balloon color	Target height	Target distance	Which video to play	Which video to play	Cool-down movements
Novel/familiar	Familiar moves (jog, lunge, roll arms) Consistent structure (whole group)	Familiar moves (throw) Familiar tune ("Farmer in the Dell")	Familiar materials (balls, cones) New materials (bats)	Familiar materials (balls for pucks, laundry basket for goal, bells) New materials (racquets, hockey stick)	New video Optional: Repeat video.	New video Optional: Repeat video.	Familiar moves (roll arms, touch toes, bend and stretch, wave goodbye)
Sustain Effort and Persistence							
Praise/ encourage	Say: *Beautiful singing voices! Keep it up!* Say: *I love how you're lunging so low to the ground!*	Say: *You're keeping your eyes on the balloon! Great job watching it!* Say: *I love how you're tapping your balloons gently!*	Say: *You hit the target! That's a home run!* Say: *What a perfect striking stance!*	Say: *GOAL! Way to go!* Say: *Wow, awesome aim! You are great at hockey!*	Say: *You really [name movement]! You have so much energy!* Say: *Excellent dancing; I love your enthusiasm!*	Say: *I love how high you're reaching your arms!* Say: *Nice, fast wiggling!*	Say: *Wow, you can reach all the way to your toes! Nice stretching!* Say: *Great, big circles with your arms!*
Vary complexity	Increase/ decrease number of moves.	Only throw and catch. Only strike and catch.	Increase/ decrease height of tee and/or size of ball.	Increase/ decrease distance from the goal.	Increase/ decrease length of video.	Increase/ decrease length of video.	Increase/ decrease number of moves.
Vary setup, directions	Sing softly/ loudly. Move slowly/ quickly.	Sing softly/ loudly. Move slowly/ quickly.	Partners do activity. Change targets (stickers, numbers).	Partners do activity. Change goal to cones or water bottles.	Vary materials (give wrist bells, scarves).	Vary materials (give wrist bells, scarves).	Vary materials (give wrist bells, scarves).

Representation

Means of Representation	Warm-Up	Core Activity 1: Balloons in the Sky	Core Activity 2: Tee-Ball	Core Activity 3: Hockey	Video 1	Video 2	Cool-Down
Forms of Communication							
Auditory	Glossary of Verbal Prompts	Glossary of Verbal Prompts Bell signals FREEZE.	Glossary of Verbal Prompts	Glossary of Verbal Prompts Bell on goal signals goal or almost a goal.	Glossary of Verbal Prompts ⟶		
Visual	Visual Support Cards ─────────────────────────────⟶						
Tactile	Give hand-over-hand instruction (hold child's hands and roll arms). ────	(hold child's hands and tap ball) Present materials when explaining activity (balloons).	(hold child's hands and tap ball) Present materials when explaining activity (bats, balls, targets).	(hold child's hands and do arm motions) Present materials when explaining activity (racquets, balls).	(as needed)	(as needed)	(hold child's hands and stretch arms)
Multiple Levels of Complexity							
Key vocabulary: define/model	jog lunge roll arms twist	freeze strike tap toss	strike (stationary object) retrieve ball	strike (stationary and moving object) retrieve ball	Instruct as needed.	Instruct as needed.	bend and stretch roll arms stretch arms touch toes wave goodbye

Action & Expression

Means of Expression	Warm-Up	Core Activity 1: Balloons in the Sky	Core Activity 2: Tee-Ball	Core Activity 3: Hockey	Video 1	Video 2	Cool-Down
Variety of responses	Sing, clap, or hum song. Move in place.	Sing, clap, or hum song. Throw and watch balloon. Throw and tap balloon just once.	Aim at variety of targets.	Aim at variety of targets.	Vary as needed.	Vary as needed.	Sing, clap, or hum song.
Complexity of responses	Accept partial movement (walk instead of jog, step instead of lunge).	Accept partial movement (touch balloon with any body part instead of tapping with hands).	Accept partial movement (touch bat to ball instead of striking).	Accept partial movement (strike ball without aiming at target).	Accept partial movement as needed.	Accept partial movement as needed.	Accept partial movement (airplane arms instead of rolling arms).

SUPPORT SCHOOL READINESS SKILLS

LANGUAGE AND LITERACY	Warm-Up	Core Activity 1: Balloons in the Sky	Core Activity 2: Tee-Ball	Core Activity 3: Hockey	Cool-Down
Expresses feelings and preferences (hot, thirsty, tired, hungry, sleepy, sweaty)	Ask: *How do you feel after warm-up? Tired? Energized?*		Ask: *How do you feel when you miss the ball? When you hit it?*	Ask: *How do you feel when you miss the ball? When you hit it?*	Ask: *How do you feel when CHAMPPS is over? Tired? Hot? Sweaty?*
Engages in active discussion (shares ideas, asks and answers questions)	Ask: *Do you have any new ideas for warm-up movements?*	Ask: *What other body parts could we use to tap the balloons?*	Ask: *Who can model the movements for ready, set, swing?*	Ask: *Who can model the movements for ready, set, swing?*	Ask: *Who can lead us in the closing song?*
Communicates personal experiences and interests	Ask: *What's your favorite warm-up move?*	Ask: *Which color balloon is your favorite?*	Ask: *Who has played tee-ball? Who has been to a baseball game?*	Ask: *Who has played hockey? Who has been to a hockey game?*	Ask: *Which activity was your favorite today? Which was your least favorite?*
Listens to/uses formal and informal language (listens to/sings songs, uses different voices)	Children listen and sing along.	Children listen and sing along.	Use baseball language: *Batter up! Home run!*	Use hockey language: *Goal!*	Children listen and sing along.
Recognizes shapes (circle, square, triangle, rectangle)	Children stand in circle.	Children stand in circle.	Use circle targets. Change shapes.	Draw attention to circles (floor markers, ball).	Draw attention to circles (floor markers, ball).
Recognizes letters	Put letters or baseball/hockey team symbols on floor markers.	Say a letter each time the balloon is struck.	Use letter targets (A, B, C, etc.).	Use letter targets (A, B, C, etc.). Write letters on goals.	Put letters on floor markers.

MATHEMATICS	Warm-Up	Core Activity 1: Balloons in the Sky	Core Activity 2: Tee-Ball	Core Activity 3: Hockey	Cool-Down
Number recognition (count, one–one correspondence)	Children count moves.	Children count taps.	Children count targets hit.	Children count the number of goals they make.	Children count stretches.
Positional words	High/low Side to side Up/down	High/low Up/down	Forward/backward High/low	Forward/backward High/low	Left/right Side to side
Ordinal language (*first, second,* etc.)	Use ordinal words for order of moves (first, twist; second, jog; third, lunge, etc.).	Use ordinal words for order of moves (first, toss balloon; second, tap balloon, etc.).	Use ordinal words for order of moves (first, stand; second, swing; third, retrieve, etc.).	Use ordinal words for order of moves (first, stand; second, swing; third, retrieve, etc.).	Use ordinal words to discuss order of moves. Ask: *What will we do first? Second? Third?*
Categorizing and sorting objects	Ask: *Look at the objects we are using today (ball, racquet, bat, star). Which objects are red/yellow/blue?*	Ask: *A balloon is a circle! Are there other circles in the room?*	Ask: *What other equipment do we use in sports?*	Ask: *What other equipment do we use in sports?*	Children sit by peers with the same shirt color, hair color, etc.

MATHEMATICS	Warm-Up	Core Activity 1: Balloons in the Sky	Core Activity 2: Tee-Ball	Core Activity 3: Hockey	Cool-Down
Patterns (recognize, describe, reproduce)	Create a movement pattern (e.g., roll arms, then lunge; repeat).	Create a movement pattern (e.g., throw, tap, clap; repeat).	Ask: *What are the steps for the tee-ball station? What do we do first? Second?*	Ask: *What are the steps for hockey station? What do we do first? Second?*	Create a movement pattern (e.g., reach up, then touch toes; repeat).

SCIENCE	Warm-Up	Core Activity 1: Balloons in the Sky	Core Activity 2: Tee-Ball	Core Activity 3: Hockey	Cool-Down
Ask/answer questions together (*Who? What? Where? How?*).	Ask: *What body parts do we stretch when we lunge? What about rolling our arms?*	Ask: *What do you see in the sky? Is it different in the day compared to at night?*	Ask: *What materials (equipment) do we need to play tee-ball?*	Ask: *What kind of surface do you use to play hockey?*	Ask: *Why do we cool-down? What body parts do we stretch?*
Make predictions together (*What if?*).	Ask: *How will our bodies feel after we jog? After we cool-down?*	Ask: *What if you weren't watching the balloon or had your eyes closed? Would the balloon be harder to hit?*	Ask: *What happens if we throw the ball harder? Gentler?*	Ask: *What happens if we hit the ball harder? Gentler?*	Ask: *How will our bodies feel after we stretch? Better? Worse?*
Understand weather/seasons, calendar/days of the week.	Ask: *Do we jog in the summer? Fall? Winter?*	Discuss how the sky looks during various weather conditions.	Ask: *In what seasons do people play baseball? (Spring!) What are other spring sports?*	Ask: *In what season do people play hockey? (Winter!) What are other winter sports?*	Let's whisper days of week/months of year while we cool down.
Discuss characteristics of living and nonliving things (*humans, animals, plants*).	Ask: *What other animals have arms? Legs? Feet? Wings?*	Ask: *What is a living thing that moves through the air like our balloons?*	Ask: *Which of these are nonliving things: baseball, horse, baseball bat?*	Ask: *Which of these are nonliving things: rabbit, hockey stick, racquet?*	Discuss taking deep breaths, feeling tired, and needing to rest.
Use sensory vocabulary.		Ask: *How do balloons feel? Light? Smooth?*	Ask: *How does the bat feel? Light? Heavy? Hard?*	Ask: *What does it sound like when you get a goal?*	Say: *Close your eyes. What do you hear? Smell? Feel?*

MOTOR	Warm-Up	Core Activity 1: Balloons in the Sky	Core Activity 2: Tee-Ball	Core Activity 3: Hockey	Cool-Down
Balance	Children twist and lunge.	Children take a stance during toss and strike.	Children maintain balance during swing.	Children maintain balance during swing.	Children bend and stretch.
Visual tracking	Children hold scarves or balls and roll their arms.	Children watch the balloon to strike it.	Children watch the ball after strike.	Children watch the ball after strike.	
Motor imitation	Children imitate leader/peers.				⟶
Body awareness	Children identify which body parts are needed for each movement.				⟶

SUPPORT SCHOOL READINESS SKILLS (continued)

MOTOR	Warm-Up	Core Activity 1: Balloons in the Sky	Core Activity 2: Tee-Ball	Core Activity 3: Hockey	Cool-Down
Body movement (stationary)	Children twist and roll their arms.	Children toss and strike.	Children strike.	Children strike.	Children roll and stretch arms, bend and stretch, touch toes, and wave goodbye.
Strength/speed/duration	Children sustain movement through the song.	Children sustain movement through the song.	Children strike ball hard or softly.	Children strike ball hard or softly.	Children slow down movement to cool down.
Coordination (eye/hand; eye/foot)	Children twist and roll arms while walking.	Children toss and strike balloon.	Children strike toward target.	Children strike toward goal.	Children hold ball while moving.
Locomotion	Children jog and lunge.	Children retrieve balloons that they do not catch.	Children retrieve balls after they hit them.	Children retrieve balls.	
Directionality (forward, backward, sidesteps)	Children switch direction (forward, backward, side to side).	Children switch direction (in front, behind).	Children switch direction (up, down, high, low).	Children switch direction (walk backward or forward to retrieve ball).	Children move side to side.
Personal space	Children use own floor marker.	Children use own floor marker.	Children use own station.	Children use own station.	Children use own floor marker.
Cross midline reach	Children pat self on opposite shoulder before and after CHAMPPS.	Children hug balloon after catching it on "Freeze."	Children swing bat across midline.	Children swing racquet or hockey stick across midline.	Children pat own shoulders to congratulate themselves, using each hand to pat opposite shoulder.
Grasp and release		Children toss and catch ball.	Children retrieve ball.	Children retrieve ball.	Children hold ball during stretch.
Motor regulation (go slow, go fast, stop)	Children sing and move slowly or quickly.	Children sing and move slowly or quickly.			Children slow down movement to cool down.

SOCIAL-EMOTIONAL	Warm-Up	Core Activity 1: Balloons in the Sky	Core Activity 2: Tee-Ball	Core Activity 3: Hockey	Cool-Down
Recognizes, describes, and regulates emotions	Ask: How's everyone feeling today for CHAMPPS?	Ask: How do you feel when you catch your balloon?	Ask: How does it feel to get a hit? home run?	Ask: How do you feel when you miss the goal?	Ask: How do you feel now that CHAMPPS is over?
Solves/prevents problems	Children stay on own floor marker.	Children stay on own floor marker.	Children stay at own station.	Children stay at own station.	Children stay on own floor marker.
Learns independence/self-help		Children gather and put away own balloons.	Children work independently.	Children work independently.	Children gather and put away their own materials.

SOCIAL-EMOTIONAL	Warm-Up	Core Activity 1: Balloons in the Sky	Core Activity 2: Tee-Ball	Core Activity 3: Hockey	Cool-Down
Takes turns/waits turn	Children move with classmates and do not speed ahead.	Children wait for song to begin before they toss balloon.	Children share a station and wait their turn.	Children share a station and wait their turn.	Children wait for all classmates to transition before they begin singing.
Helps/supports peers	Partners help one another through transitions (holding hands).	Partners help one another through transitions (holding hands).	Partners help one another through transitions (holding hands). Children retrieve balls for peers.	Partners help one another through transitions (holding hands). Children retrieve balls for peers.	Partners help one another through transitions (holding hands).
Plays cooperatively	Children plan and work collaboratively to set up materials.	Children work with a partner and take turns tossing the balloon.	Children share a station and take turns hitting ball and retrieving it.	Children share a station and take turns hitting ball and retrieving it.	Children plan and work collaboratively to put away materials.
Shares materials	One helper passes out floor markers to peers.	Ask: *What can you do if someone's balloon comes near you?*	Children share a station and tee-ball materials.	Children share a station and materials.	
Socializes with peers	Children socialize during opening CHAMPPS greeting.	Children say "Excuse me!" if a peer is in their space.	Children cheer each other on.	Children cheer each other on.	Children wave at peers and say goodbye.

APPROACHES TO LEARNING	Warm-Up	Core Activity 1: Balloons in the Sky	Core Activity 2: Tee-Ball	Core Activity 3: Hockey	Cool-Down
Transitions into/out of activities	Children return to floor markers in between movements.	Children return to floor markers when teacher says "Freeze!"	Children change between activities when directed by teacher.	Children change between activities when directed by teacher.	Children return to floor marker and transition back to class.
Listens to/follows directions	Children complete instructed movement.	→→→→→→→→→→→→→→→→→→→→→→→→			
Demonstrates focused attention	Children listen for next movement.	Children listen for "Freeze!"	Children focus on target.	Children focus on goal.	Children listen for next movement.
Demonstrates sustained attention	Children sustain movement until end of song.	Children sustain movement until end of song.	Children stay at own station.	Children stay at own station.	Children stay at own floor marker.
Demonstrates active engagement in small/large group	Children stay engaged in whole-group activity.	Children stay engaged in whole-group activity.	Children stay engaged in small-group/ independent activity (paired at stations).	Children stay engaged in small-group/ independent activity (paired at stations).	Children stay engaged in whole-group activity.
Demonstrates active engagement in independent task		Ask: *What do you do if your balloon gets away from you?*	Children engage in independent striking.	Children engage in independent striking.	

Lesson Variations

■ WARM-UP VARIATIONS

Music/Rhythm/Dance

Variation 1: Get Up and Move

Structure	Materials	Instructions
Whole group	• Floor markers • Projector with Internet access	1. Before warm-up, select a children's music video from YouTube or another online source that will get them jumping, dancing, and moving around. (See the video selection criteria on Page 269.) 2. Children imitate the music video for their warm-up.

Variation 2: Ribbon Sticks (see Unit 1, Warm-Up Variation 3)

Structure	Materials	Instructions
Whole group	• Multicolored ribbons or remnant fabric • Rulers or paint sticks (two per child)	1. Before warm-up, have children make ribbon sticks if they did not already do so in Unit 1. To make the ribbon sticks, tie or glue fabric ribbons to the paint sticks or rulers. If children already made these, bring them back out for use during warm-up and music video. 2. Each child should have two ribbon sticks. 3. Children hold and wave the ribbon sticks while they twist and roll their arms.

■ CORE ACTIVITY 1: **Balloons in the Sky** VARIATIONS

Music/Rhythm/Dance

Variation 1: Balloons in the Sky to Music

Structure	Materials	Instructions
Whole group	• Floor markers • Projector with Internet access	1. Before Core Activity 1, select a children's song to play during the activity. (See the video selection criteria on Page 271.) 2. Use the song to see if children can toss and catch or strike and catch the entire duration of the song. 3. This variation can be done at the end of Core Activity 1 to see how long children can go and if anyone can last through the whole song.

Sports/Games

Variation 2: Balloon Volleyball With a Friend

Structure	Materials	Instructions
Partners	• Floor markers • Volleyball net • Balloons	1. Before Core Activity 1, set up the volleyball net. 2. Place pairs of floor markers along either side of the net. Markers in each pair should be the same number or color, with one on each side of the net, facing the other. 3. Pair children off. 4. Each child tosses and catches or strikes and catches the balloons back and forth with their partner.

Other

Variation 3: Celebrate Balloon Day in the Classroom

Structure	Materials	Instructions
Whole group	• Balloons • Paint	1. Throughout the day, incorporate balloons into your lessons. For example: • Do art by using a balloon dipped in paint as a brush. • Explore different kinds of balloons with children, such as hot-air balloons. • Discuss with children how balloons are blown up with air and with helium. • Let children play Balloons in the Sky. 2. If possible, send a balloon home with each child.

■ CORE ACTIVITY 2: **Tee-Ball** VARIATIONS

Sports/Games

Variation 1: Tee-Ball With a Friend

Structure	Materials	Instructions
Partners	• Floor markers • Foam baseball bats • Baseballs (foam or other soft baseballs)	1. Pair children off. Partners will switch back and forth between who is batting and who is getting the ball. 2. This can promote sharing, and you can explain how baseball works with teams. 3. Make sure children evenly switch back and forth.

■ CORE ACTIVITY 3: **Hockey** VARIATIONS

Sports/Games

Variation 1: Group Hockey

Structure	Materials	Instructions
Whole group	• Ball • Racquet or hockey stick • Floor markers of various colors	1. Set up floor markers at various distances from the line-up position. Having floor markers at different distances represents different levels of difficulty. 2. Alternatively, before the children line up to play, announce what color floor marker they should aim for. 3. Children line up and take turns striking the ball (gently tapping with racquet or hockey stick) toward the chosen floor marker.

Arts and Crafts

Variation 2: Create Your Own Goal Markers

Structure	Materials	Instructions
Whole group	• Paper • Markers, crayons, or colored pencils	1. Let children decorate their own papers to serve as their goal markers. 2. Children play hockey, aiming for their own decorated goal markers on the floor.

Home Activities Record

Child: _____ Teacher: _____

Unit: _____ Week: _____

Please return by: _____

Thank you for playing with me! Please tell my teachers if we did CHAMPPS activities this week at home. Write a check (✓) if we practiced CHAMPPS at home this week. You can also write comments to tell my teachers how I did when we practiced CHAMPPS at home! Please give this form to my teacher each week.

Check (✓) if you did CHAMPPS practice.	Parent/Child Comments

Home Activities Record

Child: _____ Teacher: _____

Unit: _____ Week: _____

Please return by: _____

Thank you for playing with me! Please tell my teachers if we did CHAMPPS activities this week at home. Write a check (✓) if we practiced CHAMPPS at home this week. You can also write comments to tell my teachers how I did when we practiced CHAMPPS at home! Please give this form to my teacher each week.

Check (✓) if you did CHAMPPS practice.	Parent/Child Comments

CHAMPPS Home Activities

Hi, Family and Friends!

We are starting Unit 6 of CHAMPPS at school! I am learning all about how to strike a balloon or ball. Now I want to play CHAMPPS with you! It only takes 10–20 minutes. Thank you for playing with me!

Love, Your Little CHAMP

■ ACTIVITY 1: **Warm-Up**

Materials None
Directions Move and sing with me.

CHAMPPS Warm-Up Song

(Tune: "The Ants Go Marching")

The CHAMPPS go twisting one by one
Hurrah, hurrah!
The CHAMPPS go twisting one by one
Hurrah, hurrah!
The CHAMPPS go twisting one by one
This is the way we have some fun
And we all go twisting on, and on, and on!

Repeat with: jogging, lunging, and rolling arms.

■ ACTIVITY 2: **Balloons in the Sky**

Materials
Balloon (Alternatively, you could use a small ball, beanbag, rolled-up sock, or wadded-up paper.)

Directions

1. I stand on my floor marker. Watch as I toss the balloon up in the air.
2. I will tap the balloon to keep it in the air.
3. We'll sing "Balloons in the Sky" while we play.
4. Now you take a turn!

Balloons in the Sky

(Tune: "The Farmer in the Dell")

Balloons in the sky
Balloons in the sky
Heigh-ho, the balloons go
Balloons in the sky

■ ACTIVITY 3: **Cool-Down**

Materials None
Directions Stretch and sing with me.

CHAMPPS Cool-Down Song

(Tune: "Here We Go 'Round the Mulberry Bush")

This is the way we roll our arms
Roll our arms, roll our arms
This is the way we roll our arms
At the end of CHAMPPS

Repeat with: stretch our arms, play piano/drums, touch our toes, and wave goodbye.

stretch arms

roll arms

bend and stretch

wave goodbye

Read and move together!
Look for this book at your local library: *Thump, Thump, Rat-a-Tat-Tat* by Gene Baer.
Dance to this YouTube video: _____

Thank you for playing with me!

CHAMPPS Home Activities

Hi, Family and Friends!

I am still doing CHAMPPS Unit 6 at school! I am learning about striking a tee-ball with a bat. Now I want to play CHAMPPS with you! It only takes 10–20 minutes. Thank you for playing with me!

Love, Your Little CHAMP

■ ACTIVITY 1: **Warm-Up**

Materials None
Directions Move and sing with me.

CHAMPPS Warm-Up Song

(Tune: "The Ants Go Marching")

The CHAMPPS go twisting one by one
Hurrah, hurrah!
The CHAMPPS go twisting one by one
Hurrah, hurrah!
The CHAMPPS go twisting one by one
This is the way we have some fun
And we all go twisting on, and on, and on!

Repeat with: jogging, lunging, and rolling arms.

■ ACTIVITY 2: **Tee-Ball**

Materials
- Ball (can be rolled-up sock or newspaper, etc.)
- Toy or foam baseball bat (or empty cardboard paper towel roll, wrapping paper roll, etc.)
- Tee-ball stand (or empty large/tall cardboard box or stool)

Directions

1. Place ball on top of tee-ball stand.
2. I stand with my feet apart and hold the bat with two hands above shoulders.
3. I swing the bat forward to hit the ball.
4. Run with me to get the ball, and we'll do it again!

■ ACTIVITY 3: **Cool-Down**

Materials None
Directions Stretch and sing with me.

CHAMPPS Cool-Down Song

(Tune: "Here We Go 'Round the Mulberry Bush")

This is the way we roll our arms
Roll our arms, roll our arms
This is the way we roll our arms
At the end of CHAMPPS

Repeat with: stretch our arms, play piano/drums, touch our toes, and wave goodbye.

stretch arms

roll arms

bend and stretch

wave goodbye

Read and move together!
Look for this book at your local library: *Whoosh Around the Mulberry Bush* by Jan Ormerod and Lindsey Gardiner.

Dance to this YouTube video: _____

Thank you for playing with me!

CHAMPPS Home Activities

Hi, Family and Friends!

I am finishing up Unit 6 of CHAMPPS at school! We are learning how to play hockey with a ball! Now I want to play CHAMPPS with you! It only takes 10–20 minutes. Thank you for playing with me!

Love, Your Little CHAMP

ACTIVITY 1: **Warm-Up**

Materials None
Directions Move and sing with me.

CHAMPPS Warm-Up Song

(Tune: "The Ants Go Marching")

The CHAMPPS go twisting one by one
Hurrah, hurrah!
The CHAMPPS go twisting one by one
Hurrah, hurrah!
The CHAMPPS go twisting one by one
This is the way we have some fun
And we all go twisting on, and on, and on!

Repeat with: jogging, lunging, and **rolling arms.**

ACTIVITY 2: **Hockey**

Materials

- Puck (small ball, rolled-up sock, or rolled-up newspaper)
- Striking tool (hockey stick, broom, empty cardboard wrapping paper roll, racquet, toy or foam baseball bat, etc.)
- Goal (laundry basket, bucket, large cooking pot, large empty box placed on its side, etc.)
- Nonslip floor marker (placemat, small towel, sheet of paper, X made with masking tape)

Directions

1. Place ball on floor marker in front of goal (laundry basket).
2. I stand with my feet apart. I hold the stick with two hands, pointing it down like a golf club or hockey stick.
3. I swing the hockey stick (or other striking tool) forward to hit the ball into the goal (laundry basket).
4. Run with me to get the ball, and we'll do it again!

ACTIVITY 3: **Cool-Down**

Materials None
Directions Stretch and sing with me.

CHAMPPS Cool-Down Song

(Tune: "Here We Go 'Round the Mulberry Bush")

This is the way we roll our arms
Roll our arms, roll our arms
This is the way we roll our arms
At the end of CHAMPPS

Repeat with: stretch our arms, play piano/drums, touch our toes, and **wave goodbye.**

stretch arms

roll arms

bend and stretch

wave goodbye

Read and move together!
Look for this book at your local library: *The Animal Boogie* by Debbie Harter.

Dance to this YouTube video: _____

Thank you for playing with me!

Get Moving: CHAMPPS Motor Skills Units

Kicking

Unit Objectives

 1. **Motor Movement.** Focus on kicking. Reinforce previously learned skills such as jogging, lunging, and stretching.

 2. **Visual Tracking.** Following a moving ball.

 3. **Cooperative Play.** Focus on sharing and taking turns with friends, complimenting friends (e.g., good catch, good roll, good throw).

 4. **Force.** Kick a ball hard (with great intensity) versus soft.

 5. **Accuracy.** Kick a ball in the direction of a goal.

 6. **Distance.** Kick a ball while standing at different lengths from a goal.

 7. **Sustained Physical Activity.** Engage in continuous movement during music video.

Key Vocabulary

Body Parts	**feet, knees, toes**
Motor Movement	**dribble, kick, ride bike, tap, trap**
Concepts	**goal, pass, sports (bike ride, soccer)**
Social Emotional	**partner, team**

UNIT LESSON

Time	Activity	Focus					
3-5 min	**WARM-UP**	Gathering		Increase Heart Rate		Warm-Up Muscles	
5 min	**CORE 1:** **We Tap the Ball**	Motor Movement	Visual Tracking	Force	Accuracy	Distance	
5 min	**CORE 2:** **Tap and Trap***						
5 min	**CORE 3:** **Soccer***						
2-4 min	**PHYSICAL ACTIVITY:** Music Video (Lessons 3-6 only)	Motor Imitation & Sustained Physical Activity					
3 min	**COOL-DOWN**	Gathering		Decrease Heart Rate		Cool-Down Muscles	

*Half of the class goes to Tap and Trap stations and half goes to Soccer stations. After both small groups complete one activity, children remain with their group and the small groups switch locations/activities.

PREPARATION AND MATERIALS

Activity	Materials (class of 15 children with 2 adults)
WARM-UP **COOL-DOWN** Whole group	Numbered floor markers (1 per person) Balls of various sizes (1 per person) 1 large bucket (to hold balls)
CORE 1 **We Tap the Ball** Whole group	Numbered floor markers (1 per person) Balls of various sizes (1 per person)
CORE 2 **Tap and Trap** Small group (partners)	Numbered floor markers (enough for half the children in your class) 4 balls of various sizes
CORE 3 **Soccer** Small group (partners)	4 laundry baskets with Velcro wrist bells attached to each 4 balls of various sizes Numbered floor markers (1 per person)

Visual Support Cards
Used for these movements: stand, stand in circle, sit, jog in place, air kicks, trap ball, kick stationary object, kick moving object, roll ball, pick up ball, retrieve ball, airplane arms, bend and stretch, hug knees, ride the bike, touch toes, wave hand.
Visit the Brookes Download Hub to download and print the Visual Support Cards for Unit 7.

SETUP

Warm-Up, We Tap the Ball, and Cool-Down

1. Place floor markers in a circle.
2. Place balls of assorted sizes in a large bucket in the middle of the circle. See Figure U7.1.

Tap and Trap

1. Set up Tap and Trap station by gathering eight floor markers and four balls.
2. Place pairs of floor markers about 3 feet apart with one ball. Distance can be increased or decreased depending on individual needs. See Figure U7.2.

Soccer

1. Set up soccer goal stations by gathering four goals (laundry baskets with wrist bells attached) and four balls.
2. Place each floor marker about 3 feet from a goal (laundry basket). Distance can be increased or decreased depending on individual needs. See Figure U7.3.

Figure U7.1. Classroom setup for Warm-Up, We Tap the Ball, and Cool-Down.

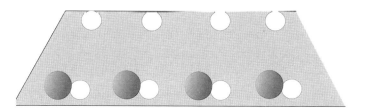

Figure U7.2. Classroom setup for Tap and Trap.

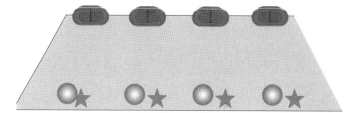

Figure U7.3. Classroom setup for Soccer.

Featured Interactive Movement Books

- *We're Going on a Bear Hunt,* written by Michael Rosen and illustrated by Helen Oxenbury. Simon and Schuster, 1989.
- *Balancing Act,* written and illustrated by Ellen Stoll Walsh. Simon and Schuster, 2010.
- *Kicking a Ball,* written by Allan Ahlberg and illustrated by Sébastien Braun. Puffin Books, 2014.

Video Content

For this unit, you will need to select two music videos, each approximately 2 minutes long, illustrating how to move to the children's songs "Head, Shoulders, Knees, and Toes" and "Hokey Pokey." Note, you can select a longer (4-minute) music video and use 2 minutes for Lesson 3, 3 minutes for Lesson 4, and the entire 4 minutes for Lessons 5 and 6.

See the recommended list of video sources on Page 265 and the criteria for video selection on Page 272.

BEFORE YOU START

1. Read through the unit. In particular, read through all of the lesson activities.

2. Identify the space where you will have CHAMPPS and how you will implement each activity with the children with whom you work.

3. Identify the school readiness skills you will focus on in each lesson activity; school readiness skills should correspond to your core curriculum.

4. Identify universal design for learning (UDL) strategies and adaptations to use for particular activities and/or to support individual children. For example, download the visual supports for use with the lesson prior to starting.

5. Review the lesson variations to determine which you will complete, if needed.

6. Plan ahead for how you will shorten the lesson, if needed (see below).

7. Complete the Planning Notes.

If you need to shorten the lesson:
Depending on the needs of the children you teach, you may choose to shorten the lesson on the first day or first two days of Unit 7 to allow children to get used to the CHAMPPS routine. For example, you could do the Warm-Up with the song, one or two core activities, and the Cool-Down with the song. Then, on the third day, you could add the third core activity.

UNIT 7 PLANNING NOTES

Motor movements to focus on:

Vocabulary to focus on:

Children who will be positioned near an adult for additional support and attention:

Children who will help with setup:

Children who will help with cleanup:

Pairs of children in Small Group 1:
(e.g., 1. Delroy and Joe, 2. Cameron and Isabella)

1.

2.

3.

4.

Pairs of children in Small Group 2:

1.

2.

3.

4.

■ WARM-UP

Structure: Whole group

Total time: 3-5 minutes

Get ready! Focus on:
- Gathering
- Increasing heart rate
- Warming up muscles

Key Vocabulary:
- **feet, knees, toes**
- **kick**

1. MOVE: Motor Movements

Children start on their floor marker, warming up their bodies while singing the "CHAMPPS Warm-Up Song" with each movement you model. Verbal prompts are provided below, if needed.

- Children jog in a circle. Say: *Remember, a jog is a **slow run.** Jog slowly **and pump your arms!***
- Children jog in place. Say: *Let's go back to our floor markers. Keep jogging, but this time, **stay in your spot.***
- Children lunge in place, toward the center of the circle. Say: *Stretch your legs with some lunges! **Step** forward and **bend** your knee! Again with the other leg!*
- Children air **kick.** Say: *Stand on your floor marker. Hands on your hips. **Lift one foot up.** Remember how we balanced? Now **kick** your foot out. **Point** your toes. Let's do it again with the other foot.*

2. ADAPT: UDL Strategies

Adapt the activity to meet the needs of the children with whom you work. See the suggestions in the following table; for additional ways to adapt, use the UDL Suggestions for Unit 7.

Engagement	Representation	Action & Expression
• Give children choices. Ask children to choose the next warm-up movement(s).	• Use verbal prompts to encourage movement. See the Glossary of Verbal Prompts. • Use visual supports. See Visual Support Cards for stand, stand in circle, lunge, sit, jog in place, and air kicks.	• Encourage the children to sing along. Give children the option to hum or clap to the melody/rhythm.

3. SUPPORT: School Readiness

Choose one to three school readiness skills to focus on. See the suggestions in the following table; for additional ways to support school readiness, turn to Page 221.

Language	Mathematics	Science
• Encourage children to sing along. • Children listen for verbal prompts. • Children identify body parts.	• Use ordinal language with children (i.e., *first, second, third*). • Use positional words with children (i.e., *forward, backward, left, right*).	• Feel heartbeat before/after warm-up. Discuss slow/fast heartbeat. • Ask: *What body parts do we stretch when we lunge?* • Ask: *We're kicking out legs toward the sky. Where is the sky? What are things we see in the sky during winter, spring, or fall?*

4. LESSON VARIATIONS

If the children you work with learn these activities quickly and need no further practice, or if you want to vary activities for review days, see Lesson Variations on Page 226.

■ CORE ACTIVITY 1: **We Tap the Ball**

Structure: Whole group

Total time: 3–5 minutes

Focus on these objectives:

- Tapping (gentle kicking)
- Dribbling
- Retrieving the ball
- Controlled movement: trapping
- Visual tracking
- Force

Key Vocabulary:

- **feet, toes**
- **dribble, tap, trap**
- **soccer**

1. MOVE: Motor Movements

- Children return to warm-up circle, standing on their floor marker with a ball.
- Model and say: *Place the ball on the floor in front of you.*
- Model and say: *Lift one foot up and **tap** the top of the ball with your **toes.** Try not to let the ball roll away. Keep it in one place.*
- Children sing "We Tap the Ball" with the movements.
- Note: Sometimes placing hands on hips helps children balance. If a child has difficulty balancing, provide a chair or table for the child to hold onto. Remind children that if their ball rolls away, they should retrieve the ball and return to their floor marker.
- At the end of the song, sing it again and have children repeat the movement with the other foot.
- Once children have practiced **tapping** the ball, move on to dribbling and **trapping**. Children gently **tap** the ball forward around the room.
- Model and say: *When we **dribble,** we lightly tap the ball and let it roll. We follow the rolling ball and lightly tap the ball again to keep the ball moving.* Do this until the song ends.
- Model and say: *When the song ends, trap the ball by placing one foot on top of the ball so the ball stops moving.*
- As children move around the room, remind them to keep their heads up so they do not bump into their friends.

2. ADAPT: UDL Strategies

Adapt the activity to meet the needs of the children with whom you work. See the suggestions in the following table; for additional ways to adapt, use the UDL Suggestions for Unit 7.

Engagement	Representation	Action & Expression
• Encourage children to sing along. Give children the option to hum or clap to the melody/rhythm. • For ball retrieval, encourage children to follow loose ball with their eyes, walk to get ball and return to floor marker.	• Model the movement(s) for children and then have them imitate. • Use verbal prompts to encourage movement. See the Glossary of Verbal Prompts. • Use visual supports. See Visual Support Cards for stand, stand in circle, tap, and trap ball.	Vary the complexity of response by offering balls of various sizes to match each child's ability level.

3. SUPPORT: School Readiness

Choose one to three school readiness skills to focus on. See the suggestions in the following table; for additional ways to support school readiness, turn to Page 221.

Language	Mathematics	Science
• Encourage children to sing along. • Ask: *What does it mean to balance on one foot?* • Ask: *What does it mean to tap/dribble/trap the ball?*	• Use ordinal language: *first kick, second trap.* • Use positional words. For example, say: *Kick the ball left; kick toward the door. Kick the ball right; kick toward the wall.* • Say: *Let's count how many taps we can do without losing the ball!*	• Ask: *Balls are round. What other things are round?* • Say: *Name some animals that tap.* • Ask: *What happens if we kick the ball harder?*

4. LESSON VARIATIONS

If the children you work with learn these activities quickly and need no further practice, or if you want to vary activities for review days, see Lesson Variations on Page 226.

◼ CORE ACTIVITY 2: **Tap and Trap**

Structure: Small group (partners)   **Total time:** 3-5 minutes

Focus on these objectives:
- Tap (gentle kicking)
- Trap
- Force
- Accuracy
- Distance
- Retrieve the ball
- Cooperative play

Key Vocabulary:
- **feet, toes**
- **kick, pass, tap, trap, dribble**
- **partner**

1. MOVE: Motor Movements

Children form two small groups. Within the small groups, pair each child with a preidentified partner. Each child in the pair stands on a floor marker facing their partner (about 3 feet apart), and one child has a ball.

To start, model and say: *Place the ball on the ground, and place one foot on top of the ball to hold it still.*

Model and say: *Look at your partner. Tap the ball (gently **kick**) to pass it to your **partner.** When the ball gets close to the **partner,** the **partner** lifts one foot to **trap** (stop) the ball. Keep going! Gently tap the ball, **passing** it back and forth to your partner.*

Note: Sometimes placing hands on hips helps children balance.

2. ADAPT: UDL Strategies

Adapt the activity to meet the needs of the children with whom you work. See the suggestions in the following table; for additional ways to adapt, use the UDL Suggestions for Unit 7.

Engagement	Representation	Action & Expression
Vary complexity of the activity by increasing or decreasing the distance between partners.	• Use verbal prompts to encourage movement. See the Glossary of Verbal Prompts. • Use visual supports. See Visual Support Cards for stand, trap ball, kick stationary object, kick moving object, roll ball, tap ball, pick up ball, and retrieve ball.	Offer a variety of responses by partnering with children who require additional support. Roll the ball to the child and have the child stop the ball with their foot (trap). Repeat.

3. SUPPORT: School Readiness

Choose one to three school readiness skills to focus on. See the suggestions in the following table; for additional ways to support school readiness, turn to Page 221.

Language and Literacy	Social	Science
• Ask: *What is a partner?* • Ask: *Who is your partner?* • Ask: *What can you say to help your partner feel good about their trapping and tapping skills?*	• Ask: *What can you do when your partner loses the ball?* • Ask: *What can you do to be a good partner?*	• Ask: *What animals can trap an object?* • Ask: *What happens when you kick the ball too hard?*

4. LESSON VARIATIONS

If the children you work with learn these activities quickly and need no further practice, or if you want to vary activities for review days, see Lesson Variations on Page 226.

■ CORE ACTIVITY 3: Soccer

Structure: Small group (partners)

Total time: 3–5 minutes

Focus on these objectives:
- Tap (gentle kicking)
- Force
- Accuracy
- Distance
- Squat
- Kneel
- Retrieve ball
- Cooperative play

Key Vocabulary:
- feet, toes
- kick
- goal, soccer
- partner, team

1. MOVE: Motor Movements

Children form small groups. Within each small group, pair each child with a preidentified partner. Each pair has their own soccer station (one ball, one floor marker, and one goal/laundry basket with bell).

Model and say to the goalie: *Squat or kneel beside the goal facing your partner. Hold the goal (basket) steady with two hands. When your partner kicks the ball into the goal, tap the basket to ring the bells.*

Model and say to kicker: *Stand on the floor marker facing the goal. Tap the ball toward the goal.*

The first child kicks the ball, aiming for the goal. If a child makes the goal, their partner shakes the basket to ring the bells. Switch roles.

2. ADAPT: UDL Strategies

Adapt the activity to meet the needs of the children with whom you work. See the suggestions in the following table; for additional ways to adapt, use the UDL Suggestions for Unit 7.

Engagement	Representation	Action & Expression
Vary the complexity of the activity by increasing or decreasing the children's distance from the goal.	• Use verbal prompts to encourage movement. See the Glossary of Verbal Prompts. • Use visual supports. See Visual Support Cards for stand, kick stationary object, pick up ball, and retrieve ball.	Offer a variety of responses such as placing one child directly in front of the goal with very little distance between the ball and the goal. Ask child to gently tap the ball into goal or push forward with their foot.

3. SUPPORT: School Readiness

Choose one to three school readiness skills to focus on. See the suggestions in the following table; for additional ways to support school readiness, turn to Page 219.

Social	Language	Math
• Children engage in cooperative play. • Children share materials and take turns. • Children assist each other in ball retrieval.	• Ask: *How do you feel when you get a goal? Miss a goal?* • Ask: *How many points do you get for a goal?* • Ask: *What can you say to cheer on your partner?*	• Use ordinal numbers: *First, tap; second, cheer!* • Say: *Count the goals!* • Say: *With your partner, measure how far you can stand from the goal and still make a goal.*

4. LESSON VARIATIONS

If the children you work with learn these activities quickly and need no further practice, or if you want to vary activities for review days, see Lesson Variations on page 226.

◼ PHYSICAL ACTIVITY: **Music Video**

Structure: Whole group   **Total time:** 2-4 minutes

Focus on this objective:
Sustained physical activity

1. MOVE: Motor Movements

Children stand on their floor marker. Spread out for enough space for floor movement. Say: **Arms out.** *Make wide,* **airplane arms.** *Make sure you are not touching a friend.*

Children move to the music video you selected.

Lesson	Video	Total Time
3	Video 1: Movements to accompany the children's song "Head, Shoulders, Knees, and Toes"	2 minutes
4	Video 2: Movements to accompany the children's song "Hokey Pokey"	3 minutes
5	Videos 1 and/or 2	4 minutes
6		

2. ADAPT: UDL Strategies

Adapt the activity to meet the needs of the children with whom you work. See the suggestions in the following table; for additional ways to adapt, use the UDL Suggestions for Unit 7.

Engagement	Representation	Action & Expression
Provide specific praise and encouragement (e.g., *I love your dance moves! Or Excellent job, keep moving!*)	• Use verbal prompts to describe movement. See the Glossary of Verbal Prompts. • Use visual supports. See Visual Support Cards for stand, stand in circle, sit, and airplane arms.	Stand in close proximity to children and model modified movements (e.g., bend knees instead of sitting).

3. SUPPORT: School Readiness

During the music video, the primary goal is to have all children maintain sustained/increased physical activity levels. To achieve this goal, teachers can provide models/prompts for motor imitation (imitate actions/songs from video, maintain personal space) and approaches to learning (active engagement, following instructions from video).

4. LESSON VARIATIONS

If the children you work with learn these activities quickly and need no further practice, or if you want to vary activities for review days, see Lesson Variations on Page 226.

■ COOL-DOWN

Structure: Whole group

Wrap up: Focus on
- Gathering
- Decreasing heart rate
- Cooling down muscles

Total time: 3–5 minutes

Key Vocabulary:
- **feet, knees, toes**
- **ride bike**

1. MOVE: Motor Movements

Children sit on their floor marker and cool-down their bodies with the movements listed below. Once you have modeled each movement, sing the "CHAMPPS Cool-Down Song" while doing the movements (see "CHAMPPS Cool-Down Song," Page 215).

- **Bend and stretch.** Model and say: *Sit with a straight back. Legs straight. Raise your arms up. Sway your arms side to side to bend and stretch.*
- **Touch toes.** Model and say: *Sit with a straight back. Arms up. Bend **forward** and slowly **reach** to touch your toes.*
- **Ride a bike.** Model and say: *Let's pretend to ride a bike. First, **lean back** on your arms. Now, **bend your knees** so you're balancing on your arms. Now, **make circles** with your feet! One after another, like riding a bike!*
- **Hug knees.** Model and say: *Lie down on your back. **Bend your knees.** Hold your knees and **squeeze them** toward your chest. Hold for 10 seconds.*
- **Wave goodbye.** Model and say: *Look at your friends. Hold out your hand and wave goodbye.*

End with yoga poses: Butterfly Pose and Child's Pose.

- Butterfly Pose. (See Figure U7.4.) Model and say: *Sit on the floor. Place the bottoms of your feet together. Breathe in and reach your arms up over your head. Breathe out and reach your hands to the floor.*
- Child's Pose. (See Figure U7.5.) Model and say: *Sit in a low kneel. Rest your bottom on your heels. Reach your arms up high and then bring them down to the ground. Spread your knees apart so your head can rest on the floor. Let's hold for 10 seconds.*

Figure U7.4. Butterfly Pose.   **Figure U7.5.** Child's Pose.

2. ADAPT: UDL Strategies

Adapt the activity to meet the needs of the children with whom you work. See the suggestions in the following table; for additional ways to adapt, use the UDL Suggestions for Unit 7.

Engagement	Representation	Action & Expression
Vary volume of voice to match the pace of movement.	• Use verbal prompts to describe movement. See the Glossary of Verbal Prompts. • Use visual supports. See Visual Support Cards for sit, bend and stretch, touch toes, ride a bike, hug knees, and wave hand.	Begin with simple movements and no singing.

3. SUPPORT: School Readiness

Choose one to three school readiness skills to focus on. See the suggestions in the following table; for additional ways to support school readiness, turn to Page 221.

Language	Mathematics	Approaches to Learning
• Encourage children to sing along. • Children listen for verbal prompts. • Children identify body parts.	• Use ordinal language (*first, second, third*). • Say: *Let's count how many times we touch our toes.* • Categorize. For example, say: *If you have on yellow or blue, touch your toes; if you have on socks, ride your bike faster.*	• Create a smooth transition for ending CHAMPPS. Say: *Let's line up quietly at the door.* • Praise children who follow directions.

4. LESSON VARIATIONS

If the children you work with learn these activities quickly and need no further practice, or if you want to vary activities for review days, see Lesson Variations on Page 226.

Walk-Around Card

CHAMPPS

1	**Warm-Up**		
	Gathering, increase heart rate, warm-up muscles		
	MATERIALS	• Numbered floor markers (1 per person) • Basket(s) • Balls of various sizes (1 per person)	
	ACTIVITIES	Sing "CHAMPPS Warm-Up Song." Children jog (around/in place), lunge, and air kick.	
2	**Core Activity 1: We Tap the Ball**		
	Physical movement, visual tracking		
	MATERIALS	Same as for Warm-Up	
	ACTIVITIES	Sing "We Tap the Ball." First: Children tap a stationary ball with one foot and then the other foot, holding ball in place. Next: Children tap ball, dribbling. When song ends, children trap the ball with one foot.	
3	**Core Activity 2: Tap and Trap**		
	Physical movement, visual tracking, force		
	MATERIALS	Set up Tap and Trap stations for a small group of preidentified paired children (half the class). Each station has 1 ball and 2 floor markers, placed 3 feet apart.	
	ACTIVITIES	First: Child taps (gently kicks) the ball to pass it to their partner. Next: Partner traps (stops) the ball with their foot. Repeat, taking turns.	
4	**Core Activity 3: Soccer**		
	Physical movement, visual tracking, force		
	MATERIALS	Set up Soccer stations for a small group of preidentified paired children (half the class). Each station has 1 goal (laundry basket with bells), 1 ball, and 1 floor marker (3 feet from goal).	
	ACTIVITIES	First: Child taps (gently kicks) ball into basket. Next: Goalie (partner) holds basket and cheers. Repeat, taking turns.	
5	**Physical Activity: Music Video**		
	Sustained physical activity		
	MATERIALS	Video, video player, wall or screen for viewing	
	Lesson 3 Video 1 (2 minutes)	**Lesson 4** Video 2 (3 minutes)	**Lessons 5 and 6** Videos 1 and/or 2 (4 minutes)
6	**Cool-Down**		
	Gathering, lower heart rate, cool-down muscles		
	MATERIALS	Floor markers	
	ACTIVITIES	First: Sing "CHAMPPS Cool-Down Song" while doing stretches. Next (optional): Do yoga poses: Butterfly Pose and Child's Pose. Then: Bend and stretch, touch toes, ride a bike, hug knees, and wave goodbye.	

Walk-Around Card

CHAMPPS

CHAMPPS Warm-Up Song
(Sung to the tune of "The Ants Go Marching")

The CHAMPPS go **jogging** one by one
Hurrah! Hurrah!
The CHAMPPS go **jogging** one by one
Hurrah! Hurrah!
The CHAMPPS go **jogging** one by one
This is the way we have some fun
And we all go **jogging** on, and on, and on, and on

(Repeat with **lunging** and **kicking**)

We Tap the Ball
(Sung to the tune of "The Farmer in the Dell")

We **tap** the ball
We **tap** the ball
Heigh-ho, the merry-o
We **tap** the ball

CHAMPPS Cool-Down Song
(Sung to the tune of "Here We Go 'Round the Mulberry Bush")

This is the way we **bend and stretch**
Bend and stretch, bend and stretch
This is the way we **bend and stretch**
At the end of CHAMPPS

(Repeat with **touch our toes, ride a bike, hug our knees,** and **wave goodbye**)

GLOSSARY OF VERBAL PROMPTS

Do (Movement)	Say (Verbal Prompt)	Use
Air kick	Bend knees	*Great! Now **bend your knees!***
	Kick, bend, kick	***Kick** one foot! Then **bend** that knee again! Good, now the other foot! **Kick! Bend! Kick!***
Bend and stretch	Reach, lean to the side, hold	*Sit with legs in front and **reach** one arm up and one arm down! Now **lean to the side** and **hold** it there! Feel the stretch! Now switch arms and repeat, stretching in the other direction!*
Dribble the ball	Tap and follow ball	*To dribble, lightly **tap the ball, follow the rolling ball,** lightly tap the ball again, and keep the ball moving.*
Hug knees	Bend knees	*Let's stretch by hugging our knees! Sit on the ground and **bend your knees.** Now **squeeze your knees** against your chest! Tight hug!*
	Squeeze knees	
Jog	Slow run	*A jog is a **slow run.***
	Pump arms	*Jog slowly and **pump your arms.***
Kick moving object	Walk and tap	*Now we're going to keep the ball moving while we kick it. Slowly **walk** forward and **tap** the ball with your feet so it moves with you. Gentle taps! **Walk and tap!***
Kick stationary object	Step, swing, kick	*First you need to **step** toward the ball! Step really close! Next, **swing** your foot at the ball! **Kick** that ball!*
Lunge	Step and bend	*Stretch your legs with some lunges! **Step** forward and **bend** your knee! Again, with the other leg!*
Pass the ball	Pass the ball	*Gently **tap (gently kick) the ball to a friend.***
Ride the bike	Lean back	*Let's pretend to ride a bike. First, **lean back** on your arms.*
	Bend knees	*Now, **bend your knees** so you're balancing on your arms.*
	Make circles	***Make circles** with your feet! One after another, like riding a bike!*
Tap the ball	Tap the ball	*Lift one foot up and **tap** the top of the ball with your **toes.** Try not to let the ball roll away.*
Touch toes	Reach forward, hold	*Sit with your legs straight! Now **reach forward** to touch your toes! **Hold** that pose!*
Trap	Stop the ball	*When we trap, we **stop the ball** by putting our foot on top of it! Keep the ball still.*

UDL SUGGESTIONS

Engagement							
Means of Engagement	**Warm-Up**	**Core Activity 1: We Tap the Ball**	**Core Activity 2: Tap and Trap**	**Core Activity 3: Soccer**	**Video 1**	**Video 2**	**Cool-Down**
Recruit Interest							
Child choice	Warm-up moves	Ball (small, medium, large)	Select color of ball.	Choose own partner.	Which video to play	Which video to play	Cool-down movements
Novel/familiar	Familiar moves (jog, lunge) Consistent structure (whole group) New moves (air kick)	Familiar materials (balls) New moves (kick)	Familiar materials (balls) Familiar structure (pairs) New moves (air kick)	Familiar materials (balls) Familiar structure (pairs) New moves (air kick)	New video Optional: Repeat video	New video Optional: Repeat video	Familiar moves (roll arms, touch toes, bend and stretch, wave goodbye)
Sustain Effort and Persistence							
Praise/ encourage	Say: *You're kicking so high into the air! Great!* Say: *That's perfect jogging! Look at you go!*	Say: *I like how you looked at the ball before kicking it!* Say: *What a nice, gentle kick!*	Say: *You got a goal! You're a soccer superstar!* Say: *I love that big strong kick! The ball went so far!*	Say: *Nice job bringing the ball right back to your partner!* Say: *Good, gentle roll to your partner's feet!*	Say: *You're a terrific dancer! Keep it up!* Say: *I love the faces you make! You're really having fun!*	Say: *Great job following all the movements!* Say: *You have so much energy! Great work!*	Say: *Wow, you can reach all the way to your toes! Nice stretching!* Say: *Great job, stretching your arms in your yoga pose!*
Vary complexity	Increase/ decrease number of moves.	Vary pace of tapping. Vary ball size/weight.	Vary distance from partner. Vary ball size/weight.	Vary distance from goal. Vary ball size/weight.	Increase/ decrease length of video.	Increase/ decrease length of video.	Increase/ decrease number of moves.
Vary setup, directions	Sing softly/ loudly. Move slowly/ fast.	Sing softly/ loudly. Move slowly/ fast.	Change group size and targets (work in groups of three or four; aim at wall instead of partner).	Change targets (aim at floor markers or target instead of goal/ buckets).	Vary materials (give instruments, scarves).	Vary materials (give instruments, scarves).	Vary materials (give balls, beanbags, scarves).

UDL SUGGESTIONS *(continued)*

Representation

Means of Representation	Warm-Up	Core Activity 1: We Tap the Ball	Core Activity 2: Tap and Trap	Core Activity 3: Soccer	Video 1	Video 2	Cool-Down
Forms of Communication							
Auditory	Glossary of Verbal Prompts ————————————————————————→						
Visual	Visual Support Cards ————————————————————————→						
Tactile	Give hand-over-hand instruction (hold child's hands and pull forward gently to lunge). ——→	(hold child's hands or have them hold chair for balance) Present materials when explaining activity (ball).	(hold child's hands and retrieve ball) Present materials when explaining activity (ball).	(hold child's hands and roll ball) Present materials when explaining activity (ball, basket).	(as needed)	(as needed)	(move child's feet in circles with hands for bike exercise)
Multiple Levels of Complexity							
Key vocabulary: define/model	jog (in place, around) lunge air kick	kick ball retrieve ball trap ball	kick ball retrieve ball trap ball	kick ball retrieve ball trap ball roll ball	Instruct as needed.	Instruct as needed.	bend and stretch touch toes ride the bike hug knees wave goodbye

Action & Expression

Means of Representation	Warm-Up	Core Activity 1: We Tap the Ball	Core Activity 2: Tap and Trap	Core Activity 3: Soccer	Video 1	Video 2	Cool-Down
Variety of responses	Sing, clap, or hum song. Move in place.	Sing, clap, or hum song. Move in place.	Kick with any part of foot (toe, inner foot).	Kick with any part of foot (toe, inner foot). Partners kick ball back and forth, rather than roll.	Vary as needed.	Vary as needed.	Sing, clap, or hum song.
Complexity of responses	Accept partial movement (step forward instead of lunge).	Accept partial movement (touch foot to ball instead of kicking).	Accept partial movement (kick ball in any direction).	Accept partial movement (touch foot to ball instead of kicking)	Accept partial movement as needed.	Accept partial movement as needed.	Accept partial movement (touch knees instead of toes).

SUPPORT SCHOOL READINESS SKILLS

LANGUAGE AND LITERACY	Warm-Up	Core Activity 1: We Tap the Ball	Core Activity 2: Tap and Trap	Core Activity 3: Soccer	Cool-Down
Expresses feelings and preferences (hot, thirsty, tired, hungry, sleepy, sweaty)	Ask: *How do you feel after warm-up? Do you feel your heart beating faster?*	Ask: *Who likes to balance on one foot?*	Ask: *How can you help your partner feel good? (For example, pat on the back, shake hands.)*	Ask: *How do you feel when you kick the ball? When you get a goal? When you miss a goal?*	Ask: *How do you feel when CHAMPPS is over? Tired? Hot? Sweaty?*
Engages in active discussion (shares ideas, asks and answers questions)	Ask: *Do you have any new ideas for warm-up movements?*	Ask: *Who can tap one foot on the ground? Show me!*	Ask: *What other kinds of balls might you trap? Beach ball? Nerf ball?*	Ask: *What is a goal? What does it mean to score?*	Ask: *What are your ideas for cool-down? Who wants to do yoga moves?*
Communicates personal experiences and interests	Ask: *What's your favorite warm-up move?*	Ask: *When have you kicked a ball before? What other games involve kicking?*	Ask: *Have you played or worked with a partner before? When?*	Ask: *Who has played soccer? Who has been to a soccer game?*	Ask: *Which activity was your favorite today? Which was your least favorite?*
Listens to/uses formal and informal language (listens to/sings songs, uses different voices)	Children listen and sing along.	Children listen and sing along.	Ask: *What can you say to help your partner? (For example, "Great kick!" or "Try again!")*	Use soccer language: *Goal! Score! Assist!*	Children listen and sing along.
Recognizes shapes (circle, square, triangle, rectangle)	Children stand in a square.	Children stand in a square.	Children stand in a square.	Children stand in a square.	Children sit in an oval.
Recognizes letters	Have each child hold four previously introduced letters for stretches. Call out letter: *Everyone with K jog around circle. Now everyone with D lunge around circle.*	Add letters to floor markers. Children name their lettered floor marker.	Add letters (partner letters).	Add letters to baskets. Children identify their letter.	Have each child hold four previously introduced letters for stretches. Call out a letter: *Everyone with K reach for toes. Now everyone with D reach for toes.*
Vocabulary	air kick, bend, foot, jog, knee, lunge	balance on one foot, kick, tap, trap	tap, trap, retrieve	tap, trap, retrieve, goal, goalie, knees, bend	arms, bend, bike, feet, hands, hug, knees, point, shoulder, stretch, toes, waist, wave, wiggle

MATHEMATICS	Warm-Up	Core Activity 1: We Tap the Ball	Core Activity 2: Tap and Trap	Core Activity 3: Soccer	Cool-Down
Number recognition (count, one-one correspondence)	Children count moves (lunges, kicks).	Add numbers (on floor markers).	Children match numbers.	Say: *Count the goals!* Place numbers on baskets.	Children count stretches.

SUPPORT SCHOOL READINESS SKILLS *(continued)*

MATHEMATICS	Warm-Up	Core Activity 1: We Tap the Ball	Core Activity 2: Tap and Trap	Core Activity 3: Soccer	Cool-Down
Positional words	Forward/backward Up/down	Behind/in front Forward/backward	Ask: *Where is the ball: under your foot, beside your foot, or in front of your foot?*	Say to goalie: *Are you kneeling in front of, behind, or beside the goal?*	Left/right Side to side
Ordinal language (*first, second,* etc.)	Use ordinal words for order of moves (first, jog; second, lunge; third, air kick, etc.).	Use ordinal words for order of moves (first, tap; second, dribble, etc.).	Use ordinal words for order of moves (first, tap; second, trap, etc.).	Use ordinal words for order of moves (first, kick; second, cheer, etc.).	Use ordinal words to discuss order of moves.
Categorizing, sorting, measuring	Children stand by shirt color, hair color, etc.	Say, for example: *Children on the right side, move to the red floor marker!*		Say: *With your partner, measure how far you can stand from the goal and make a goal.* Say, for example: *Number 2 partners, move to the red soccer goal!*	Children sit near a friend with the same color shirt, same color shoes, etc.
Patterns (recognize, describe, reproduce)	Create a movement pattern (e.g., lunge, then kick; repeat).	Create a movement pattern (e.g., tap, dribble, clap; repeat).	Say: *Let's try this pattern: tap, tap, kick, trap.*		Create a movement pattern (e.g., hug knees, then touch toes).

SCIENCE	Warm-Up	Core Activity 1: We Tap the Ball	Core Activity 2: Tap and Trap	Core Activity 3: Soccer	Cool-Down
Ask/answer questions together (*Who? What? Where? How?*).	Ask: *What body parts do you stretch when you lunge? What about when you do an air kick?*	Say: *Balls are round! What else in nature is round?* (seeds, fruit, rocks)	Ask: *Whose turn is it to kick? How far can you kick?*	Ask: *What will you do when you miss the goal?*	Ask: *Why do we cool-down? What body parts do we stretch?*
Make predictions together (*What if?*).	Ask: *How will our bodies feel after we warm-up?*	Ask: *What if the ball was heavier? What if we kicked the ball harder? Softer?*	Ask: *What if the ball was smaller? What if we kicked the ball with our left foot?*	Ask: *What if the ball was larger, like a beach ball? What if we kicked a baseball instead?*	Ask: *What if we moved faster during cool-down? How would that make us feel when we return to the classroom?*
Understand weather/seasons, calendar/days of the week.	Say: *We're kicking into the sky! What do you see in the sky in winter? In fall?*	Ask: *What days do we have CHAMPPS?*	Ask: *What CHAMPPS games will you play this weekend with your family?*	Ask: *In what season do we play soccer?*	Ask: *When might you do cool-down stretches at home?* (at night, before bed, after school)

SCIENCE	Warm-Up	Core Activity 1: We Tap the Ball	Core Activity 2: Tap and Trap	Core Activity 3: Soccer	Cool-Down
Discuss characteristics of living things (*humans, animals, plants*).	Children feel their heartbeats before and after warm-up. Discuss how heartbeats get faster.	Ask: *What other animals tap?* (beaver, woodpecker)	Ask: *What animals can trap a ball?* (dog, cat, seal)	Ask: *Can you play soccer indoors? Outdoors? How is outdoors different from indoors?*	Discuss taking deep breaths, feeling tired, and needing to rest.
Use sensory vocabulary.	Have children feel their heartbeats.	Have children close their eyes, feel different objects with their foot, and describe them.		Ask: *What do you hear when you get a goal? (A bell!)*	Have children place a hand to their chest and breathe slowly.

MOTOR	Warm-Up	Core Activity 1: We Tap the Ball	Core Activity 2: Tap and Trap	Core Activity 3: Soccer	Cool-Down
Balance	Children maintain balance and lunge.	Children maintain balance during tap.	Children maintain balance during trap.	Children maintain balance during kick.	Children maintain balance as they bend and stretch, ride bike, and hug knees.
Visual tracking	Children hold scarves during warm-up.	Children watch and retrieve the ball.	Children watch and retrieve the ball.	Children watch and retrieve the ball.	
Motor imitation	Children imitate leader/peers.				→
Body awareness	Children identify which body parts are needed for the movement.				→
Body movement (stationary)	Children jog in place and do air kicks.	Children tap a stationary ball.	Children tap.	Children kick from a stationary position.	Children bend and stretch, touch toes, ride bike, hug knees, and wave goodbye.
Strength/speed/duration	Children sustain movement throughout the song.	Children tap ball hard or softly.	Children tap ball hard or softly.	Children kick ball hard or softly.	Children slow down movement to cool-down.
Coordination (eye/hand; eye/foot)		Children tap ball while moving slowly.	Children tap and trap a ball with a partner.	Children kick ball toward target.	Children hold ball while moving.
Locomotion	Children jog and lunge.	Children kick moving ball and retrieve it.	Children tap and trap moving ball and retrieve ball.	Children kick moving ball and retrieve it.	
Directionality (forward, backward, sidesteps)	Children switch direction (*forward, backward*).	Children switch how they tap ball (*forward, backward, sideways*).	Children switch how they tap and trap (*forward, backward, sideways*).		Children switch direction (*up, down, around*).

SUPPORT SCHOOL READINESS SKILLS *(continued)*

MOTOR	Warm-Up	Core Activity 1: We Tap the Ball	Core Activity 2: Tap and Trap	Core Activity 3: Soccer	Cool-Down
Personal space	Children use own floor marker.	Children use shared space.	Children use shared space.	Children use shared space.	Children use own floor marker.
Cross midline reach	Children pat self on opposite shoulder before and after CHAMPPS.				Children pat own shoulders to congratulate themselves, using each hand to pat opposite shoulder.
Grasp and release	Children grasp/ release hands of friends as they step backward to make circle larger.	Children retrieve ball.	Children retrieve ball.	Children retrieve ball.	Children grasp and release their ankles, shins, toes, etc.
Motor regulation (go slow, go fast, stop)	Children sing and move slowly or quickly.	Children sing and tap slowly or quickly.	Children walk quickly (speed walk) to retrieve balls.	Children walk quickly (speed walk) to retrieve balls.	Children move slowly through cool-down movements.
Music and dance	Children sing and dance calmly.	Children sing song together.			Children sing song together.

SOCIAL-EMOTIONAL	Warm-Up	Core Activity 1: We Tap the Ball	Core Activity 2: Tap and Trap	Core Activity 3: Soccer	Cool-Down
Recognizes, describes, and regulates emotions	Ask: *How do you feel today? How do you feel about CHAMPPS?*	Ask: *How does it feel to tap the ball gently?*	Ask: *How do you feel when your partner traps the ball? Misses the ball?*	Ask: *How does it feel to kick the ball hard?*	Ask: *How do you feel now that CHAMPPS is over?*
Solves/prevents problems	Children stay on own floor marker.	Ask: *What do you do when the ball gets away from you?*	Children use corresponding numbers with partner.	Children stay at own station.	Children stay on own floor marker.
Learns independence/ self-help	Each child sings independently.	Children gather and put away their own balls.	Children retrieve their loose ball and return to station.	Children retrieve their loose ball and return to station.	Children help gather and put away materials.
Takes turns/ waits turn	Children move with classmates and not speed ahead.	Children wait until all children are ready before they begin tapping the ball.	Children watch and wait their turn while partner kicks ball or traps ball.	Children take turns making goals and retrieving balls.	Children wait for all classmates to transition before they begin singing.
Helps/supports peers	Have partners help one another through transitions (holding hands).		Ask: *What can you say to support your friend? Good try! Try again! Great kick!*	Partners help one another by holding basket steady for each other.	Have partners help one another through transitions (holding hands).

SOCIAL-EMOTIONAL	Warm-Up	Core Activity 1: We Tap the Ball	Core Activity 2: Tap and Trap	Core Activity 3: Soccer	Cool-Down
Plays cooperatively	Children go to vacant floor marker and share space with peers.	Children stay at own floor marker.	Children work with a partner.	Children work with a partner to play soccer and cheer for one another.	Children help put away play materials together.
Shares materials		Children assist in passing out balls.	Children share materials.	Children share materials.	When balls are used during Cool-Down, children share balls with peers.
Socializes with peers	Children socialize during opening CHAMPPS greeting.	Children compliment one another's kicks.	Children work with a partner.	Children work with a partner and cheer partner on.	Children wave at peers and say goodbye.

APPROACHES TO LEARNING	Warm-Up	Core Activity 1: We Tap the Ball	Core Activity 2: Tap and Trap	Core Activity 3: Soccer	Cool-Down
Transitions into/out of activities	Children return to floor markers in between movements.	Children return to floor markers in between movements.	Children move between Core Activity 2 and Core Activity 3 with partner.	Children move between Core Activity 2 and Core Activity 3 with partner.	Children return to floor marker and transition back to class.
Listens to/follows directions	Children complete instructed movement.				→
Demonstrates focused attention	Encourage children to listen for next movement.	Encourage children to listen for start and end of song.	Children switch roles (tap/trap).	Children switch roles (kick/cheer).	
Demonstrates sustained attention	Encourage children to sustain movement until end of song.	Children sustain movement until end of song.	Children stay with partner.	Children stay with partner.	Children sustain movement until end of song.
Demonstrates active engagement in small/large group	Children stay engaged in whole-group activity.	Children stay engaged in whole-group activity.	Children stay engaged in partner work.	Children stay engaged in partner work.	Children stay engaged in whole-group activity.
Demonstrates active engagement in independent task		Children independently tap and retrieve ball.	Children independently tap ball to pass to partner, who traps ball. Partners pass ball back and forth.	Children independently tap (gently kick) ball to goal and retrieve ball.	

Lesson Variations

◼ WARM-UP VARIATIONS

Music/Rhythm/Dance

Variation 1: Dance Around

Structure	Materials	Instructions
Whole group	• Floor markers • Projector with Internet access	1. Before warm-up, select a music video from YouTube or another online source that will get children jumping, dancing, and moving around. (See the video selection criteria on Page 272.) 2. Children imitate the music video for their warm-up.

◼ CORE ACTIVITY 1: **We Tap the Ball** VARIATIONS

Music/Rhythm/Dance

Variation 1: Tap the Ball and Freeze

Structure	Materials	Instructions
Whole group or partners	• Floor markers • Projector with Internet access • Balls of various sizes	1. Before the activity, select a children's music video from YouTube or another online source. 2. Play music as children tap the ball. 3. When the music stops, children must stop and trap the ball.

Sports/Games

Variation 2: Tap and Count

Structure	Materials	Instructions
Whole group	• Balls of various sizes	1. Have the children tap the ball for a certain number of taps. For example, everyone can do three taps together, or each child can be given an individual number of taps to try. 2. If children are able, they could also count how many taps they can do on the ball.

◼ CORE ACTIVITY 2: **Tap and Trap** VARIATIONS

Sports/Games

Variation 1: Group Roll and Kick

Structure	Materials	Instructions
Whole group	• Balls of various sizes	1. Place children in groups of three instead of pairs for them to practice rolling and kicking in other directions. 2. Alternatively, gather the entire class in a circle. Have each child say a friend's name and then try to roll the ball to that friend across the circle.

Arts and Crafts

Variation 2: Decorate Goals

Structure	Materials	Instructions
Whole group	• Small plastic buckets or shoeboxes (smaller goals for greater challenge) • Crayons, markers, or colored pencils	1. Children decorate smaller buckets or shoeboxes to aim for when they are rolling and kicking. 2. Alternatively, they could also decorate paper plates to aim for or decorate other items in the classroom that could serve as a goal marker toward which they can kick the ball (e.g., overturned chair).

■ CORE ACTIVITY 3: **Soccer** VARIATIONS

Sports/Games

Variation 1: Classroom Soccer

Structure	Materials	Instructions
Small groups	• Painter's tape • Basket • Floor markers • Soccer pinnies in various colors • Balls of various sizes	1. Have a classroom soccer game. To set up the room, create a large rectangle using painter's tape. Place two baskets on two opposite sides of the rectangle. Place floor markers spread out throughout rectangle. 2. Place children in two small groups; each group wears a different-colored shirt/pinny. 3. Each child stands on a floor marker. Make sure team members are spread apart. 4. Children pass a ball to team members and until they reach a basket. 5. Then, the last child taps ball into basket to score a goal. 6. For an added challenge, do not use floor markers. Children dribble and pass the ball.

Home Activities Record

CHAMPPS

Child: _____   Teacher: _____
Unit: _____   Week: _____
Please return by: _____

Thank you for playing with me! Please tell my teachers if we did CHAMPPS activities this week at home. Write a check (✓) if we practiced CHAMPPS at home this week. You can also write comments to tell my teachers how I did when we practiced CHAMPPS at home! Please give this form to my teacher each week.

Check (✓) if you did CHAMPPS practice.	Parent/Child Comments

Home Activities Record

CHAMPPS

Child: _____   Teacher: _____
Unit: _____   Week: _____
Please return by: _____

Thank you for playing with me! Please tell my teachers if we did CHAMPPS activities this week at home. Write a check (✓) if we practiced CHAMPPS at home this week. You can also write comments to tell my teachers how I did when we practiced CHAMPPS at home! Please give this form to my teacher each week.

Check (✓) if you did CHAMPPS practice.	Parent/Child Comments

CHAMPPS Home Activities

Hi, Family and Friends!
We are starting Unit 7 of CHAMPPS at school! I am learning all about how to kick a ball. Now I want to play CHAMPPS with you! It only takes 10–20 minutes. Thank you for playing with me!
Love, Your Little CHAMP

◼ ACTIVITY 1: **Warm-Up**

Materials None
Directions Move and sing with me.
CHAMPPS Warm-Up Song
(Tune: "The Ants Go Marching")

The CHAMPPS go jogging one by one
Hurrah, hurrah!
The CHAMPPS go jogging one by one
Hurrah, hurrah!
The CHAMPPS go jogging one by one
This is the way we have some fun
And we all go jogging on, and on, and on!

Repeat with: lunging and **kicking.**

◼ ACTIVITY 2: **We Tap the Ball**

Materials
- Ball (can be wadded-up newspaper wrapped with different color duct tape or masking tape)
- Floor marker (placemat, towel, or sheet of paper taped on floor)

Directions
1. We both stand on floor marker. I place the ball on the floor.
2. Watch as I tap the ball very gently with one foot. The ball does not move. We'll sing "We Tap the Ball" as we play.
3. After tapping the ball, we dribble it by tapping the ball a little harder, so it rolls around the room. I follow the ball and keep tapping it.
4. When the song ends, I place one foot on top of the ball to trap it (stop it).
5. Now you take a turn!

We Tap the Ball
(Tune: "The Farmer in the Dell")

We tap the ball
We tap the ball
Heigh-ho, the merry-o
We tap the ball

◼ ACTIVITY 3: **Cool-Down**

Materials None
Directions Stretch and sing with me.
CHAMPPS Cool-Down Song
(Tune: "Here We Go 'Round the Mulberry Bush")

This is the way we bend and stretch
Bend and stretch, bend and stretch
This is the way we bend and stretch
At the end of CHAMPPS

Repeat with: touch our toes, ride a bike, hug our knees, and **wave goodbye.**

touch toes

ride the bike

hug your knees

wave goodbye

Read and move together!
Look for this book at your local library: *We're Going on a Bear Hunt* by Michael Rosen.
Dance to this YouTube video: _____

Thank you for playing with me!

CHAMPPS: CHildren in Action Motor Program for PreschoolerS by Paddy C. Favazza and
Michaelene M. Ostrosky with Melissa Stalega, Hsiu-Wen Yang, Katherine Aronson-Ensign, Martin Block,
W. Catherine Cheung, and Yusuf Akemoglu. Copyright © 2023 by Paul H. Brookes Publishing Co., Inc. All rights reserved.

CHAMPPS Home Activities

Hi, Family and Friends!
I am still doing CHAMPPS Unit 7 at school! I am learning about rolling and kicking a ball with a partner to pass it back and forth. Now I want to play CHAMPPS with you! It only takes 10–20 minutes. Thank you for playing with me!
Love, Your Little CHAMP

■ ACTIVITY 1: **Warm-Up**

Materials None
Directions Move and sing with me.

CHAMPPS Warm-Up Song
(Tune: "The Ants Go Marching")

The CHAMPPS go jogging one by one
Hurrah, hurrah!
The CHAMPPS go jogging one by one
Hurrah, hurrah!
The CHAMPPS go jogging one by one
This is the way we have some fun
And we all go jogging on, and on, and on!

Repeat with: lunging and **kicking.**

■ ACTIVITY 2: **Tap and Trap**

Materials

• Ball (can be rolled-up sock or newspaper, etc.)
• Floor marker (placemat, towel, sheet of paper taped on floor, etc.)

Directions

1. We both stand on floor marker. I place the ball on the floor and place one foot on top to hold it in place.
2. Watch as I look at you and tap (gently kick) the ball to you.
3. You lift one foot to trap (stop) the ball. We will repeat to pass the ball back and forth.

■ ACTIVITY 3: **Cool-Down**

Materials None
Directions Stretch and sing with me.

CHAMPPS Cool-Down Song
(Tune: "Here We Go 'Round the Mulberry Bush")

This is the way we bend and stretch
Bend and stretch, bend and stretch
This is the way we bend and stretch
At the end of CHAMPPS

Repeat with: touch our toes, ride a bike, hug our knees, and **wave goodbye.**

touch toes

ride the bike

hug your knees

wave goodbye

Read and move together!
Look for this book at your local library: *Balancing Act* by Ellen Stoll Walsh.

Dance to this YouTube video: _____

Thank you for playing with me!

CHAMPPS Home Activities

Hi, Family and Friends!

I am finishing up Unit 7 of CHAMPPS at school. I am getting so good at kicking a ball that now I can play soccer with a partner! Now I want to play CHAMPPS with you! It only takes 10–20 minutes. Thank you for playing with me!

Love, Your Little CHAMP

■ ACTIVITY 1: **Warm-Up**

Materials None
Directions Move and sing with me.

CHAMPPS Warm-Up Song

(Tune: "The Ants Go Marching")

The CHAMPPS go jogging one by one
Hurrah, hurrah!
The CHAMPPS go jogging one by one
Hurrah, hurrah!
The CHAMPPS go jogging one by one
This is the way we have some fun
And we all go jogging on, and on, and on!

Repeat with: lunging and **kicking.**

■ ACTIVITY 2: **Soccer**

Materials

• Ball (can be wadded up newspaper wrapped with colored duct tape or masking tape)
• Bucket (or laundry basket, large cooking pot, shoe box turned on its side, etc.)
• Floor marker (placemat, small towel, or sheet of paper taped to floor)

Directions

1. Place ball on floor marker in front of bucket.
2. I kick the ball into the bucket.
3. Give me high-fives and say, "Great kick; you got a goal!" or "That's okay; try again!"
4. Run with me to get the ball and do it again!

■ ACTIVITY 3: **Cool-Down**

Materials None
Directions Stretch and sing with me.

CHAMPPS Cool-Down Song

(Tune: "Here We Go 'Round the Mulberry Bush")

This is the way we bend and stretch
Bend and stretch, bend and stretch
This is the way we bend and stretch
At the end of CHAMPPS

Repeat with: touch our toes, ride a bike, hug our knees, and **wave goodbye.**

touch toes

ride the bike

hug your knees

wave goodbye

Read and move together!
Look for this book at your local library: *Kicking a Ball* by Allan Ahlberg.
Dance to this YouTube video: _____

Thank you for playing with me!

Additional Resources

Included in this section are the following resources:

- *Skill Leveling Guide.* This is the most comprehensive resource in this section, with detailed guidance related to the motor skills taught in Units 1–7. It describes what you will see when a child is performing each skill at a beginner, intermediate, or established level; tips for teaching the skill; and lists of references and resources for learning more.

- *Classroom Inventory for Motor Play Materials, With Resources.* Use this document to take inventory of motor play materials you have available for use with CHAMPPS. Web resources are listed here so you can find any materials you may need.

- *Resources for Musical Motor Activities—Videos.* Use this list as a starting point for finding YouTube music videos and DVDs you may wish to use with CHAMPPS.

- *Criteria for Selecting Physical Activity Music Videos.* Use this document to evaluate music videos you may wish to use with CHAMPPS.

- *Criteria for Selecting Preschool Interactive Movement Books.* Use this document to evaluate books you may wish to use with CHAMPPS.

Skill Leveling Guide

This guide begins with tips about general resources on motor skills available from the Singapore Sports Council's My Active Singapore website. This is followed by detailed guidance about how to note a child's skill level and suggestions for supporting specific skills addressed in CHAMPPS. For each skill, a definition is provided, along with information about how to determine a child's skill level (beginner, intermediate, or established), what to emphasize when teaching the skill, and where to find additional resources and references. CHAMPPS skills covered here include

- Walking

- Running

- Balance—static and dynamic balance

- Jumping—jumping for height, jumping from a height, and jumping for distance

- Hopping

- Catching

- Throwing—overhand throwing, underhand throwing and rolling, and two-handed throwing

- Striking—overhand and two-handed striking of a stationary object and striking a moving object

- Kicking—kicking a stationary object

Note: All web resources and URLs included in this section are current at the time of this writing but subject to change. If you are unable to access one of these resources based on the information provided here, use your search engine either to visit the site's home page and explore, or to search for comparable resources.

GENERAL RESOURCES

The Singapore Sports Council My Active Singapore website provides a wealth of information on motor skills, including several comprehensive guides listed below.

Locomotor Skills

Visit the Singapore Sports Council My ActiveSG web page on Locomotor Skills for Kids: https://www.myactivesg.com/read/2016/11/locomotor-skills

Click the Locomotor Skills link to download a complete locomotor skills guide covering multiple skills in the CHAMPPS curriculum. Explore the additional links on this page to find PDF guides focused on specific motor skills such as walking and running; these are also noted below in the Skill Leveling resource lists for those motor skills.

Stability Skills

Visit the Singapore Sports Council My ActiveSG web page on Stability Skills for Kids: https://www.myactivesg.com/read/2016/11/stability-skills

Click the Stability Skills link to download a complete guide covering static balance, dynamic balance, and other skills related to stability. Explore the additional links on this page to find PDF guides focused on specific stability skills; these are also noted below in the Skill Leveling resource lists for those skills.

Object Control Skills

Visit the Singapore Sports Council My ActiveSG web page on Object Control Skills for Kids: https://www.myactivesg.com/read/2016/11/object-control-skills

Click the Object Control Skills link to download a complete skills guide covering multiple object control skills in the CHAMPPS curriculum. Explore the additional links on this page to find PDF guides focused on specific object control skills such as throwing and catching; these are also noted below in the Skill Leveling resource lists for those motor skills.

SKILL LEVELING: WALKING

Walking: Child engages in an upright movement of both feet that requires the transfer of body weight from one foot to the other. One foot always remains in contact with the ground.

	Beginner	Intermediate	Established
Balance	• Child has difficulty maintaining balance when moving.	• Child has somewhat steady balance.	• Child maintains balance when going up/down steps.
Arms	• Child moves arms or holds out arms to maintain balance. • Child may reach out to hold hand or furniture to maintain balance.	• Child's arms remain close to trunk, and child exhibits minimal swinging of arms.	• Child's arms swing smoothly with each step. As left arm swings forward, child steps forward with right foot. As right arm swings forward, child steps forward with left foot.
Steps	• Child's feet might be too far apart to maintain balance. • Child shows inconsistent distance between steps and takes short and flat-footed steps. • Child steps forward on toes rather than using a heel-to-toe movement (placing heel down first).	• Child takes somewhat consistent steps forward. • Child takes many steps that include heel-to-toe movement (as opposed to only toe-walking).	• All of child's steps are consistent in length and width, and child walks with a steady stride. • All of child's steps are heel-to-toe walking; child's heel touches ground first, then middle of foot, then toe.

Sources: Block, 2016; KIDDO, 2019; Singapore Sports Council, 2016a.

What to Emphasize for Walking

What to Emphasize	How to Teach (It is important to first demonstrate or model each movement.)	What to Say (verbal prompts)
Upright posture to maintain balance	• Use verbal prompts.	*Stand tall like a giraffe.*
Heel-to-toe movement	• Do stretching exercises with feet. • Lay a ladder on the floor, or draw lines with painter's tape, for child to step over. • Place a ladder on the floor, or draw lines with chalk or tape, for child to step over. • Simplify each movement: 1) rest heel on floor and hold, 2) rock foot forward so toes touch floor and hold, and 3) repeat in rhythm. • Use verbal prompts.	*Heel first, then toe.* *Heel to toe.* *Swing arms as you step.*
Swinging arms	• Swing alternating arms at side while stepping forward.	*Swing arms as you step.*

Sources: Block, 2016; KIDDO, 2019; Singapore Sports Council, 2016a.

SKILL LEVELING: RUNNING

Running: Child moves swiftly on foot with a *flight phase,* which is when both feet momentarily leave the ground at same time.

	Beginner	Intermediate	Established
Arms	• Child has straight arms. • Child keeps arms straight beside their body or sometimes moves arms to the side or across midline. • Child does not use arms to propel forward.	• Child has slightly bent arms. • Arms sometimes move opposite of forward foot. • Child sometimes moves arms slightly forward and backward, holding them close to body.	• Child has bent, L-shaped arms. • Child swings bent arms forward and back (pumping) close to body. • Child consistently moves opposite arm of forward foot.
Feet, legs, steps	• Child takes uneven steps or flat-footed steps that might resemble fast walking. • Child's stance appears to have feet wide apart for balance. • Child appears to keep one foot on the ground at all times.	• Child attains small lift off ground. • Child displays some extension of trailing leg.	• Child pushes off ball of foot. • Child displays evident lift (flight) between strides when both feet are off the ground. • Child's trailing leg has full extension. • Child leans as forward leg bends with higher knee lift and straightens with each step, pushing body forward. • Step has extension of trailing leg.

Sources: Block, 2016; KIDDO, 2019; Singapore Sports Council, 2016a.

What to Emphasize for Running

What to Emphasize	How to Teach (It is important to first demonstrate or model each movement.)	What to Say (verbal prompts)
Pushing off balls of feet	• Have children walk on toes to help them find the balls of their feet. • Transition from toe-walking to running.	n/a
Swinging arms backward and forward	• Use verbal prompts.	*Pump your arms!*
Slowing down arms and legs when ready to stop	• Have children jog and practice starting and stopping. • Then, slowly increase speed of the jog until child is running.	*Let's jog in place!* *Jog fast! Jog slowly!* *Stop!*

Sources: Block, 2016; KIDDO, 2019; Singapore Sports Council, 2016a.

SKILL LEVELING: BALANCE

STATIC BALANCE

Static balance: Child's body maintains a stable center of gravity and does not move or fall over while balancing on one foot or performing another task (e.g., standing on a moving bus, riding an escalator, getting dressed).

	Beginner	Intermediate	Established
Eyes	• Child's eyes are closed, eyes are focused on feet (looking down), or gaze is unfocused, looking away.	• Child's eyes are open, and eye gaze is focused forward or eyes are looking ahead, focused more on an object, apparatus, or target. • Child may lose balance with closed eyes.	• Child's eyes are focused forward on an external object. • Child maintains balance with eyes closed. • Head is stable.
Arms	• Child displays excessive arm movement. • Child can only balance with support (e.g., hand holding, touching or leaning against wall, touching furniture).	• Child keeps arms tight against body and tense, occasionally raising them for balance.	• Child displays no excessive arm movements and uses arms to counterbalance. • Child uses no object for support while maintaining balance (e.g., holding a hand, touching or leaning on wall).
Torso	• Child's torso wiggles, attaining balance sporadically.	• Child's torso wiggles less; child loses balance less frequently or can maintain balance for longer duration.	• Child keeps trunk stable and upright and maintains balance for duration of task (standing on one foot, putting on clothes).
Legs	• Child exhibits no dominant leg preference when standing on one foot.	• Child begins to show dominant leg preference when standing on one foot.	• Child keeps support leg still and foot flat on ground. • Child's nonsupport leg is raised, bent back, and not touching the support leg.
Feet	• Child cannot stand (maintain stationary balance) on one foot for more that 1–3 seconds without having both feet on the ground.	• Raised foot of nonsupporting leg begins to stay off ground and only touches ground sporadically. • Child's nonsupport foot is resting on the other foot or touching the support leg.	• Child keeps foot of supporting leg flat on the ground for longer duration when completing tasks (standing on one foot, putting on clothing, hopping).

Sources: Block, 2016; Council for the Curriculum, Examinations & Assessment, 2019; KIDDO, 2019; Singapore Sports Council, 2016c.

What to Emphasize for Static Balance

What to Emphasize	How to Teach (It is important to first demonstrate or model each movement.)	What to Say (verbal prompts)
Maintaining level of gravity	• Demonstrate bending knees or arms to lower the center of gravity. • Increase width of base if child is balancing on an object. • Demonstrate focusing eyes on an object. • Demonstrate tightening (contracting) muscles to hold balance.	n/a
Keeping eyes focused forward	• Provide an object or target for child to focus on (e.g., "Look at the clock"). • Use verbal prompts.	*Focus eyes.* *Eyes straight ahead.*
Holding arms still or extended to maintain balance	• To begin, provide a wall or object for child to lean palm against for support; gradually start to remove supporting object. • Use verbal prompts.	*Airplane arms.*
Sources: Block, 2016; Council for the Curriculum, Examinations & Assessment, 2019; KIDDO, 2019; Singapore Sports Council, 2016c.		

DYNAMIC BALANCE

Dynamic balance: Child maintains balance while the body is moving (e.g., while walking, running upstairs, dribbling a ball).

	Beginner	Intermediate	Established
Eyes	• Child's eyes are unfocused or focused on feet.	• Child's eyes are focused downward.	• Child's eyes are focused forward.
Arms	• Child's arms require support of either an object or hand-hold assistance to maintain balance.	• Child's arms move excessively, and momentary balance is attained but not sustained (balance is easily lost).	• Child's arms are outstretched for balance as needed, with very little stability lost.
Torso	• Child's torso is tense and rigid.	• Child's torso is tense and rigid, or torso is wiggling to maintain balance.	• Child's torso is upright and stable, facing forward while maintaining steady balance.
Feet	• Child's feet shuffle-step and remain on the ground or very close to the ground. • Child's dominant foot leads.	• Child begins to demonstrate alternating foot pattern. • Child displays poor spacing of feet.	• Child consistently uses alternating foot pattern. • Child does not pause in between steps (walks fluidly).
Sources: Block, 2016; Council for the Curriculum, Examinations & Assessment, 2019; KIDDO, 2019; Singapore Sports Council, 2016c.			

What to Emphasize for Dynamic Balance

What to Emphasize	How to Teach (It is important to first demonstrate or model each movement.)	What to Say (verbal prompts)
Using arms to maintain balance	• Hold child's arms out to the side and walk in front of or behind them. • Use verbal prompts.	*Airplane arms.*
Alternating feet	• Place footprints or markers along beam or object on which child is walking and balancing. • Increase or decrease the width of line or beam that child is walking and balancing on. • Use verbal prompts.	*Heel-toe.*
Sources: Block, 2016; Council for the Curriculum, Examinations & Assessment, 2019; KIDDO, 2019; Singapore Sports Council, 2016c.		

SKILL LEVELING: JUMPING

JUMPING FOR HEIGHT

Jumping for height: Child makes a vertical jump that requires a one- or two-foot upward takeoff to gain height.

	Beginner	Intermediate	Established
Head and eyes	• Child's head lifts little or not at all, and eye gaze is unfocused.	• Child's head is up and faces forward slightly. • Child's eye gaze is sometimes focused upward.	• Child's head is up. • Child's eye gaze is consistently focused forward.
Arms	• Child's arms may hang loosely down by side when jumping. • Child does not use arms to propel jump or for balance; arms are not coordinated with trunk and leg movement.	• Child's arms move slightly backward and forward when jumping; arms are minimally used to attain consistent balance.	• Child lifts arms upward during flight. • Child's arms move in a fluid and coordinated fashion with the rest of the child's body movements.
Upper body	• Child's upper body is not stretched out at takeoff.	• Child's upper body does not stretch fully during jump. • Child's upper body might lean forward too much, resulting in a forward movement or falling when landing.	• Child's upper body pushes upward into a full-body stretch.
Knees	• Child's knees are stiff and barely bend on takeoff or when landing. • Child is in unstable or wobbly crouch.	• Child bends knees, exceeding 90 degrees, during takeoff and landing. • Child's knees do not thrust upward when extending upward to jump.	• Child's knees are deeply bent (between 60 and 90 degrees) with simultaneous bend at hips. • Child's knees straighten at flight phase.
Feet	• Child lifts only heels of feet or child's feet achieve little height off the ground. • Child's movement looks like a jump forward as opposed to jumping for greater height.	• Child makes two-foot takeoff. • Child's makes an unsteady landing on feet or foot, landing in a different spot from where they began.	• Child pushes off with both feet simultaneously. • Child makes a steady landing on or near the spot where they began.
Sources: Block, 2016; Council for the Curriculum, Examinations & Assessment, 2019; KIDDO, 2020a; Singapore Sports Council, 2016a.			

What to Emphasize for Jumping for Height

What to Emphasize	How to Teach (It is important to first demonstrate or model each movement.)	What to Say (verbal prompts)
Taking off with both feet	• Child can bounce up and down on both feet like a kangaroo. • When bouncing upward, have child raise both hands as if netting a basketball. • Child can bounce on small trampoline. • Use verbal prompts.	*Feet together.* *Jack in the box* (to encourage height).
Bending knees 60 to 90 degrees during crouch	• Encourage bending knees (in crouch position) to jump up to reach a hanging target. • Child can squat up and down without lifting feet off ground to get comfortable with crouch. • Hold child at waist and gently lift child up on count of 3. • Use verbal prompts.	*Bend knees.*
Straightening knees at takeoff and lifting arms upward	• Use verbal prompts.	*Reach for the sky.* *Shoot your rocket into the sky.*
Tilting head upward with eyes fixed ahead	• Hang a target above child's outstretched hands. • Use verbal prompts.	*Eyes ready.* *Head up.* *Look over the fence.*
Controlled landing with two feet close to takeoff point	• Place a floor marker on ground at takeoff and landing point. • Use verbal prompts.	*Feet together.* *Soft landing.* Or: *Quiet feet.*
Sources: Block, 2016; Council for the Curriculum, Examinations & Assessment, 2019; KIDDO, 2020a; Singapore Sports Council, 2016a.		

JUMPING FROM HEIGHT

Jumping from height: Child makes a vertical jump down from an elevated surface that involves taking off and landing on two feet.

	Beginner	Intermediate	Established
Head and eyes	• Child lifts head a little or not at all. • Child's head is down, and eye gaze may be unfocused.	• Child's head is up and faces forward slightly. • Child's eye gaze is focused downward and forward.	• Child's head is up. • Child's eye gaze is consistently focused on target (line, spot on ground).
Arms	• Child's arms hang loosely down by side when jumping. • Child waves arms (or holds onto others) for balance.	• Child's arms flail or move inconsistently in order to achieve balance.	• Child lifts arms upward and out to propel jump while easily maintaining balance. • Child's arms swing forward on landing.
Knees	• Child's knees remain straight with minimal bend.	• Child bends knees slightly, displaying wobbling knees when feet touch ground.	• Child's knees consistently bend for takeoff and then extend straight while jumping. • Child's knees bend slightly upon landing.
Feet	• Child uses one foot to step down. The lead foot touches the ground, while the opposite foot stays in place and then touches the ground.	• Child uses two feet to jump down, but one foot takes the lead in landing on the ground first. • Child uses one foot to land on ground, immediately followed by landing the opposite foot.	• Child uses two feet to jump down and lands on the ground. • Both of child's feet are in air at the same time, and both feet land on the ground at the same time with toes touching the ground first. • Child has a steady landing with feet positioned approximately shoulder-width apart.

Sources: Block, 2016; Council for the Curriculum, Examinations & Assessment, 2019; KIDDO, 2020a; Singapore Sports Council, 2016a.

What to Emphasize for Jumping From Height

What to Emphasize	How to Teach (It is important to first demonstrate or model each movement.)	What to Say (verbal prompts)
Lifting arms outward and then forward during flight phase	• Use verbal prompts.	*Airplane arms.* (arms out) *Reach.* (swing arms forward)
Jumping off with two feet and landing with two feet with toes touching first	• Children pretend that their feet are "glued together." • Place a target on ground for child to jump onto (floor marker). • Use verbal prompts.	*Feet together.*
Extending knees straight during flight and bending upon landing	• Use verbal prompts.	*Feet apart.* *Land on the spot.*

Sources: Block, 2016; Council for the Curriculum, Examinations & Assessment, 2019; KIDDO, 2020a; Singapore Sports Council, 2016a.

JUMPING FOR DISTANCE

Jumping for distance: Child makes a horizontal jump in which they launch themselves forward, taking off and landing on two feet.

	Beginner	Intermediate	Established
Head and eyes	• Child's head is down or turned to the side. • Child's eye gaze is downward rather than forward, or eyes are closed.	• Child's head is up and slightly facing forward. • Child's eye gaze is sometimes focused forward toward target.	• Child's head is up. • Child's eye gaze is consistently focused forward toward target.
Arms	• Child's arm swing is limited. • Child's arms hang loosely by sides when jumping, or arms are "wild" in the air in an attempt to maintain balance.	• Child sometimes uses arms a little to propel jump, moving arms in a backward-upward swing when starting the jump. • Child also may extend arms for balance.	• Child consistently swings arms back and above waist level when starting the jump. • Child swings arms forward and high during the jump.
Upper body	• Body is pushed upward with little emphasis on the length of the jump.	• Body stretches forward slightly to emphasize length of the jump.	• Body is kept at 45 degrees during takeoff with full emphasis on achieving distance. • Child leans slightly forward when landing.
Knees	• Child does not bend knees at all or has limited bend in knees at onset of jump. • Child may land jump with straight legs or minimal knee bend.	• Child more consistently bends knees lower. • Child may try to land jump with straight knees and does not absorb impact.	• Child's knees are consistently bent low in a crouched position at the beginning of the jump. • Child lands with knees slightly bent.
Legs	• Child's legs are not fully stretched at the beginning of the jump.	• Child's legs are sometimes fully stretched at the beginning of the jump.	• Child's legs are fully stretched at the beginning and during the jump.
Feet	• Child's landed feet may appear more like the child is jumping in place as opposed to jumping forward for distance. • Child has difficulty jumping with both feet simultaneously at onset and landing of jump.	• Child may let one foot slightly lead at the beginning of the jump. • Child jumps with a one-footed landing. • Child may make heavy or wobbly landing or fall back on bottom for landing.	• Child uses both feet to push at the beginning of the jump. • Child lands on two feet (toe-ball-heel) in a different spot than where they started. • Child makes gentle landing.

Sources: Block, 2016; Council for the Curriculum, Examinations & Assessment, 2019; KIDDO, 2020a; Singapore Sports Council, 2016a.

What to Emphasize for Jumping for Distance

What to Emphasize	How to Teach (It is important to first demonstrate or model each movement.)	What to Say (verbal prompts)
Bending knees in preparatory crouch and upon landing	• Use verbal prompts.	*Ready position.* *Bend knees.*
Keeping head up, eyes (gaze) forward	• Hold an object a short distance in front of child above eye level. • Use verbal prompts.	*Catch the fly.* *Head up.* *Eyes forward.*
Eye, arm, and knee coordination	• Set up low obstacles on ground and hold a target in front of child. • Child jumps over obstacles while touching the target. • Use verbal prompts.	*Feet apart.* *Land on spot (floor marker).*
Lifting knees and straightening during flight to encourage jumping long distance	• Place a low hurdle in front of child. • Practice taking off from bouncing equipment (e.g., small trampoline).	n/a
Jumping and/or landing on two feet simultaneously	• Have child jump in place with a bean bag or ball in between ankles to encourage jumping with two feet. • Scatter hoops a short distance apart. • Child jumps (with a two-foot takeoff) from one hoop to another. • Use verbal prompts.	*Quiet feet.* *Sticky feet.* *Feet together.* *Heels off floor.*

Sources: Block, 2016; Council for the Curriculum, Examinations & Assessment, 2019; KIDDO, 2020a; Singapore Sports Council, 2016a.

SKILL LEVELING: HOPPING

Hopping: Child takes off on one foot and lands on the same foot in a continuous and rhythmic movement.

	Beginner	Intermediate	Established
Torso	• Child may raise torso or shoulders without actually hopping, make a two-footed jump, or make one or two wobbly hops. • Child's body may appear rigid and straight, or child may overextend (lean to the right or left or forward) in an effort to maintain balance.	• Child's body begins to lean forward, but child lacks full balance.	• Child's body remains in a steady upright position, leaning forward to attain distance while maintaining full balance.
Arms	• Child may hold bent arms to their side or hold a person's hand or wall for balance. • Child may unsuccessfully use arms for balance (may fall).	• Child may flail arms (move arms out or up and down) to maintain balance without holding onto someone or the wall.	• Child swings bent arms while maintaining one-footed balance. • Child swings nonsupporting (bent) leg forward and back to push self off ground and forward.
Legs	• Child may not lift support leg off ground. • Child exhibits a lift and bend of nonsupport leg. • Child's nonsupport leg and thigh remain parallel to floor.	• Child raises nonsupport (bent) leg in front of support (straight) leg.	• Child uses support (straight) leg to push off with the ball of foot.
Feet	• Child tries to push off on balls of feet, making one or two hops with minimal distance or height. • Child may put nonsupporting (bent) leg down after each hop instead of keeping it raised and bent. • Child may lose balance often without support (holding someone's hand or touching wall).	• Child pushes off balls of feet more frequently when using their dominant foot but not with nondominant foot. • Child makes limited number of hops (one to three hops) with inconsistent balance.	• Child can make several (four or more) one-footed hops with each foot without losing balance. • Child's feet land securely on ground, achieving greater distance than previously attained.

Sources: Block, 2016; KIDDO, 2018g; Singapore Sports Council, 2016a.

What to Emphasize for Hopping

What to Emphasize	How to Teach (It is important to first demonstrate or model each movement.)	What to Say (verbal prompts)
Keeping torso straight, leaning slightly forward, and using arms to maintain balance	• Child can use a wall, stable table or chair to lean their lower arms against. • Leader can lend arm or hand for support and walk alongside child as they hop.	n/a
Hopping on one foot	• Arrange footprint markers, floor markers, or poly dots for child to hop on, ensuring that they are spaced close enough for child to hop. • Start with hopping in place (hop twice on left foot, rest, hop twice on right foot). • Child can hold up nonhopping foot. • Use verbal prompts.	*Spring up.* *One foot.* *Lift up* (for supporting foot).
Hopping for distance rather than height	• Place object on ground to hop over (e.g., tape on ground, line in sand, stick or ruler, mini-hurdle). • Place lines or markers on ground as a "goal" for child to reach. • Use verbal prompts.	*Eyes forward.*
Sources: Block, 2016; KIDDO, 2018g; Singapore Sports Council, 2016a.		

SKILL LEVELING: CATCHING

Catching: Child grasps a rolled or thrown object using their fingers and hands. **Note:** *It is important to gradually change the size of the ball or thrown object, starting with objects that are more graspable (e.g., bean bag, underinflated ball), and vary the size of the target and the distance to the person throwing the ball.*

	Beginner	Intermediate	Established
Head and eyes	• Child's head is turned away. • Child's eyes are closed, or their gaze is not on ball (looking away).	• Child's head sometimes faces forward with eyes open for majority of the time the ball is coming. • Child's gaze is sometimes on ball.	• Child's head is consistently facing forward with eyes open, and gaze is always focused on ball.
Arms	• Child's arms hang straight at sides, or arms are close to chest. • Child uses arms to scoop ball close to chest.	• Child's arms are slightly bent and extended slightly in front of chest. • Child "hugs" ball rather than catches it.	• Child's arms are extended in front of them, with elbows bent. • Child extends arms further as ball comes closer to them.
Hands	• If the child's arms are extended, their hands may be in front of their face to block the oncoming ball, or the child may have hands out straight with palms facing up toward the ceiling.	• Child's outstretched hands are positioned in front of them (width of their body) with palms pointing inward. • Child uses chest (not hands) to hold onto the ball after catching it; it looks like child is "hugging" the ball.	• Child extends hands to catch the ball as ball is approaching. • Child's hands may rotate with the ball. • Child uses hands and fingers to support the caught ball.
Fingers	• Child does not use fingers to grasp ball; child may use forearm to catch ball.	• Child uses their whole hand to catch the ball; child may "clap" hands around the ball rather than grasping ball with fingers.	• Child's fingers grasp the ball tightly (fingers curl/bend and fold around the caught ball). • Child catches ball with fingers pointing away from chest.
Feet	• Child's feet are together while standing upright.	• Child has one foot slightly ahead of the other foot while still standing upright. Knees may be slightly bent.	• Child stands with one foot ahead of the other foot and with both knees clearly bent; child is standing balanced in a "ready" position.

Sources: Block, 2016; KIDDO, 2018a, 2018f; Singapore Sports Council, 2016b.

What to Emphasize for Catching

Note: It is important to gradually change the size of the ball or thrown object, starting with objects that are more graspable (e.g., bean bag, underinflated ball), and vary the size of the target and the distance to the person throwing the ball.

What to Emphasize	How to Teach (It is important to first demonstrate or model each movement.)	What to Say (verbal prompts)
Sitting or standing with hands held out in "ready" position	• Scaffold: First catch a rolled ball in seated position, with adult close to child.	*Ready* (hands and/or feet ready).
If standing, keeping one foot slightly ahead of the other in a balanced stance	• Gradually move further away from child. • Repeat with child in a standing position. • Use verbal prompts.	*Set* (eyes on ball). *Catch.*
Keeping eyes focused on ball or thrown object	• Scaffold: Introduce a larger ball and then introduce smaller ones as the child becomes more proficient. • Scaffold: Introduce soft and/or slower-moving objects first, such as stuffed animal, scarves or balloons, to encourage comfort with a moving object. • Scaffold: Introduce underinflated balls (or bean bags) that are more easily grasped than fully inflated balls. • Sit or stand in front of child, in close proximity, and begin by simply passing object back and forth, rather than throwing it. • Use verbal prompts.	*Ready* (hands and/or feet ready). *Set* (eyes on ball). *Catch.*
Extending hands outward to meet the ball	• Count down with child before tossing: *Five, four, three, two, one, catch!* • Use verbal prompts.	*Ready* (hands and/or feet ready). *Set* (eyes on ball). *Catch.*
Wrapping fingers around ball to grasp and pull closer toward chest	Child practices grasping by using squishy/stress ball to squeeze tightly and then relaxes grip in a continuous motion without releasing ball. Note, if the child has difficulty grasping and releasing the ball, consult an occupational therapist for additional grasp-and-release games.	*Grasp* (fingers curl around object). *Release* (fingers uncurl as object is dropped or held in open hand).
Sources: Block, 2016; KIDDO, 2018a, 2018f; Singapore Sports Council, 2016b.		

SKILL LEVELING: OVERHAND THROWING

Overhand throwing: Child throws with hand on top of object. Throwing involves a vertical arm wind up, stepping forward, following through with thrusted object, and a slight knee bend.

	Beginner	Intermediate	Established
Eyes	• Child's gaze is away from target.	• Child's gaze alternates from on target to away from target.	• Child's gaze is consistently on target.
Trunk	• Child's trunk makes no spinal rotation while throwing	• Child's trunk makes a little spinal rotation.	• Child's trunk makes full spinal rotation.
Knees and legs	• Child does not bend knees at all, and legs remain together without stepping forward.	• Child's front knee is slightly bent and legs are slightly separated as they step forward.	• Child's front knee clearly bends during throw; child's knee straightens after throw. • Child's legs are clearly separated as child steps into throw.
Hands and arms	• Child raises hand vertically, holding ball at chest level or beside their head before release of ball. • Child's elbows are tight beside body. • Child's hand/fingers release ball down in front of them or with very little force.	• Child raises hand for a high-arm windup with the ball held behind head. • Child moves, throwing arm forward and down and releasing ball with some force.	• Child uses high-arm windup (leads throw with elbow). • Child bends and holds elbow back behind ear.
Shoulders	• Child does not rotate shoulders at all when throwing.	• Child slightly rotates shoulder of throwing arm a little.	• Child rotates shoulder of throwing arm back so opposite shoulder is in line with target when throwing.
Feet	• Child is balanced with feet together and planted firmly (no stepping forward or transfer of weight from one foot to the other).	• While throwing, child steps forward on the same leg as throwing arm.	• While throwing, child steps with opposite foot, transferring weight from one foot to the other foot.

Sources: Block, 2016; KIDDO, 2018d, 2018k; Singapore Sports Council, 2016b.

What to Emphasize for Overhand Throwing

Note: *It is important to gradually change the size of the ball or thrown object, starting with objects that are more graspable (e.g., bean bag, underinflated ball), and vary the size of the target and the distance to target.*

What to Emphasize	How to Teach (It is important to first demonstrate or model each movement.)	What to Say (verbal prompts)
Preparing for throw	• Have child focus on target with body slightly turned away. • Throwing hand remains behind object, and foot opposite from throwing arm remains forward. • Bring throwing arm back (touch ear) to front. Child performs motion without holding object and then performs motion while holding object without releasing.	n/a
Drawing object back, then pushing object forward while simultaneously stepping opposite foot forward	• Use verbal prompts for drawing object back/pushing forward. • Guide child to step with opposite foot. • Child practices rocking motion. • Place markers on floor where child should step. Place same-color tape on each shoulder, to align with steps. (Throwing arm and opposite foot have blue tape; other arm and foot have red tape.) • Use verbal prompts for stepping with opposite foot.	*Swing back, swing forward.* *Step.* *Other foot.*
Bending front knee when throwing	• Use verbal prompts.	*Bend* (bend front knee).
Aiming at target	• Encourage child to point at target and then throw, to promote aim.	n/a
Following overhand throw sequence: step back, bend elbow and lift arm to behind ear, step forward, release	• Use verbal prompts.	*Ready* (bend and hold elbow back at shoulder height behind ear). *Step* (place opposite foot on floor marker). *Bend* (bend front knee). *Throw* (throw object into bucket/hula hoop).

Sources: Block, 2016; KIDDO, 2018d, 2018k; Singapore Sports Council, 2016b.

SKILL LEVELING: UNDERHAND THROWING AND ROLLING

Underhand throwing/rolling: Child uses a backward-to-forward swing of the hand to release object, while lunging slightly downward, legs spaced apart (vertically), and with knees slightly bent.

	Beginner	Intermediate	Established
Eyes	• Child's eyes remain on ball.	• Child's eyes alternate between looking at ball/throwing object and looking at target.	• Child's eyes remain focused on target.
Trunk	• Child's trunk bends at the waist and body straightens upon release of ball.	• Child's trunk bends slightly and body straightens after throwing.	• Child's trunk slightly turns with throw.
Arms	• Child's arm straightens and swings backward-forward.	• Child's arm swings forward as ball is released between knee and waist level.	• Child's arm swings behind body to waist level and then swings forward for the follow-through with throw (upon release of the ball).
Hands	• Child's hands hold ball on both sides with palms facing each other.	• Child has one hand on top of ball/throwing object and the other hand on bottom of ball.	• Child holds ball, swinging hand/arm with the ball backward and then forward. • Child is holding the ball in hand on opposite side of forward foot.
Feet	• Child remains stationary with feet kept apart.	• Child sometimes steps forward, using foot opposite of hand used to throw ball.	• Child consistently steps forward using foot that is opposite of the hand used to throw the ball. • Child transfers weight from the heel of forward foot to the ball of foot when stepping forward and releasing ball.

Sources: Block, 2016; KIDDO, 2018d, 2018k; Singapore Sports Council, 2016b.

What to Emphasize for Underhand Throwing and Rolling

Note: *It is important to gradually change the size of the ball or thrown object, starting with objects that are more graspable (e.g., bean bag, underinflated ball), and vary the size of the target and the distance to target.*

What to Emphasize	How to Teach (It is important to first demonstrate or model each movement.)	What to Say (verbal prompts)
Facing the direction of the target and focusing on the target	• Instruct child to point at target and then throw or roll.	*Point at target* (aim).

Stepping forward with foot opposite from throwing arm	• Place a line on floor to indicate where to stand. Place a marker on the floor in front of line to indicate where the child should step when throwing or rolling.
	• Teach this sequence:
	  • Hold ball in throwing hand (dominant hand).
	  • Step forward (step on floor marker with nondominant foot).
	  • Swing (arm swings up and back near ear if throwing).
	  • Throw (arm swings forward, releases object with force).
	  • Roll or throw (ball/object rolls or moves toward target).
	• Use verbal prompts for stepping with opposite foot.
	• Use verbal prompts for sequence of moves.
		Step forward (step on floor marker with nondominant foot, opposite of throwing arm).
		Swing (arm swings up and back, near ear).
		Throw (arm swings forward, releases object with force).
		Roll or *throw* (ball/object rolls or moves toward target).
		Step and throw/roll. Once child knows the sequence, prompt can be shortened to *step and throw/roll.*

Snapping wrist forward upon release of ball (or throwing object)	• Simplify underhand throwing movement by having child begin sitting down instead of standing.
	  • Child sits down and rolls underhand.
	  • Child sits with legs straddled and then rolls ball toward target with both hands.
	• Use verbal prompts.
		Palm up (hold ball with palm up, thumb outside).
		Thumb up (turn thumb from outside to top of ball).
		Open up (open hand to release ball at waist).

Following through in the direction of target after throw and release	• Use colorful targets that appeal to child. • Create lanes or lines using rope and/or painter's tape to guide child.	n/a

Sources: Block, 2016; KIDDO, 2018d, 2018k; Singapore Sports Council, 2016b.

SKILL LEVELING: TWO-HANDED THROWING

Two-handed throwing: Child uses a forward swing with weight transfer from rear to front foot, releasing ball at knee level or below.

	Beginner	Intermediate	Established
Eyes	• Child's trunk is still and rigid with no hip rotation; trunk of body leans backward before flexing forward.	• Child's trunk has a little hip rotation; body leans slightly backward before releasing ball.	• Trunk has full hip rotation; body swings forward with full weight transfer.
Trunk	• Child's knees are not bent, and legs remain in upright position.	• Child sometimes has slightly bent knees, lunging forward.	• Child consistently has slightly bent knees when weight transfers to front foot as ball is released.
Knees	• Child's trunk is still and rigid with no hip rotation; trunk of body leans backward before flexing forward.	• Child's trunk has little hip rotation; body leans slightly backward before releasing ball.	• Trunk has full hip rotation; body swings forward with full weight transfer.
Hands and arms	• Child sometimes holds ball high (near head) or low (below waist) with both hands/elbow slightly bent.	• Child sometimes holds ball in front of chest. • During throw, child's arms straighten and ball is slightly pushed or released.	• Child consistently holds ball in front of chest. • During throw, child uses arms to strongly push ball out at chest level, transferring force from shoulder to arms to hand.
Feet	• Child remains stationary with feet slightly apart. Feet are not stationary.	• Child's feet are somewhat stationary as child leans forward to throw ball.	• Child consistently steps forward with one foot while throwing.
Sources: Block, 2016; Singapore Sports Council, 2016b.			

What to Emphasize for Two-Handed Throwing

Note: It is important to gradually change the size of the ball or thrown object, starting with objects that are more graspable (e.g., bean bag, underinflated ball), and vary the size of the target and the distance to target.

What to Emphasize	How to Teach (It is important to first demonstrate or model each movement.)	What to Say (verbal prompts)
Holding ball to chest	• Child performs motion without holding object and then holding object without releasing • Use verbal prompts.	*Ball to chest* (bend elbows, hands to chest).
Bending knees, then leaning forward	• Use verbal prompts.	*Bend* (bend at the knee).
Stepping with front foot	• Child performs motion and rocks back and forth • Place markers on the floor. Child places front foot on the floor marker while leaning forward. • Use verbal prompts.	*Step* (one foot steps forward).
Aiming at target	• Encourage child to point at target and then throw to promote aim.	*Point at target* (aim).
Following two-hand throw sequence	• Child lifts ball to chest, bends at the knees, steps forward, and throws. • Use verbal prompts.	*Ball to chest* (bend elbows, hands to chest). *Bend* (bend at the knee). *Step* (one foot steps forward). *Throw* (child throws object into bucket/ hula hoop).
Sources: Block, 2016; Singapore Sports Council, 2016b.		

SKILL LEVELING: TWO-HANDED STRIKING OF A STATIONARY OBJECT

Two-handed striking: Child swings an object, such as a bat or racquet, at an object and makes contact with enough force to move the object.

	Beginner	Intermediate	Established
Head and eyes	• Child's head is turned away. • Child's eyes are closed, or eye gaze is not focused on object (ball on T-ball stand).	• Child's head is sometimes facing the ball on T-ball stand. • Child's eyes are open, and eye gaze is sometimes focused on the object.	• Child's head faces the T-ball stand. • Child's eye gaze is consistently on the object.
Feet	• Child's feet are close together.	• Child's feet are sometimes shoulder-length apart.	• Child's feet are consistently shoulder-length apart.
Knees	• Child's knees are straight/stiff (not bent).	• Child's knees are sometimes bent.	• Child's knees are consistently bent.
Arms and elbows	• Child's arms remain stationary while holding bat. • Child's arms move downward in chopping motion during swing.	• Child's arms are close to body while holding bat. • Child's arms move horizontally during swing.	• Child's arms raise to hold bat at shoulder level. • Child's elbows are bent at 90 degrees. • Child's arms follow through with swing.
Hands and fingers	• Child's fingers of one or both hands loosely grasp the bat.	• Child's fingers (of both hands) grasp the bat. • Child's wrists/hands follow the swing but without rotation.	• Child's fingers of both hands firmly grasp bat. • Child's fingers of nondominant hand are below the first hand. • Child's wrists/hands follow through (rotate) with the swing.
Trunk and hips	• Child's trunk and hips remain stationary with no transfer of weight.	• Child sometimes rotates trunk and hips while striking ball. • Child's trunk movement is uncoordinated, or child loses balance. • Child's trunk turns away from ball before swing.	• Child consistently rotates trunk, hips, and shoulders smoothly with swing; there is transfer of weight from back to front with swing. • Child has trunk rotation with follow-through while completing swing.

Sources: Block, 2016; Jelly Bean Sports, 2017; Kayden, 2020; Singapore Sports Council, 2016b.

What to Emphasize for Two-Handed Striking of a Stationary Object

What to Emphasize	How to Teach (It is important to first demonstrate or model each movement.)	What to Say (verbal prompts)
Facing the direction of the object and focusing on the object	• Use a preferred object, such as a ball that is the child's favorite color or allow the child to choose the object. • Use stickers, tape, or markers to put a target or bullseye on the ball. • Use verbal prompts.	*Eyes on the ball!*
Aiming and making bat-ball contact	• Use a large stationary ball held in place on a cone, then a small stationary ball held in place on a cone, and then a large moving ball (e.g., beach ball, playground ball). • Children who have trouble aiming can practice while sitting in a chair.	n/a
Standing steadily with feet slightly apart	• Place floor markers where the child's feet should be.	n/a
Bending elbows before swinging	• Use verbal prompts.	*Have chicken wing arms! Cluck, cluck!*
Practicing the individual movements of striking until movements can be done smoothly	• Use verbal prompts.	*Ready* (eyes on ball, feet apart). *Set* (bend knees, raise bat over shoulder). *Swing* (step, swing).
Following through with the swing	• Use verbal prompts.	*Chase the ball with your bat!*
Sources: Block, 2016; Jelly Bean Sports, 2017; Kayden, 2020; Singapore Sports Council, 2016b.		

SKILL LEVELING: KICKING A STATIONARY OBJECT

Kicking: Child uses their foot to exert force on an object.

	Beginner	Intermediate	Established
Head and eyes	• Child's head is turned, child shies away from ball, eyes are closed, or gaze is not focused on object.	• Child's head sometimes faces downward with open eyes, and gaze is sometimes focused on ball.	• Child's head faces downward. • Child's gaze is consistently on the ball.
Hips and trunk	• Child's trunk remains stationary. • Child's hips are not turned to the side.	• Child's hips and trunk slightly turn to the side. • Child's trunk shows no follow-through with kick.	• Child consistently turns hips and trunk to the side. • Child's trunk follows through with kick.
Arms	• Child's arms hang down straight by side, or arms are held close to chest.	• Child's arms sway slightly to the side, or arms sway close to chest.	• Child's arms sway to the side, and arms sway loosely by chest in opposition to legs.
Legs and knees	• Child's legs are stationary, or dominant (kicking) leg is lifted but not extended outward, or dominant (kicking) leg is lifted and briefly/barely extended.	• Child keeps one leg somewhat stationary. • Child's dominant leg is lifted and slightly extended outward. • Child extends dominant leg out. • Child's legs and knees show little to no follow-through.	• Child firmly plants one leg. • Child's dominant leg is lifted and extended outward. • Child bends knee back before swinging forward. • Child's leg follows through with kick.
Feet	• Child's foot does not connect with ball. • Child kicks using toes.	• Child's foot sometimes makes contact with ball. • Child's foot is pointed outward; bottom of foot faces ball.	• Child's foot consistently strikes ball. • Child's dominant foot is pointed outward and toward the object. • Child kicks using inside of foot. • Child's nondominant foot is beside or slightly behind ball.

Sources: Block, 2016; KIDDO, 2020b; Singapore Sports Council, 2016b; Sturridge, 2015.

What to Emphasize for Kicking a Stationary Object

What to emphasize	How to teach (It is important to first demonstrate/ model each movement.)	What to say (verbal prompts)
Extending one leg outward and pointing foot toward object	• Provide practice while using verbal prompts. • Use verbal prompts.	*Kick!*
Keeping eyes on the ball and extending toes when kicking	• Tie a ribbon around the child's shoe or put a sticker on their shoelaces. • Tell the child to kick the ball with the ribbon/sticker.	n/a
Aiming for the center of the ball	• Put a sticker or piece of tape in the middle of the ball, where the child should aim.	n/a
Practicing each stage of kicking	• Demonstrate each movement. • Use verbal prompts.	*Step* (place nondominant foot beside ball). *Swing* (swing dominant foot at ball while balancing on nondominant foot). *Kick* (with inside of foot or shoelaces).
Sources: Block, 2016; KIDDO, 2020b; Singapore Sports Council, 2016b; Sturridge, 2015.		

RESOURCES FOR PRESCHOOL MOTOR DEVELOPMENT: GENERAL

A Teacher's Guide to Adapted Physical Education, Fourth Edition (book and downloadable resources)
Block, M. E. (2016). *A teacher's guide to adapted physical education* (4th ed.). Paul H. Brookes Publishing Co.

Active Start: A Statement of Physical Activity Guidelines for Children From Birth to Age 5, Third Edition
Visit this link to obtain this resource from the Digital Download Library of the Society of Health and Physical Educators (SHAPE) America: https://www.shapeamerica.org/standards/guidelines/activestart.aspx

Active Start—Physical Activity Guidelines for Children Birth to 5 Years
Visit this link to obtain this resource created by the National Association for Sport and Physical Education (NASPE): https://cecpdonline.org/wp-content/uploads/2016/05/08-NAPSE-Guidelines.pdf

Active Start—Why Active Play Is So Important
Visit this link to read this article from the Interprovincial Sport and Recreation Council of Manitoba, Canada: https://sportforlife.ca/wp-content/uploads/2016/12/Why-Active-Play-is-so-Important-Active-Start.pdf

Early Childhood Activities
Visit this link to obtain activity guides for infants, toddlers, and preschoolers, available from the Digital Download Library of SHAPE America: https://www.shapeamerica.org//publications/resources/downloads-earlyChildhood.aspx

Kid Sense: Gross Motor Activities and Gross Motor Developmental Checklist
Visit this link to read the Kid Sense Child Development Corporation web page on gross motor activities: https://childdevelopment.com.au/areas-of-concern/gross-motor-skills/gross-motor-activities/

Visit this link on the same website for a developmental checklist for gross motor skills: https://childdevelopment.com.au/resources/child-development-charts/gross-motor-developmental-checklist/

KIDDO Challenge: Online Fundamental Movement Skills Assessment and Reporting Tool
Visit the link to watch a video about how to use this assessment from KIDDO, created by professionals in exercise and sports science in the School of Human Sciences at the University of Western Australia (August 19, 2019): https://www.youtube.com/watch?v=drMusOG3-vA

National Association for Sport and Physical Education (NASPE): Appropriate Practices in Movement Programs for Children Ages 3–5
Visit the California Association for Health, Physical Education, Recreation, and Dance web page on NASPE Appropriate Practices: https://www.cahperd.org/Public/Advocacy/NASPE_Appropriate_Practices

Click on the first link on this page to download a PDF of appropriate practices for children ages 3–5.

Singapore Ministry of Education: Preschool Motor Skills Development
Visit the Singapore Ministry of Education's web page on the Nurturing Early Learners (NEL) Framework: https://www.moe.gov.sg/preschool/curriculum

Review the information on this page about motor skills development.

RESOURCES FOR SPECIFIC SKILLS

Walking

My Active Singapore: Walking
Visit the Singapore Sports Council: My ActiveSG web page on Locomotor Skills for Kids: https://www.myactivesg.com/read/2016/11/locomotor-skills

Click on the Walking link for a PDF guide on walking.

Running

Active for Life: Sprinting
Visit the link to read the article "Running: How to Teach Kids to Sprint Correctly" at the Active for Life website: https://activeforlife.com/teach-kids-to-sprint-correctly/

Developing Fundamental Movement Skills: Sprint Run

Visit the Council for the Curriculum, Examinations and Assessment (2019) website for Northern Ireland, Curriculum page: https://ccea.org.uk/about/what-we-do/curriculum

Follow the links to curricula for the foundation stage (ages 4–6). Click on Physical Development and Movement, and then click to explore the resources for Developing Fundamental Movement Skills. These resources include a PDF guide on sprinting.

KIDDO Challenge: Learn How to Run

Visit the link to watch the video "Learn How to Run" from KIDDO, created by professionals in exercise and sports science in the School of Human Sciences at the University of Western Australia (June 20, 2018): https://www.youtube.com/watch?v=Ly-Zh-rXeh4

My Active Singapore: Running

Visit the Singapore Sports Council: My ActiveSG web page on Locomotor Skills for Kids: https://www.myactivesg.com/read/2016/11/locomotor-skills

Click on the Running link for a PDF guide on running.

Singapore Ministry of Education: Preschool Motor Skills Development

Visit the Singapore Ministry of Education's web page on the Nurturing Early Learners (NEL) Framework: https://www.moe.gov.sg/preschool/curriculum

Review the information on this page about motor skills development. Click on the Running link for a PDF guide on running.

Balance

Active Start–Developing Agility, Balance, and Coordination

Visit this link to read an article from the Interprovincial Sport and Recreation Council of Manitoba, Canada: https://www.gov.mb.ca/mh/activeliving/tools_resources/early_years/active_start1.pdf

Developing Fundamental Movement Skills: Balance

Visit the Council for the Curriculum, Examinations and Assessment website for Northern Ireland, Curriculum page: https://ccea.org.uk/about/what-we-do/curriculum

Follow the links to curricula for the foundation stage (ages 4–6). Click on Physical Development and Movement, and then click to explore the resources for Developing Fundamental Movement Skills (https://ccea.org.uk/learning-resources/developing-fundamental-movement-skills).

This resource includes a PDF guide on balance: https://ccea.org.uk/document/1762

KIDDO Challenge: Learn How to Balance

Visit the link to watch the video "Learn How to Balance" from KIDDO, created by professionals in exercise and sports science in the School of Human Sciences at the University of Western Australia (June 21, 2018): https://www.youtube.com/watch?v=Ly-Zh-rXeh4

My Active Singapore: Static Balance

Visit the Singapore Sports Council: My ActiveSG web page on Stability Skills for Kids: https://www.myactivesg.com/read/2016/11/stability-skills

Click on the Static Balance link for a PDF guide on static balance.

My Active Singapore: Dynamic Balance

Visit the Singapore Sports Council: My ActiveSG web page on Stability Skills for Kids: https://www.myactivesg.com/read/2016/11/stability-skills

Click on the Dynamic Balance link for a PDF guide on dynamic balance.

The Inspired Treehouse: The Best Balance Activities for Kids

Visit this link to read the article "The Best Balance Activities for Kids" at the website The Inspired Treehouse: https://theinspiredtreehouse.com/child-development-balance/

Jumping

Developing Fundamental Movement Skills: Jump for Distance

Visit the Council for the Curriculum, Examinations and Assessment (2019) website for Northern Ireland, Curriculum page: https://ccea.org.uk/about/what-we-do/curriculum

Follow the links to curricula for the foundation stage (ages 4–6). Click on Physical Development and Movement, and then click to explore the resources for Developing Fundamental Movement Skills (https://ccea.org.uk/learning-resources/developing-fundamental-movement-skills).

This resource includes a PDF guide on jumping for distance: https://ccea.org.uk/document/1765

Developing Fundamental Movement Skills: Jump for Height

Visit the Council for the Curriculum, Examinations and Assessment (2019) website for Northern Ireland, Curriculum page: https://ccea.org.uk/about/what-we-do/curriculum

Follow the links to curricula for the foundation stage (ages 4–6). Click on Physical Development and Movement, and then click to explore the resources for Developing Fundamental Movement Skills (https://ccea.org.uk/learning-resources/developing-fundamental-movement-skills).

This resource includes a PDF guide on jumping for height: https://ccea.org.uk/document/1766

KIDDO Challenge Videos on Jumping Skills

Visit the following links to watch videos on jumping skills from KIDDO, created by professionals in exercise and sports science in the School of Human Sciences at the University of Western Australia.

"Learn How to Jump" (June 20, 2018): https://www.youtube.com/watch?v=P1jGqZFtJ9I

"Developing the Skill of Jumping" (January 7, 2020): https://www.youtube.com/watch?v=Hoz2m7gvroo

"Learn How to Hop" (June 21, 2018): https://www.youtube.com/watch?v=R8VABKvS3c0

My Active Singapore: Jumping for Height

Visit the Singapore Sports Council: My ActiveSG web page on Locomotor Skills for Kids: https://www.myactivesg.com/read/2016/11/locomotor-skills

Click on the Jumping for Height link for a PDF guide on this skill.

My Active Singapore: Jumping From Height

Visit the Singapore Sports Council: My ActiveSG web page on Locomotor Skills for Kids: https://www.myactivesg.com/read/2016/11/locomotor-skills

Click on the Jumping From Height link for a PDF guide on this skill.

My Active Singapore: Jumping for Distance

Visit the Singapore Sports Council: My ActiveSG web page on Locomotor Skills for Kids: https://www.myactivesg.com/read/2016/11/locomotor-skills

Click on the Jumping for Distance link for a PDF guide on this skill.

The Gumbo Gang–Lesson: Jumping and Landing

Visit the Gumbo Gang website for a lesson in basic jumping and landing skills: http://gumbogang.com/lesson-jumping-landing/

Hopping

Visit the Council for the Curriculum, Examinations and Assessment (2019) website for Northern Ireland, Curriculum page: https://ccea.org.uk/about/what-we-do/curriculum

Follow the links to curricula for the foundation stage (ages 4–6). Click on Physical Development and Movement, and then click to explore the resources for Developing Fundamental Movement Skills (https://ccea.org.uk/learning-resources/developing-fundamental-movement-skills).

This resource includes a PDF guide on jumping and hopping.

KIDDO Challenge Videos on Hopping Skills

Visit the following link to watch a video on hopping skills from KIDDO, created by professionals in exercise and sports science in the School of Human Sciences at the University of Western Australia.

"Learn How to Hop" (June 21, 2018): https://www.youtube.com/watch?v=R8VABKvS3c0

My Active Singapore: Hopping

Visit the Singapore Sports Council: My ActiveSG web page on Locomotor Skills for Kids: https://www.myactivesg .com/read/2016/11/locomotor-skills

Click on the Hopping link for a PDF guide on this skill.

Catching

Developing Fundamental Movement Skills: Catch

Visit the Council for the Curriculum, Examinations and Assessment (2019) website for Northern Ireland, Curriculum page: https://ccea.org.uk/about/what-we-do/curriculum

Follow the links to curricula for the foundation stage (ages 4–6). Click on Physical Development and Movement. Then, click to explore the resources for Developing Fundamental Movement Skills (https://ccea.org.uk/learning-resources/ developing-fundamental-movement-skills).

This resource includes a PDF guide on catching: https://ccea.org.uk/document/1763

Developmental Steps to Teaching Your Child to Catch

Visit the North Shore Pediatric Therapy website to read "7 Developmental Steps to Teaching Your Child to Catch" by Lindsey Moyer, available at the following link: http://nspt4kids.com/parenting/7-developmental-steps-to-teaching-your-child-to-catch/

KIDDO Challenge Videos on Catching

Visit the following links to watch videos on catching from KIDDO, created by professionals in exercise and sports science in the School of Human Sciences at the University of Western Australia.

"Learn How to Catch" (June 21, 2018): https://www.youtube.com/watch?v=toiCHNtXVKw

"Assessing the Fundamental Movement Skill of Catching" (June 25, 2018): https://www.youtube.com/ watch?v=JiTfq98CEgk

My Active Singapore: Catching

Visit the Singapore Sports Council: My ActiveSG web page on Locomotor Skills for Kids: https://www.myactivesg .com/read/2016/11/locomotor-skills

Click on the Catching link for a PDF guide on this skill.

Throwing

Ball Skills

Visit the following web page on the Australian Capital Territory Government's website for a PDF on ball skills: https:// health.act.gov.au/sites/default/files/2019-08/AP%20Ball%20Skills.pdf

KIDDO Challenge Videos on Throwing

Visit the following links to watch videos on catching from KIDDO, created by professionals in exercise and sports science in the School of Human Sciences at the University of Western Australia.

"Learn How to Throw" (June 20, 2018): https://www.youtube.com/watch?v=vi8NGXOqZlg

"Assessing the Fundamental Movement Skill of Throwing" (June 25, 2018): https://www.youtube.com/ watch?v=YqouziDKCoM

My Active Singapore: Overhand Throw

Visit the Singapore Sports Council: My ActiveSG web page on Object Control Skills for Kids: https://www.myactivesg .com/read/2016/11/object-control-skills

Click on the Overarm Throwing link for a PDF guide on this skill.

My Active Singapore: Two-Handed Throwing

Visit the Singapore Sports Council: My ActiveSG web page on Object Control Skills for Kids: https://www.myactivesg.com/read/2016/11/object-control-skills

Click on the Two-handed Throwing link for a PDF guide on this skill.

My Active Singapore: Underarm Throwing

Visit the Singapore Sports Council: My ActiveSG web page on Object Control Skills for Kids: https://www.myactivesg.com/read/2016/11/object-control-skills

Click on the Underarm Throwing link for a PDF guide on this skill.

My Active Singapore: Underarm Rolling

Visit the Singapore Sports Council: My ActiveSG web page on Object Control Skills for Kids: https://www.myactivesg.com/read/2016/11/object-control-skills

Click on the Underarm Rolling link for a PDF guide on this skill.

Queensland School Council: Throwing and Catching Module

Visit the Queensland Curriculum and Assessment Authority website for Queensland Government, Australia: https://www.qcaa.qld.edu.au

Resources for educators (available at https://www.qcaa.qld.edu.au/downloads/p_10) include a link to an instructional module PDF for throwing and catching: https://www.qcaa.qld.edu.au/downloads/p_10/kla_hpe_sbm_207.pdf

Striking

Visit the How They Play website to read Brad Kayden's article "How to Teach Young Children to Hit a Baseball": https://howtheyplay.com/team-sports/How-to-Teach-Young-Children-to-Hit-a-Baseball

Visit the link to watch the following video on teaching young children to hit a baseball, created by Jelly Bean Sports.

"How to Teach Young Children to Hit a Baseball" (February 22, 2017): https://www.youtube.com/watch?v=nSpMrNEWkYU

My Active Singapore: Two-Handed Sidearm Striking

Visit the Singapore Sports Council: My ActiveSG web page on Object Control Skills for Kids: https://www.myactivesg.com/read/2016/11/object-control-skills

Click on the Two-Handed Sidearm Striking link for a PDF guide on this skill.

Kicking

KIDDO Challenge Videos on Kicking

Visit the following links to watch videos on kicking from KIDDO, created by professionals in exercise and sports science in the School of Human Sciences at the University of Western Australia.

"Developing the Skill of Kicking" (January 7, 2020): https://www.youtube.com/watch?v=oUn5wJZJm-M

"Assessing the Fundamental Movement Skill of Kicking (Soccer)" (June 25, 2018): https://www.youtube.com/watch?v=MnP9GkdhEQg

My Active Singapore: Kicking

Visit the Singapore Sports Council: My ActiveSG web page on Object Control Skills for Kids: https://www.myactivesg.com/read/2016/11/object-control-skills

Click on the Kicking link for a PDF guide on this skill.

How to Kick a Ball

Visit *The Guardian*'s website to read English football player Daniel Sturridge's 2015 article "How to Kick a Ball," available at this link: http://www.theguardian.com/lifeandstyle/2015/jun/20/daniel-sturridge-how-to-kick-a-ball

Classroom Inventory for Motor Play Materials, With Resources

Check items that you have in your classroom or school that can be used during CHAMPPS.

Teacher's Name: _____ Number of Children: _____ Number of Adults: _____

	Materials **Note:** Examples of materials we have found helpful are listed below. Most are available through retailers that provide exercise equipment for children (Flaghouse.com, Gymhouse.com) or through general online retailers such as Amazon or Sears. Most items are available in various sizes; choose the sizes that best fit the needs of the children you teach.	Substitution List or circle materials you have that can be used as a substitute for the item listed under Materials. Use the listed examples to spark ideas.	Check (√) each item you have in your class or school (to share with other teachers).
1	Nonskid floor markers (to indicate where to stand or a trail to follow) *Brand names: Various*		
2	Cones (to mark a designated spot or to make hurdles) *Brand names: Alyoen and Flaghouse*	Milk jug filled with sand/pebbles	
3	Nonskid stepping blocks (low and high heights) for hurdles *Brand name: Makarci*	Yoga blocks	
4	Poles (two), to attach to blocks or cones for hurdles *Brand name: Agora*	Yard stick, gift wrap roll, jump rope, string, yarn	
5	Balance beam *Brand name: Zeny*	Tape on floor, drawn line on ground, cardboard strip	
6	Large hula hoops (to crawl through) *Brand name: WZHHYY*	Cardboard boxes, kitchen table, two chairs with a blanket between them to form a tunnel	
7	Small hoops (to throw balls and beanbags through) *Brand name: Alyoen*	Inner tubes, tires, pool noodle circles	
8	Scarves *Brand name: HKACSTHI*	Ribbon wands, cloth napkins, kitchen towels, pompoms	
9	Beanbags *Brand names: Alyoen, GSI, Educational Insights*	Small stuffed animals, yarn balls, sand-filled balloons, sand-/pebble-filled socks or mittens	
10	Large- and medium-sized balls *Brand names: Various*	Soccer balls, playground balls	
11	Small-sized balls *Brand names: Rhode Island Novelty and others*	Tennis balls, Nerf balls, soft rubber balls	
12	Inflatable balls *Brand names: VCOSTORE beach balls and others*	Beach balls	
13	Paddles, Bats, Hockey Sticks (for striking) *Brand names: Gym Closet Foam Lollipop Paddles, Flaghouse Softee Hockey Stick, Flaghouse Heavy Duty Plastic Rainbow Giant Bat Set*	Short sticks, wiffle bats, plastic bats, hockey sticks appropriate for preschool age children (e.g., small grip, shortened length)	

Classroom Inventory for Motor Play Materials, With Resources (continued)

	Materials	Substitution List or circle materials you have that can be used as a substitute for the item listed under Materials. Use the listed examples to spark ideas.	Check (√) each item you have in your class.
1	CD player; tape or record player	Karaoke machine, computer with speakers	
2	Music tapes/CDs/records of at least three different music styles (e.g., jazz, classical, children's music)	Songs taught to children without CD, tape, or record player	
3	Musical/rhythm instruments (enough for each child to have one)	Maracas, music sticks, jingle sticks, bells, mini tambourines	
4	Internet access (for YouTube videos)		
5	iPad		
6	Smartboard	Projector with Internet connection, screen or sheet attached to wall	

Resources for Musical Motor Activities—Videos

Search online for the following recommended video resources, available for free via YouTube or for purchase on DVD. The content creators Patty Shukla, Children Love to Sing, and The Learning Station have extensive musical resources, available for purchase on DVD or CD, that you may wish to explore further.

Unit	Online Video Resources
Unit 1 Foundational Skills: Body Awareness, Motor Imitation, and Visual Tracking	"Shake and Move" (DVD) From Shukla, P. (2011). *Musical PE for you and me, volume 1* [DVD]. Shukla Music. "Stand Up, Sit Down" (DVD) From Shukla, P. (2011). *Musical PE for you and me, volume 1* [DVD]. Shukla Music. "Move and Freeze" (YouTube video) The Learning Station. (2016, November 17). *Move and freeze* [Video]. YouTube. https://www.youtube.com/watch?v=gE7zCfxJ7bE
Unit 2 Walking and Running	"Hearty Fun" (YouTube video) Children Love to Sing. (2013, May 12). *Hearty fun* [Video]. YouTube. https://www.youtube.com/watch?v=GzvJhCBH80U "Cruisin' Down the Freeway" (YouTube video) Children Love to Sing. (2008, October 10). *Cruisin' down the freeway* [Video]. YouTube. https://www.youtube.com/watch?v=FrkK7gPvWiY
Unit 3 Balance, Jumping, and Hopping	"JUMP!" From Shukla, P. (2011). *Musical PE for you and me, volume 1* (DVD). Shukla Music. "Cool Sports Fitness Song" (YouTube video) Children Love to Sing. (2013, July 30). *Cool Sports Fitness Song* [Video]. YouTube. https://www.youtube.com/watch?v=tlORtqkZoFk
Unit 4 Catching	"The Penguin Song" (YouTube video) The Learning Station. (2014, December 30). *The Penguin Song* [Video]. YouTube. https://www.youtube.com/watch?v=_FEpPjhVtdc "Touch the Stars" (YouTube video) Children Love to Sing. (2009, October 6). *Touch the stars* [Video]. YouTube. https://youtu.be/UIaUoKRE4vc
Unit 5 Throwing	"Happy Dance" (YouTube video) The Learning Station. (2015, February 20). *Happy dance* [Video]. YouTube. https://youtu.be/cQ6BPWyIueQ?t=14s "Swimming Song" (YouTube video) The Learning Station. (2015, May 29). *Swimming song* [Video]. YouTube. https://youtu.be/ZsaywRY5iP0?t=14s
Unit 6 Striking	"Do Your Chores" (YouTube video) Children Love to Sing. (2013, February 18). *Do your chores* [Video]. YouTube. https://youtu.be/w_gpl2SDApc "Rumba Dance" (YouTube video) The Learning Station. (2014, April 22). *Rumba dance* [Video]. YouTube. https://youtu.be/7R64sBEi-7I?t=14s
Unit 7 Kicking	"Head, Shoulders, Knees & Toes" (YouTube video) The Learning Station. (2017, April 21). *Head, shoulders, knees & toes* [Video]. YouTube. https://youtu.be/7R64sBEi-7I?t=14s "Hokey Pokey Kids' Dance Song" (YouTube video) The Learning Station. (2014, January 28). *Hokey Pokey Kids' dance song* [Video]. YouTube. https://youtu.be/iZinb6rVozc?t=13s

Criteria for Selecting Physical Activity Music Videos

Unit 1   Foundational Skills: Body Awareness, Motor Imitation, and Visual Tracking

Criteria: Insert check (√) if the video meets the criteria.	Video	Video	Video
1. **Insert name or link** to video (YouTube or other online source).			
2. The video is **age appropriate for preschool children** (content, vocabulary).			
3. The **movements are modeled** by people or cartoons/characters.			
4. The **movements seen match the words or directions used** in the video.			
5. The video incorporates different **positional words** (*over, under, up, down*). **List** positional concepts used.			
6. The video incorporates different **body parts** (e.g., fingers, toes, knees, legs, arms). **List** body parts used.			
7. The video uses **action words or vocabulary** (*kick, throw, catch, walk*) that **match the unit objectives. List** action words used.			
8. The video is current, representing **diversity** in images (e.g., if children are present in video, children represent human differences). **List** all examples of diversity that apply: race (R), ethnicity (E), abilities (A), languages (L), gender (G), and (O) other.			
9. The video **encourages only acceptable behaviors** and **does not** encourage behaviors that might be considered violent, scary, unsafe, or offensive in some families (e.g., jumping on bed, hitting others).			
10. The video is **at least 2 minutes** in duration with **continuous movement but does not exceed 4 minutes.**			
11. Is the video available as a **DVD? Insert link** to purchase.			

Criteria for Selecting Physical Activity Music Videos *(continued)*

Unit 2   Walking and Running

Criteria: Insert check (√) if the video meets the criteria.	Video	Video	Video
1. Insert name or link to video (YouTube or other online source).			
2. The video is age appropriate for preschool children (in content, vocabulary).			
3. The movements are modeled by people or cartoons/ characters.			
4. The movements seen match the words or directions used in the video.			
5. The video incorporates different positional words (over, under, up, down). List positional concepts used.			
6. The video incorporates different body parts (e.g., fingers, toes, knees, legs, arms). List body parts used.			
7. The video uses action words or vocabulary (kick, throw, catch, walk) that matches the unit objectives. List action words used.			
8. The video is current, representing diversity in images (e.g., if children are present in video, children represent human differences). List all examples of diversity that apply: race (R), ethnicity (E), abilities (A), languages (L), and gender (G).			
9. The video encourages only acceptable behaviors and does not encourage behaviors that might be considered violent, scary, unsafe, or offensive in some families (e.g., jumping on bed, hitting others).			
10. The video is at least 2 minutes in duration with continuous movement but does not exceed 4 minutes.			
11. Is the video available as a DVD? Insert link to purchase.			

Criteria for Selecting Physical Activity Music Videos *(continued)*

Unit 3 Balance, Jumping, and Hopping

Criteria: Insert check (√) if the video meets the criteria.	Video	Video	Video
1. **Insert name or link** to video (YouTube or other online source).			
2. The video is **age appropriate for preschool children** (in content, vocabulary).			
3. The **movements are modeled** by people or cartoons/characters.			
4. The **movements seen match the words or directions used** in the video.			
5. The video incorporates different **positional words** (*over, under, up, down*). **List** positional concepts used.			
6. The video incorporates different **body parts** (e.g., fingers, toes, knees, legs, arms). **List** body parts used.			
7. The video uses **action words or vocabulary** (*kick, throw, catch, walk*) that **matches the unit objectives. List** action words used.			
8. The video is current, representing **diversity** in images (e.g., if children are present in video, children represent human differences). **List** all examples of diversity that apply: race (R), ethnicity (E), abilities (A), languages (L), and gender (G).			
9. The video **encourages only acceptable behaviors** and **does not** encourage behaviors that might be considered violent, scary, unsafe, or offensive in some families (e.g., jumping on bed, hitting others).			
10. The video is **at least 2 minutes** in duration with **continuous movement** but does not exceed 4 minutes.			
11. Is the video available as a **DVD? Insert link** to purchase.			

Criteria for Selecting Physical Activity Music Videos *(continued)*

Unit 4 Catching

Criteria: Insert check (√) if the video meets the criteria.	Video	Video	Video
1. **Insert name or link** to video (YouTube or other online source).			
2. The video is **age appropriate for preschool children** (in content, vocabulary).			
3. The **movements are modeled** by people or cartoons/characters.			
4. The **movements seen match the words or directions used** in the video.			
5. The video incorporates different **positional words** (*over, under, up, down*). **List** positional concepts used.			
6. The video incorporates different **body parts** (e.g., fingers, toes, knees, legs, arms). **List** body parts used.			
7. The video uses **action words or vocabulary** (*kick, throw, catch, walk*) that **matches the unit objectives. List** action words used.			
8. The video is current, representing **diversity** in images (e.g., if children are present in video, children represent human differences). **List** all that examples of diversity that apply: race (R), ethnicity (E), abilities (A), languages (L), and gender (G).			
9. The video **encourages only acceptable behaviors** and **does not** encourage behaviors that might be considered violent, scary, unsafe, or offensive in some families (e.g., jumping on bed, hitting others).			
10. The video is **at least 2 minutes** in duration with **continuous movement but does not exceed 4 minutes.**			
11. Is the video available as a **DVD? Insert link** to purchase.			

Criteria for Selecting Physical Activity Music Videos *(continued)*

Unit 5 Throwing

Criteria: Insert check (√) if the video meets the criteria.	Video	Video	Video
1. **Insert name or link** to video (YouTube or other online source).			
2. The video is **age appropriate for preschool children** (in content, vocabulary).			
3. The **movements are modeled** by people or cartoons/characters.			
4. The **movements seen match the words or directions used** in the video.			
5. The video incorporates different **positional words** (*over, under, up, down*). **List** positional concepts used.			
6. The video incorporates different **body parts** (e.g., fingers, toes, knees, legs, arms). **List** body parts used.			
7. The video uses **action words or vocabulary** (*kick, throw, catch, walk*) that **matches the unit objectives. List** action words used.			
8. The video is current, representing **diversity** in images (e.g., if children are present in video, children represent human differences). **List** all examples of diversity that apply: race (R), ethnicity (E), abilities (A), languages (L), and gender (G).			
9. The video **encourages only acceptable behaviors** and **does not** encourage behaviors that might be considered violent, scary, unsafe, or offensive in some families (e.g., jumping on bed, hitting others).			
10. The video is **at least 2 minutes** in duration with **continuous movement** but does not exceed 4 minutes.			
11. Is the video available as a **DVD? Insert link** to purchase.			

Criteria for Selecting Physical Activity Music Videos *(continued)*

Unit 6   Striking

Criteria: Insert check (√) if the video meets the criteria.	Video	Video	Video
1. **Insert name or link** to video (YouTube or other online source).			
2. The video is **age appropriate for preschool children** (in content, vocabulary).			
3. The **movements are modeled** by people or cartoons/ characters.			
4. The **movements seen match the words or directions used** in the video.			
5. The video incorporates different **positional words** (*over, under, up, down*). **List** positional concepts used.			
6. The video incorporates different **body parts** (e.g., fingers, toes, knees, legs, arms). **List** body parts used.			
7. The video uses **action words or vocabulary** (*kick, throw, catch, walk*) that **matches the unit objectives. List** action words used.			
8. The video is current, representing **diversity** in images (e.g., if children are present in video, children represent human differences). **List** all examples of diversity that apply: race (R), ethnicity (E), abilities (A), languages (L), and gender (G).			
9. The video **encourages only acceptable behaviors** and **does not** encourage behaviors that might be considered violent, scary, unsafe, or offensive in some families (e.g., jumping on beds, hitting others).			
10. The video is **at least 2 minutes** in duration with **continuous movement but does not exceed 4 minutes.**			
11. Is the video available as a **DVD? Insert link** to purchase.			

Criteria for Selecting Physical Activity Music Videos *(continued)*

Unit 7 Kicking

Criteria: Insert check (√) if the video meets the criteria.	Video	Video	Video
1. **Insert name or link** to video (YouTube or other online source).			
2. The video is **age appropriate for preschool children** (in content, vocabulary).			
3. The **movements are modeled** by people or cartoons/characters.			
4. The **movements seen match the words or directions used** in the video.			
5. The video incorporates different **positional words** (*over, under, up, down*). **List** positional concepts used.			
6. The video incorporates different **body parts** (e.g., fingers, toes, knees, legs, arms). **List** body parts used.			
7. The video uses **action words or vocabulary** (*kick, throw, catch, walk*) that **matches the unit objectives. List** action words used.			
8. The video is current, representing **diversity** in images (e.g., if children are present in video, children represent human differences). **List** all examples of diversity that apply: race (R), ethnicity (E), abilities (A), languages (L), and gender (G).			
9. The video **encourages only acceptable behaviors** and **does not** encourage behaviors that might be considered violent, scary, unsafe, or offensive in some families (e.g., jumping on bed, hitting others).			
10. The video is **at least 2 minutes** in duration with **continuous movement but does not exceed 4 minutes.**			
11. Is the video available as a **DVD? Insert link** to purchase.			

Criteria for Selecting Preschool Interactive Movement Books

	Book Title/Author		
Criteria: Insert check (√) if the book meets the criteria below.			
1. The story is **age appropriate for preschool children** (in content, length, and vocabulary). This includes picture books with no written vocabulary words.			
2. The story is **interactive.** It has some element that supports or encourages the child to move in different ways.			
3. The story incorporates different **positional words** (*over, under, up, down*). **List** positional concepts used.			
4. The story incorporates different **body parts** (e.g., fingers, toes, knees, legs, arms). **List** body parts used.			
5. The story incorporates **action words or vocabulary** (*kick, throw, catch, gallop, tiptoe, walk, jump, run, march, hop, hide, smell, sing*). **List** words used.			
6. The story emphasizes **cooperative play** with friends/family as opposed to competition. The story shows children (or animals or animated characters) playing with friends (FR) and/or family (F).			
7. Story is **current** in its images and terminology.			
8. The story represents **diversity** in images, showing children who represent a wide range of characteristics engaged in movement activities. Which representation of diversity is seen in the story? **List** all that apply: race (R), ethnicity (E), abilities (A), languages (L), gender (G) or other (O).			
9. The story **does not** encourage behaviors or include themes that might be considered violent, scary, unsafe, or unacceptable in some families (e.g., jumping on bed, kicking balls in the house, hitting others, monsters chasing children).			
10. The **size of the book is suitable** (e.g., pictures visible) for reading to a class of 15-20 children.			
11. The book is **affordable.** Note the cost of the book.			
12. **List other strengths** of the story or book.			

References

Ackerman, D. J., & Barnett, W. S. (2005). *Prepared for kindergarten: What does "readiness" mean?* National Institute for Early Childhood Research.

American Academy of Pediatrics. (2020). *Making physical activity a way of life: AAP policy explained.* https://www.healthychildren.org/English/healthy-living/fitness/Pages/Making-Fitness-a-Way-of-Life.aspx

Australian Capital Territory Government. (n.d.). *Ball skills.* https://health.act.gov.au/sites/default/files/2019-08/AP%20Ball%20Skills.pdf

Block, M. E. (2016). *A teacher's guide to adapted physical education* (4th ed.). Paul H. Brookes Publishing Co.

Bradley, R. H., & Corwyn, R. F. (2002). Socioeconomic status and child development. *Annual Review of Psychology, 53,* 371–399.

Brady, L. (2005). Teaching strategies for young children with special needs. In R. Garguilo, J. Kilgo, & S. Graves (Eds.), *Young children with special needs: An introduction to early childhood special education* (pp. 270–305). Delmar.

Brian, A., Goodway, J., Logan, J., & Sutherland, S. (2017). SKIPing with teachers: An early years motor skill intervention. *Physical Education and Sport Pedagogy, 2*(3), 270–282. doi: 10.1080/17408989.2016.1176133

Brown, W., Pfeiffer, K., McIver, K., Dowda, M., Addy, C., & Pate, R. (2009). Social and environmental factors associated with preschoolers' nonsedentary physical activity. *Child Development, 80*(1), 45–58.

Brown, W., Schenkelberg, M., McIver, K., O'Neill, J., Howie, E., Pfeiffer, K., Saunders, R., Dowda, M., Addy, C., & Pate, R. (2016). Physical activity and young children with developmental delays. In S. L. Odom, B. Reichow, B. Boyd, & E. Barton (Eds.), *Handbook on early childhood special education* (pp. 487–500). Springer International Publishing.

Buchanan, A., & Briggs, J. (1998). Making cues meaningful: A guide for creating your own. *Teaching Elementary Physical Education, 9*(3), 16–18.

Buckingham, J., Wheldall, K., & Beaman-Wheldall, R. (2013). Why poor children are more likely to become poor readers: The school years. *Australian Journal of Education, 57*(3), 190–213.

California Association for Health, Physical Education, Recreation, and Dance. (n.d.). *National Association for Sport and Physical Education (NASPE): Appropriate practices in movement programs for children ages 3–5.* https://www.cahperd.org/Public/Advocacy/NASPE_Appropriate_Practices

CAST. (2018). *About universal design for learning.* https://www.cast.org/impact/universal-design-for-learning-udl

Center on Education Policy. (2008). *Instructional time in elementary schools: A closer look at changes for specific subjects.* Center on Education Policy.

Children Love to Sing. (2008, October 10). *Cruisin' down the freeway* [Video]. YouTube. https://www.youtube.com/watch?v=FrkK7gPvWiY

Children Love to Sing. (2009, October 6). *Touch the stars* [Video]. YouTube. https://youtu.be/UIaUoKRE4vc

Children Love to Sing. (2013, February 18). *Do your chores* [Video]. YouTube. https://youtu.be/w_gpI2SDApc

Children Love to Sing. (2013, May 12). *Hearty fun* [Video]. YouTube. https://www.youtube.com/watch?v=GzvJhCBH80U

Children Love to Sing. (2013, July 30). *Cool sports fitness song* [Video]. YouTube. https://www.youtube.com/watch?v=tIORtqkZoFk

Choi, J. K., Wang, D., & Jackson, A. P. (2019). Adverse experiences in early childhood and their longitudinal impact on later behavioral problems of children living in poverty. *Child Abuse & Neglect, 98,* 104–181.

Clark, J. E. (1994). Motor development. In V. S. Ramachandran (Ed.), *Encyclopedia of human behavior* (3rd ed., pp. 245–255). Academic Press.

Clark, J. E. (2005). From the beginning: A developmental perspective on movement and mobility. *Quest, 57*(1), 37–45.

Clark, J. E., & Metcalfe, J. S. (2002). The mountain of motor development: A metaphor. *Motor Development: Research and Reviews, 2,* 163–190.

Cook, R. E., Klein, M. D., & Chen, D. (2016). *Adapting early childhood curricula for children with special needs.* Pearson.

Council for the Curriculum, Examinations & Assessment. (2019). *Northern Ireland, curriculum (online).* https://ccea.org.uk/about/what-we-do/curriculum

Council for Exceptional Children's Division for Early Childhood & National Association for the Education of Young Children. (2009). *Early childhood inclusion: A joint position statement of the Division for Early Childhood (DEC) and the National Association for the Education of Young Children (NAEYC).* The University of North Carolina, FPG Child Development Institute. https://www.naeyc.org/sites/default/files/globally-shared/downloads/PDFs/resources/position-statements/ps_inclusion_dec_naeyc_ec.pdf

Cunconan-Lahr, R. (2006). Inclusive childcare begins with universal design. *Pennsylvania Early Intervention, 18*(1), 1–3.

Dickey, K., Castle, K., & Pryor, K. (2016). Reclaiming play in schools. *Childhood Education, 92*(2), 111–117.

Division for Early Childhood of the Council for Exceptional Children. (2014). DEC recommended practices in early intervention/early childhood special education, 2014. http://www.dec-sped.org/recommendedpractices

Elkind, D. (2007). *The power of play: How spontaneous, imaginative activities lead to happier, healthier children.* Da Capo Press.

Emck, C., Bosscher, R., Beek, P., & Doreleijers, T. (2009). Gross motor performance and self-perceived motor competence in children emotional, behavioral, and pervasive developmental disorders: A review. *Developmental Medicine and Child Neurology, 51*(7), 501–517.

Favazza, P. C., & Siperstein, G. N. (2016). Motor skills interventions for young children with disabilities. In B. Reichow, B. Boyd, E. Barton, & S. L. Odom (Eds.), *Handbook on early childhood special education* (pp. 225–246). Springer International Publishing.

Favazza, P. C., Siperstein, G. N., Ghio, K. G., Wairimu, J., & Masila, S. (2016). The Young Athletes Curriculum: Impact on children with disabilities in Kenya. *Journal of Research in Childhood Education, 30*(1), 113–127.

Favazza, P. C., Siperstein, G. N., Zeisel, S., Odom, S. L., Sideris, J. H., & Moskowitz, A. (2013). Young Athletes Intervention: Impact on motor development. *Adapted Physical Activity Quarterly, 30,* 235–253.

Fedewa, A. L., & Ahn, S. (2011). The effects of physical activity and physical fitness on children's achievement and cognitive outcomes: A meta-analysis. *Research Quarterly for Exercise and Sport, 82*(3), 521–535.

Ginsburg, K. (2007). The importance of play in promoting healthy child development and maintaining strong parent-child bonds. *Pediatrics, 119*(1), 182–191.

GO WITH YOYO: Fitness Fun for Kids. (2010, April 13). *Noodle balance: Preschool fitness games!* [Video]. YouTube. https://www.youtube.com/watch?v=WPsUQusTWyc

Goodway, J. D., & Branta, C. F. (2003). Influence of a motor skill intervention on fundamental motor skill development of disadvantaged preschool children. *Research Quarterly for Exercise and Sport, 74*(1), 36–46.

Goodway, J. D., Crowe, H., & Ward, P. (2003). Effects of motor skill instruction on fundamental motor skill development. *Adapted Physical Activity Quarterly, 20*(3), 298–314.

Gowen, E., & Hamilton, A. (2013). Motor abilities in autism: A review using a computational context. *Journal of Autism and Developmental Disorders, 43*(2), 323–344.

Groft, M., & Block, M. E. (2006). General teaching strategies when working with students with autism in physical education. *Teaching Elementary Physical Education, 17*(6), 25–28.

Grow, L. L., Carr, J. E., Gunby, K. V., Charania, S. M., Gonsalves, L., Ktaech, I. A., & Kisamore, A. N. (2009). Deviations from prescribed prompting procedures: Implications for treatment integrity. *Journal of Behavioral Education, 18,* 142–156.

Gumbo Gang. (n.d.). *Lesson: Jumping and landing.* http://gumbogang.com/lesson-jumping-landing/

Haiback-Beach, P., Reid, G., & Collier, D. (2018). *Motor learning and development* (2nd ed.). Human Kinetics.

Hartman, E., Houwen, S., Scherder, E., & Visscher, C. (2010). On the relationship between motor performance and executive functioning in children with intellectual disabilities. *Journal of Intellectual Disability Research, 54,* 468–477.

Haywood, K., & Getchell. N. (2014). *Lifespan motor development* (6th ed.). Human Kinetics.

Hnatiuk, J. A., Salmon, J., Hinkley, T., Okely, A. D., & Trost, S. (2014). A review of preschool children's physical activity and sedentary time using objective measures. *American Journal of Preventive Medicine, 47*(4), 487–497.

Horn, E. M., Palmer, S. B., Butrea, G. D., & Lieber, J. (2016). *Six steps to inclusive preschool curriculum: A UDL-based framework for children's school success.* Paul H. Brookes Publishing Co.

Howard, E. C. (2011). *Moving forward with kindergarten readiness assessment: A position paper of the Early Childhood State Collaborative on Assessment and Student Standards.* Council of Chief State School Offices.

Interprovincial Sport and Recreation Council of Manitoba, Canada. (n.d.). *Active Start—Why active play is so important.* https://sportforlife.ca/wp-content/uploads/2016/12/Why-Active-Play-is-so-Important-Active-Start.pdf

Iverson, J. (2010). Developing language in a developing body: The relationship between motor development and language development. *Journal of Child Language, 37,* 229–261.

Jelly Bean Sports. (2017, February 22). *How to teach young children to hit a baseball* [Video]. YouTube. https://www.youtube.com/watch?v=nSpMrNEWkYU

Jiang, Y., & Koball, H. (2018). *Basic facts about low-income children: Children under 18 years, 2016.* National Center for Children in Poverty, Columbia University Mailman School of Public Health.

Johnston, S., Nelson, C., Evans, J., & Palazolo, K. (2003). The use of visual supports in teaching young children with autism spectrum disorder to initiate interactions. *AAC: Augmentative and Alternative Communication, 19,* 86–104.

Kagan, S. L., Moore, E., & Bredekamp, S. (1995). *Reconsidering children's early development and learning: Toward common views and vocabulary.* National Education Goals Panel, Goal 1 Technical Planning Group.

Kayden, B. (2020). *How to teach young children to hit a baseball.* How They Play. https://howtheyplay.com/team-sports/How-to-Teach-Young-Children-to-Hit-a-Baseball

Ketcheson, L., Hauck, J., & Ulrich, D. (2017). The effects of an early motor skill intervention on motor skills, levels of physical activity, and socialization in young children with autism spectrum disorder: A pilot study. *Autism: The International Journal of Research and Practice, 21*(4), 481–492. https://doi.org/10.1177/1362361316650611

Kid Sense Child Development Corporation. (2015a). *Fine motor developmental chart.* http://www.childdevelopment.com.au/home/183

Kid Sense Child Development Corporation. (2015b). *Gross motor developmental chart.* http://www.childdevelopment.com.au/home/184

Kid Sense Child Development Corporation. (n.d.). *Gross motor activities.* https://childdevelopment.com.au/areas-of-concern/gross-motor-skills/gross-motor-activities/

KIDDO. (2018a, June 25). *KIDDO challenge: Assessing the fundamental movement skill of catching* [Video]. YouTube. https://www.youtube.com/watch?v=JiTfq98CEgk

KIDDO. (2018b, June 25). *KIDDO challenge: Assessing the fundamental movement skill of kicking (soccer)* [Video]. YouTube. https://www.youtube.com/watch?v=MnP9GkdhEQg

KIDDO. (2018c, June 25). *KIDDO challenge: Assessing the fundamental movement skill of striking (teeball)* [Video]. YouTube. https://www.youtube.com/watch?v=_jMsp9mIF3c

KIDDO. (2018d, June 25). *KIDDO challenge. Assessing the fundamental movement skill of throwing* [Video]. YouTube. https://www.youtube.com/watch?v=YqouziDKCoM

KIDDO. (2018e, June 21). *KIDDO challenge: Learn how to balance* [Video]. YouTube. https://www.youtube.com/watch?v=Ly-Zh-rXeh4

KIDDO. (2018f, June 21). *KIDDO challenge: Learn how to catch* [Video]. YouTube. https://www.youtube.com/watch?v=toiCHNtXVKw

KIDDO. (2018g, June 21). *KIDDO challenge: Learn how to hop* [Video]. YouTube. https://www.youtube.com/watch?v=R8VABKvS3c0

KIDDO. (2018h, June 20). *KIDDO challenge: Learn how to jump* [Video]. YouTube. https://www.youtube.com/watch?v=P1jGqZFtJ9I

KIDDO. (2018k, June 20). *KIDDO challenge: Learn how to throw* [Video]. YouTube. https://www.youtube.com/watch?v=vi8NGXOqZlg

KIDDO. (2019, August 19). *KIDDO challenge: Online fundamental movement skills assessment and reporting tool* [Video]. YouTube. https://www.youtube.com/watch?v=drMusOG3-vA

KIDDO. (2020a, January 7). *KIDDO challenge: Developing the skill of jumping* [Video]. YouTube. https://www.youtube.com/watch?v=R8VABKvS3c0

KIDDO. (2020b, January 7). *KIDDO challenge: Developing the skill of kicking* [Video]. YouTube. https://www.youtube.com/watch?v=oUn5wJZJm-M

Landin, D. (1994). The role of verbal cues in skill learning. *Quest, 46,* 299–313.

Lee, R., Zhai, F., Brooks-Gunn, J., Han, W. J., & Waldfogel, J. (2014). Head start participation and school readiness: Evidence from the Early Childhood Longitudinal Study—Birth Cohort. *Developmental Psychology, 50*(1), 202–215. https://doi.org/10.1037/a0032280

Lerner, R. M. (1976). *Theories of development: An overview in concepts and theories of human development* (pp. 136–155). Addison-Wesley.

Libby, M. E., Weiss, J. S., Bancroft, S., & Ahearn, W. H. (2008). A comparison of most-to-least and least-to-most prompting on the acquisition of solitary play skills. *Behavioral Analysis in Practice, 1,* 37–43.

Logan, S., Robinson, L., Wilson, A., & Lucas, W. (2011). Getting the fundamentals of movement: A meta-analysis of the effectiveness of motor skill intervention in children. *Child: Care, Health and Development, 38*(3), 305–315.

Logan, S. W., Webster, E. K., Getchell, N., Pfeiffer, K. A., & Robinson, L. E. (2015). Relationship between fundamental motor skill competence and physical activity during childhood and adolescence: A systematic review. *Kinesiology Review, 4*(4), 416–426.

MacDonald, M., Lord, C., & Ulrich, D. (2013). The relationship of motor skills and adaptive behavior skills in young children with autism spectrum disorders. *Research in Autism Spectrum Disorders, 7*(11), 1383–1390.

MacDonald, M., Ross, S., McIntyre, L. L., & Tepfer, A. (2017). Relations of early motor Skills on age and socialization, communication, and daily living in young children with developmental disabilities. *Adapted Physical Activity Quarterly, 34*(2), 179–194.

Massey, G., & Wheeler, J. (2000). Acquisition and generalization of activity schedules and their effects on task engagement in a young child with autism in an inclusive preschool classroom. *Education and Training in Mental Retardation and Developmental Disabilities, 35,* 326–335.

McDuffie, A., Turner, L., Stone, W., Yoder, P., Wolery, M., & Ulman, T. (2007). Developmental correlates of different types of motor imitation in young children with autism spectrum disorders. *Journal of Autism and Developmental Disorders, 37*(3), 401–412.

McPhillips, M., & Jordan-Black, J. (2007). The effect of social disadvantage on motor development in young children: A comparative study. *Journal of Child Psychology, 48*(12), 1214–1222.

Meadan, H., Ostrosky, M. M., Santos, R. M., & Snodgrass, M. (2013). How can I help? Prompting procedures to support children's learning. *Young Exceptional Children, 16*(4), 31–39.

Milteer, R. M., Ginsburg, K. R., Council on Communications and Media, & Committee on Psychosocial Aspects of Child and Family Health. (2012). The importance of play in promoting healthy child development and maintaining strong parent-child bond: Focus on children in poverty. *Pediatrics, 129*(1), e204–e213. doi: 10.1542/peds.2011-2953

Morrison, R., Sainato, D., BenChaaban, D., & Endo, S. (2002). Increasing play skills of children with autism using activity schedules and correspondence training. *Journal of Early Intervention, 25,* 58–72.

Moyer, L. (n.d.). *7 developmental steps to teaching your child to catch.* North Shore Pediatric Therapy. http://nspt4kids.com/parenting/7-developmental-steps-to-teaching-your-child-to-catch/

National Association for Education of Young Children. (2020). *NAEYC Position Statement.* https://www.naeyc.org/sites/default/files/globally-shared/downloads/PDFs/resources/position-statements/dap-statement_0.pdf

National Center for Physical Development and Outdoor Play. (2010). *From playpen to playground: The importance of physical play for the motor development of young children.* Head Start National Center for Physical Development and Outdoor Play.

National Physical Activity Plan Alliance. (2016). The 2016 United States report card on physical activity for children and youth. Retrieved from http://www.physicalactivityplan.org/reportcard/2016FINAL_USReportCard.pdf

Newell, K. (1984). Physical constraints to development of motor skills. In J. Thomas (Ed.), *Motor development during preschool and elementary years* (pp. 105–120). Burgess.

Newell, K. (1986). Constraints on the development of coordination. In G. Wade & H. T. Whiting (Eds.), *Motor development in children: Aspects of coordination and control* (pp. 341–360). Nijhoff.

Office of Disease Prevention and Health Promotion (ODPHP). (2018). *Shape America: Society of Health and Physical Educators: Active Start: A Statement of Physical Activity Guidelines for Children Birth to Age 5, 2nd Edition.* https://health.gov/our-work/physical-activity/current-guidelines/top-10-things-know

Oja, L., & Jorimae, T. (2002). Physical activity, motor ability, and school readiness of 6-yr.-old children. *Perceptual and Motor Skills, 95*(2), 407–415.

Orkwis, R. (2003). *Universally designed instruction.* ERIC/OSEP Digest. https://files.eric.ed.gov/fulltext/ED475386.pdf

Parker, R., & Thomsen, B. S. (2019). *Learning through play at school: A study of playful integrated pedagogies that foster children's holistic skills development in the primary school classroom.* The LEGO Foundation.

Payne, G., & Isaacs, L. (2012). *Human motor development: A lifespan approach.* McGraw Hill.

Petty, K. (2010). *Developmental milestones of young children.* Redleaf Press.

Piek, J. P., Dawson, L., Smith, L. M., & Gasson, N. (2008). The role of early fine and gross motor development on later motor and cognitive ability. *Human Movement Science, 27*(5), 668–681.

Provost, B., Heimerl, S., & Lopez, B. (2007). Levels of gross and fine motor development in young children with autism spectrum disorder. *Physical and Occupational Therapy in Pediatrics, 27*(3), 21–36.

Provost, B., Lopez, B., & Heimerl, S. (2007). A comparison of motor delays in young children: Autism spectrum disorder, developmental delay, and developmental concerns. *Journal of Autism and Developmental Disorders, 37*(2), 321–328.

Queensland Curriculum and Assessment Authority. (n.d.). *Home page.* https://www.qcaa.qld.edu.au

Reinders, N. J., Branco, A., Wright, K., Fletcher, P. C., & Bryden, P. J. (2019). Scoping review: Physical activity and social functioning in young people with autism spectrum disorder. *Frontiers in Psychology, 10,* 120. https://doi.org/10.3389/fpsyg.2019.00120

Riethmuller, A., Jones, R., & Okely, A. (2009). Efficacy of interventions to improve motor development in young children: A systematic review. *Pediatrics, 124*(4), 782–792.

SHAPE America. (2020). *Active start: A statement of physical activity guidelines for children from birth to age 5* (3rd ed.). https://www.shapeamerica.org/standards/guidelines/activestart.aspx

SHAPE America. (n.d.). *Digital download library: Early childhood activities.* https://www.shapeamerica.org//publications/resources/downloads-earlyChildhood.aspx

Shukla, P. (2011). *Musical PE for you and me, volume 1* [DVD]. Shukla Music.

Singapore Sports Council: My ActiveSG. (2016a). *Locomotor skills for kids.* https://www.myactivesg.com/read/2016/11/locomotor-skills

Singapore Sports Council: My ActiveSG. (2016b). *Object control skills for kids.* https://www.myactivesg.com/read/2016/11/object-control-skills

Singapore Sports Council: My ActiveSG. (2016c). *Stability skills for kids.* https://www.myactivesg.com/read/2016/11/stability-skills

Sturridge, D. (2015). How to kick a ball. *The Guardian.* http://www.theguardian.com/lifeandstyle/2015/jun/20/daniel-sturridge-how-to-kick-a-ball

The Inspired Treehouse. (n.d.). *The best balance activities for kids.* https://theinspiredtreehouse.com/child-development-balance/

The Learning Station. (2014, January 28). *Hokey Pokey kids' dance song* [Video]. YouTube. https://youtu.be/iZinb6rVozc?t=13s

The Learning Station. (2014, April 22). *Rumba dance* [Video]. YouTube. https://youtu.be/7R64sBEi-7I?t=14s

The Learning Station. (2014, December 30). *The penguin song* [Video]. YouTube. https://www.youtube.com/watch?v=_FEpPjhVtdc

The Learning Station. (2015, February 20). *Happy dance* [Video]. YouTube. https://youtu.be/cQ6BPWyIueQ?t=14s

The Learning Station. (2015, May 29). *Swimming song* [Video]. YouTube. https://youtu.be/ZsaywRY5iP0?t=14s

The Learning Station. (2016, November 17). *Move and freeze* [Video]. YouTube. https://www.youtube.com/watch?v=gE7zCfxJ7bE

The Learning Station. (2017, April 21). *Head, shoulders, knees & toes* [Video]. YouTube. https://youtu.be/7R64sBEi-7I?t=14s

Trawick-Smith, J. (2010). *From playpen to playground: The importance of physical play for the motor development of young children.* Head Start Body Start, National Center for Physical Development and Outdoor Play.

Trevlas, E., Matsouka, O., & Zachopoulou, E. (2003). Relationship between playfulness and motor creativity in preschool children. *Early Child Development and Care, 173*(5), 535–543.

Tucker, P. (2008). The physical activity levels of preschool-aged children: A systematic review. *Early Childhood Research Quarterly, 23*(4), 547–558.

United Nations Children's Fund (UNICEF). (2015). *Millennium development goals (MDG) monitoring.* https://www.un.org/millenniumgoals/2015_MDG_Report/pdf/MDG%202015%20rev%20(July%201).pdf

United Nations Children's Fund (UNICEF). (2021). *Seen, counted, included: Using data to shed light on the well-being of children with disabilities.* https://data.unicef.org/resources/children-with-disabilities-report-2021/

U.S. Department of Education. (2014). *Thirty-sixth annual report to Congress on the implementation of the Individuals with Disabilities Education Act, Parts B and C, 2014.* https://files.eric.ed.gov/fulltext/ED557419.pdf

U.S. Department of Health and Human Services. (2018). *Physical activity guidelines for Americans* (2nd ed.). https://health.gov/paguidelines/second-edition/pdf/Physical_Activity_Guidelines_2nd_edition.pdf

Uzgiris, I. C. (1999). Imitation as activity. In J. Nadel & G. Butterworth (Eds.), *Imitation in infancy* (pp. 186–206). Cambridge University Press.

Valentini, N. (2004). Visual cues, verbal cues, and child development strategies. *Journal for Physical and Sport Educators, 17*(3), 21–23.

Venetsanou, F., & Kambas, A. (2010). Environmental factors affecting preschoolers' motor development. *Early Childhood Education Journal, 37*(3), 319–327.

Vuijk, P. J., Hartman, E., Scherder, E., & Visscher, C. (2010). Motor performance of children with mild intellectual disability and borderline intellectual functioning. *Journal of Intellectual Disability Research, 54*(11), 955–965.

Wassenberg, R., Feron, F., Kessels, A., Hendriksen, J., Kalff, A., Kroes, M., & Vles, J. (2005). Relation between cognitive and motor performance in 5- to 6-year-old children: Results from a large scale cross sectional study. *Child Development, 76*(5), 1092–1103.

World Health Organization. (2011). *World report on disability.* https://www.who.int/disabilities/world_report/2011/report

Wuang, Y., Wang, C., Huang, M., & Su, C. (2008). Profiles and cognitive predictors of motor functions among early school-age children with mild intellectual disabilities. *Journal of Intellectual Disability Research, 52*(12), 1048–1060.

Index

Page numbers followed by *t* and *f* indicate tables and figures, respectively.